From World City to the World in One City

Studies in Urban and Social Change

Published

From World City to the World in One City: Liverpool through Malay Lives
Tim Bunnell

Urban Land Rent: Singapore As A Property State
Anne Haila

Globalised Minds, Roots in the City: Urban Upper-middle Classes in Europe
Alberta Andreotti, Patrick Le Galès and Francisco Javier Moreno-Fuentes

Confronting Suburbanization: Urban Decentralization in Post-Socialist Central and Eastern Europe
Kiril Stanilov and Luděk Sýkora (eds.)

Cities in Relations: Trajectories of Urban Development in Hanoi and Ouagadougou
Ola Söderström

Contesting the Indian City: Global Visions and the Politics of the Local
Gavin Shatkin (ed.)

Iron Curtains: Gates, Suburbs and Privatization of Space in the Post-socialist City
Sonia A. Hirt

Subprime Cities: The Political Economy of Mortgage Markets
Manuel B. Aalbers (ed.)

Locating Neoliberalism in East Asia: Neoliberalizing Spaces in Developmental States
Bae-Gyoon Park, Richard Child Hill and Asato Saito (eds.)

The Creative Capital of Cities: Interactive Knowledge of Creation and the Urbanization Economics of Innovation
Stefan Krätke

Worlding Cities: Asian Experiments and the Art of Being Global
Ananya Roy and Aihwa Ong (eds.)

Place, Exclusion and Mortgage Markets
Manuel B. Aalbers

Working Bodies: Interactive Service Employment and Workplace Identities
Linda McDowell

Networked Disease: Emerging Infections in the Global City
S. Harris Ali and Roger Keil (eds.)

Eurostars and Eurocities: Free Movement and Mobility in an Integrating Europe
Adrian Favell

Urban China in Transition
John R. Logan (ed.)

Getting Into Local Power: The Politics of Ethnic Minorities in British and French Cities
Romain Garbaye

Cities of Europe
Yuri Kazepov (ed.)

Cities, War, and Terrorism
Stephen Graham (ed.)

Cities and Visitors: Regulating Tourists, Markets, and City Space
Lily M. Hoffman, Susan S. Fainstein, and Dennis R. Judd (eds.)

Understanding the City: Contemporary and Future Perspectives
John Eade and Christopher Mele (eds.)

The New Chinese City: Globalization and Market Reform
John R. Logan (ed.)

Cinema and the City: Film and Urban Societies in a Global Context
Mark Shiel and Tony Fitzmaurice (eds.)

The Social Control of Cities? A Comparative Perspective
Sophie Body-Gendrot

Globalizing Cities: A New Spatial Order?
Peter Marcuse and Ronald van Kempen (eds.)

Contemporary Urban Japan: A Sociology of Consumption
John Clammer

Capital Culture: Gender at Work in the City
Linda McDowell

Cities After Socialism: Urban and Regional Change and Conflict in Post-Socialist Societies
Gregory Andrusz, Michael Harloe and Ivan Szelenyi (eds.)

The People's Home? Social Rented Housing in Europe and America
Michael Harloe

Post-Fordism
Ash Amin (ed.)

*The Resources of Poverty: Women and Survival in a Mexican City**
Mercedes Gonzal de la Rocha

Free Markets and Food Riots
John Walton and David Seddon

*Fragmented Societies**
Enzo Mingione

*Urban Poverty and the Underclass: A Reader**
Enzo Mingione

Forthcoming

Cities and Ethno-National Conflict: Empires, Nations and Urban Processes
James Anderson and Liam O'Dowd

Paradoxes of Segregation: Urban Migration in Europe
Sonia Arbaci

From Shack to House to Fortress
Mariana Cavalcanti

The Making of Urban Africa: Contesting and Negotiating the Colonial and Postcolonial State
Laurent Fourchard

Urban Social Movements and the State
Margit Mayer

Cities and Social Movements: Immigrant Rights Struggles in Amsterdam, Paris, and Los Angeles
Walter Nicholls and Justus Uitermark

Fighting Gentrification
Tom Slater

*Out of print

From World City to the World in One City

Liverpool through Malay Lives

Tim Bunnell

WILEY Blackwell

This edition first published 2016

Registered Office
John Wiley & Sons, Ltd, The Atrium, Southern Gate, Chichester, West Sussex, PO19 8SQ, UK

Editorial Offices
350 Main Street, Malden, MA 02148-5020, USA
9600 Garsington Road, Oxford, OX4 2DQ, UK
The Atrium, Southern Gate, Chichester, West Sussex, PO19 8SQ, UK

For details of our global editorial offices, for customer services, and for information about how to apply for permission to reuse the copyright material in this book please see our website at www.wiley.com/wiley-blackwell.

Library of Congress Cataloging-in-Publication Data

Names: Bunnell, Tim, author.
Title: From world city to the world in one city : Liverpool through Malay lives / Tim Bunnell.
Description: Chichester, UK ; Malden, MA : John Wiley & Sons, 2016. |
Includes bibliographical references and index.
Identifiers: LCCN 2015035652 (print) | LCCN 2015044489 (ebook) | ISBN 9781118827741 (cloth) | ISBN 9781118827734 (pbk.) | ISBN 9781118827710 (ePub) |
ISBN 9781118827727 (Adobe PDF)
Subjects: LCSH: Malay Club (Liverpool)–History. | Merchant mariners–Malaysia. |
Malays (Asian people)–England–Liverpool. | Liverpool (England)–History–20th century.
Classification: LCC HD8039.S42 M438 2016 (print) | LCC HD8039.S42 (ebook) |
DDC 305.899/28042753–dc23
LC record available at http://lccn.loc.gov/2015035652

A catalogue record for this book is available from the British Library.

Cover image: 'Red Ensign on Mersey Ferry, 2007' © Colin McPherson.

Set in 10.5/12pt New Baskerville by SPi Global, Pondicherry, India

Printed and bound in Malaysia by Vivar Printing Sdn Bhd

1 2016

Contents

Series Editors' Preface

The Wiley Blackwell *Studies in Urban and Social Change* series is published in association with the *International Journal of Urban and Regional Research.* It aims to advance theoretical debates and empirical analyses stimulated by changes in the fortunes of cities and regions across the world. Among topics taken up in past volumes and welcomed for future submissions are:

- connections between economic restructuring and urban change
- urban divisions, difference, and diversity
- convergence and divergence among regions of east and west, north, and south
- urban and environmental movements
- international migration and capital flows
- trends in urban political economy
- patterns of urban-based consumption

The series is explicitly interdisciplinary; the editors judge books by their contribution to intellectual solutions rather than according to disciplinary origin. Proposals may be submitted to members of the series Editorial Committee, and further information about the series can be found at www.suscbookseries.com.

Jenny Robinson
Manuel Aalbers
Dorothee Brantz
Patrick Le Galès
Chris Pickvance
Ananya Roy
Fulong Wu

List of Figures

Figures

Abbreviations and Acronyms

ARTIS	Angkatan Revolusi Tentera Islam Singapura (Singapore Islamic Revolutionary League)
BL	The British Library
BT	Board of Trade (archival sources held at The National Archives of the UK, Kew, London)
CMIO	Chinese-Malay-Indian-Others
CO	Colonial Office (archival sources held at The National Archives of the UK, Kew, London)
EEC	European Economic Community
EU	European Union
FMS	Federated Malay States
GAPENA	Gabungan Persatuan Penulis Nasional Malaysia (Malaysian National Writers' Association)
GDP	gross domestic product
GPS	global positioning system
ha	hectare
IOR	India Office Records (held at the British Library, London)
ISA	Internal Security Act
km	kilometre
MDC	Merseyside Development Corporation
MSA	Merseyside Malaysian and Singapore Community Association
MV	Motor Vessel
NEP	New Economic Policy (Malaysia)
NUS	National University of Singapore
OA	Ocean Steamship Company archive (held at the Maritime Archives and Library, Merseyside Maritime Museum, Liverpool)
P&O	Peninsular and Oriental Steam Navigation Company
PAP	People's Action Party (Singapore, est. 1954)

PAS	Parti Islam Se-Malaysia (Pan-Malaysian Islamic Party, est. 1951)
PMPMUK	Persatuan Masyarakat Pekerja Malaysia United Kingdom (Malaysian Workers' Association of the United Kingdom)
RM	Malaysian Ringgit
RTM	Radio Televisyen Malaysia
SMA	Sekretariat Melayu Antarabangsa (International Malay Secretariat)
SS	Steamship (single screw)
SSC	Straits Steamship Company
UMNO	United Malays National Organisation (Malaysia, est. 1946)

Glossary of Non-English Terms

Non-English terms are Malay except where noted as Arabic (Ar), Chinese (Ch), Hokkien (Hk), Persian (Per), Portuguese (Port) or Urdu (Urd)

adat	customary law
alam Melayu	Malay world region in Southeast Asia
anak raja	royalty
ayah	father
babi	pork
bahasa Melayu	Malay language
bahasa Melayu pasar	marketplace Malay language
baju Melayu	traditional Malay shirt
balik kampung	return trip
bandar sejarah	historic town
boleh maju	can prosper or succeed
Bumiputera	lit. 'son of the soil'; used since 1970s by the Malaysian government to implement racially based affirmative action policies for ethnic Malays and other, smaller 'indigenous' (*bumiputera*) groups
bunga	flower
ceramah	public talk
dakwah	lit. 'to proclaim' (as in the proselytizing and preaching of Islam)
darah keturunan Arab	Arabic ancestral blood
dunia Melayu	Malay world (as in either regional realm in Southeast Asia or extended world of Malay historical and diasporic connections)
Dunia Melayu movement	Malay World movement
Eid al-Fitr (Ar)	Religious holiday marking the end of the Islamic fasting month of Ramadan

Eropah	Europe
feng shui (Ch)	Chinese philosophical system of harmonizing human existence with the surrounding environment
ghaut serang	land-based intermediary agent or broker who was an authorized crew supplier
halal (Ar)	lit. 'permissible' objects or courses of action for Muslims according to Islamic law; commonly but not exclusively in relation to consumption of food and drink
Haj(j)i (Ar)	honorific title given to Muslim person who completes Islamic pilgrimage (*hajj*) to Mecca
Hari Raya	'Great day'; national holiday in Malaysia marking the day of breaking of fast (Eid al-Fitr or Aidilfitri) at the end of Ramadan
imam	person who leads prayers in a mosque
induk	mother (territorially meaning motherland)
jamban	traditional squat latrine
jurang budaya	cultural gap
kain kafan	burial clothes
kaki	friend
kampung/kampong	village or community
kawan	friend
Kelab Melayu	Malay Club (Liverpool)
Kelab UMNO Liverpool	Liverpool UMNO Club
kelasi	seafarer
kelasi kapal	sailor
kenduri	feast
kerbau	buffalo
kereta lembu	bullock cart
ketuanan Melayu	Malay lordship (political reference to ethnic Malay pre-eminence or supremacy in contemporary Malaysia)
khalasi (Ar)	seaman or dockyard worker
kopitiam (Hk)	traditional coffee shop
kris	dagger
kuno	antiquated
lascar (Per)	Indian Ocean seafarer
lashkar (Urd)	army or camp
lashkari (Port)	soldier
laskar	soldier
lepak	hang out
makan	eat

Melayu baru	new Malay
membandarkan	urbanize
merajuk	lit. sulk, implying having problems or being hurt
merantau	circular migration
Merdeka	independence (of Federation of Malaya, est. 31 August 1957)
nusantara	Malay world region or archipelago in Southeast Asia
orang kulit berwarna	coloured people
orang puteh	white people
Pak Cik	honorific title for male elder
penghulu	village head, orig. subdistrict chief
peon	servant boy or menial labourer
perantau	migrant or sojourner
raja	hereditary ruler or king
Ramadan (Ar)	ninth month of the Islamic calendar, observed by Muslims as the month of fasting
rantau	region
ronggeng	Malay dance
rumpun Melayu	Malay stock
selamat tinggal	goodbye
sepak raga	kick volleyball
songkok	rimless cap
syurga dunia	heaven on earth
tahlil dan doa arwah	prayers for the deceased
tanah Melayu	Malay homeland, referring to what is today peninsular (West) Malaysia
tanah merah	red earth
tandas	bathroom
teh tarik	frothy, sweet, milky tea
tokoh-tokoh	figures
tudung	headscarf
ustaz (Ar)	male Muslim scholar and teacher of Islam (female, *ustazah*)
zawiyah (Ar)	Islamic religious school

Acknowledgements

It has taken me much longer than expected to complete this book, but that is certainly not because of any lack of assistance along the way. In part, it may be precisely because so many people have helped me – with often irresistible suggestions of additional sources and alternative possible directions – that research and writing have been such prolonged processes. This does not mean that I am blaming anyone (or everyone) else for my meanderings, and I alone, of course, am responsible for any shortcomings in the end product. But it does mean that I have many people in many places to thank – not only with regard to material that constitutes the book but also for positioning me in much wider worlds of knowledge and experience, only a small subset of which is captured in the chapters that follow.

I am grateful, first of all, to Zaharah Othman whose own writing about and concern for Malay ex-seafarers in Britain inspired my research. It was also through Zaharah that I met Sharidah Sharif and her family in Liverpool. Sharidah and Wahab were my main contact points in 'the field' between 2004 and 2008, and I thank them for their kindness in feeding me with lots of information and sustenance. (How wonderful that I came to eat *petai* more often in Liverpool than I do in Southeast Asia!) During field research in 2004 I received institutional support from the Department of Geography at the University of Liverpool – thanks to David Sadler and Dave Featherstone for arranging that. Dave also kindly furnished me with several important archival references from his own historical work on subaltern transnationalisms. My fieldwork from 2004 to 2006 was generously funded by a National University of Singapore (NUS) grant, 'Malay Routes: Life histories and geographies of Malayness in Liverpool' (R-109-000-058-112).

NUS has provided a very stable anchorage and supportive home base for my Malay Routes research over more than a decade. I am grateful to the Faculty of Arts and Social Sciences for staff research support scheme funds to carry out additional fieldwork in Liverpool in 2009. I held a joint appointment in the Asia Research Institute from that year until 2014, and benefited from opportunities to present my work there, although the Department of Geography has always been my main home. Strands of my Liverpool research have been enriched through discussion in the department's Social and Cultural Geography research group, as well as by more direct contributions over the years from Elaine Ho, Lisa Law, Anant Maringanti, Chris McMorran, Sarah Moser, Hamzah Muzaini, Ong Chin Ee, Natalie Oswin, Noorashikin Abdul Rahman, Vani S., Pam Shurmer-Smith and James Sidaway. Aspects of my Malay Routes work have been inflicted upon several cohorts of geography honours students, and some of them (Faizal bin Abdul Aziz, Guo Hefang and Lo Dening) kindly carried out research assistance for me. Lee Li Kheng is to thank for the book's cartographic work. Beyond the Department of Geography, other NUS-ers past and present whom I wish to thank for varied contributions to my research are Daniel Goh, Phil Kelly, Lai Chee Kien, Hussin Mutalib, Alice Nah, Kris Olds, Dahlia Shamduddin and Eric Thompson. My thinking about the Malay world also benefited from comments and suggestions made by scholars and students who attended a seminar I gave in the Malay Studies programme in 2007.

While my home institution remains a great place to do research in human geography and urban studies as well as on the Malay world, I am also grateful for NUS support of sabbatical leave elsewhere. My sabbatical in 2008 started in Malaysia at the Institute of the Malay World and Civilization (ATMA), Universiti Kebangsaan Malaysia. Thanks to Jim Collins for supporting my fellowship there and to both Zawawi Ibrahim and Shamsul A.B. for sharing their considerable insights. Other Malaysians and/or Malaysianists who have supported my work during and beyond that sabbatical period include Tan Sri Ismail Hussein, Joel Kahn, Sumit Mandal, Izham Omar, Meghann Ormond and Mansor Puteh. My sabbatical leave ended in Indonesia and there I have to thank Neogroho Andy H. for sharing memories of his late grandfather. For the main component of the sabbatical in the northwest of England, I was based institutionally at the University of Manchester's School of Environment and Development where the collegiality of Neil Coe and Martin Hess was much appreciated. In Liverpool during that same period I am grateful for help and support from Ronnie and Cathy Bujang, Farida Chapman, Dave Featherstone (again), Paul Fadzil, Erwina A. Ghafar, Teddy Lates, Rosita Mohamed, Wan Mohamed Rosidi Hussein, Sharidah Sharif (again) and Nick White.

Among assistance that I received at various archives and repositories in Malaysia and Singapore as well as in Britain (all of which are listed in the Archival and Documentary Sources section at the back of the book), my particular thanks to helpful folks at the Maritime Archives and Library at Merseyside Maritime Museum and at the Liverpool Record Office. In addition, presentations at the following institutions during my sabbatical year all, in different ways, provided new ideas and suggestions for which I am grateful: the Contemporary Urban Centre in Liverpool, the London Urban Salon, the Seafarers' International Research Centre at the University of Cardiff, the 'International Conference on Diasporas' at Hong Kong University, and seminars in the geography programmes at the University of Plymouth and at Trinity College, Ireland.

Beyond the sabbatical year, my thinking has been shaped by various presenting and writing experiences. Papers that I presented at the conference on 'Geographies of Transnational Networks' held at the University of Liverpool in 2005, and at the symposium on 'Migration and Identities in Asia' held at Yonsei University in 2009 were revised and published in *Global Networks* and *Pacific Affairs* respectively. The only existing publication from my Malay Routes work that includes material in a form that is recognizable in this book (in Chapter 8) is a paper that appeared in *Transactions of the Institute of British Geographers* in 2008 (vol. 33, pp. 251–67), and I am grateful to the Royal Geographical Society (with the Institute of British Geographers) for permitting this. Thanks to Zane Kripe and Peter Pels for the invitation to present at the 'Futurities' conference in Leiden in June 2014 as this helped me to rethink the framing of Chapter 6.

Overall framing of the book was strongly influenced by the (very) challenging comments I received from members of the editorial board of the Wiley Blackwell Studies in Urban and Social Change series. Thanks to Jenny Robinson for agreeing to proceed with the project. The reviews I received from Richard Phillips and Ananya Roy provided excellent, complementary sets of suggestions as to how to improve the manuscript. Jenny provided very clear editorial guidance as well as lots of helpful suggestions from her own careful reading. Two other people have kindly read and helped to nuance the entire text: Michelle Miller and Gareth Richards. An NUS Faculty of Arts and Social Sciences book grant funded excellent editing and formatting services from Impress Creative and Editorial Sdn Bhd. I thank Jacqueline Scott and Allison Kostka at Wiley for their efficiency and patience.

In the context of a process of research and writing which has seen a blurring of boundaries between informants, on the one hand, and friends and family, on the other, I have deliberately left two sets of thanks until last. The first go to the Malay 'elders' (the Pak Cik-Pak Cik) across whose lives the urban geographies of this book are mapped. I am privileged and very grateful to have had opportunities to converse with many ex-seafaring men and members of their families. Thanks to Pak

Cik Ali, Pak Cik Jaafar and especially to Pak Cik Mat Nor for sharing so much with me. In Pak Cik Mat Nor's case this extended over multiple interviews and conversations in three different countries. Perhaps the only ex-seaman with whom I conversed more was the late Pak Cik Fadzil who kindly welcomed me to Saturday morning breakfasts with his family.

Special thanks, second, to members of my family, the composition of which has changed significantly over the past decade. Zep, Xavi and Bea have all been born since 2011. While they have not sped up my writing, they are three wonderful excuses for all the delays. I have been 'finishing' this book for as long as the kids' mummy has known me. Michelle: I am so lucky to have a wife who is so encouraging, loving, patient … and a meticulous editor! My parents, Megan and Craig, remain models of what supportive parenting means. Finally, during several stints of fieldwork in Liverpool I stayed with my grandmother, Doreen Owen, enjoying her company, cooking and memories of Liverpool's dance halls after the Second World War. She died in November 2014, and is now buried next to my granddad at the top of the cemetery in Hawarden, North Wales, from where it is possible to see over to Liverpool on a clear day.

Tim Bunnell
Singapore

Prologue

This book is about people who met at Liverpool's Malay Club over a period of more than half a century. It examines, in particular, the maritime linkages that made possible the formation of the Malay Club and the worlds of connection that the club in turn sustained. Research for the book formally began at the National University of Singapore in 2004, but the genesis of my 'Malay Routes' project lay in a couple of seemingly unconnected events over the preceding three years. First, during a research trip to Kuala Lumpur in 2001, I watched a Malay-language film that implanted in my mind the possibility of a long-standing Malay seafaring presence in England. The main characters in *Dari Jemapoh ke Manchester* (From Jemapoh to Manchester) are two teenage boys, Yadi and Mafiz, who leave behind the sleepy village of Jemapoh in the 1960s in a red Volvo, and head for the great port of Singapore – maritime gateway to lands beyond the Malay world. Yadi dreams of meeting his football idol, George Best, and of watching 'Manchestee Uni-ted'. Mafiz, by contrast, is no football fan, but is motivated to hit the road and sea lanes by the prospect of tracking down his seafaring father (*ayah*). Where is Mafiz's *ayah*? They are not sure, but the last contact was a postcard, from Liverpool …

The second event, a year after I watched *Dari Jemapoh ke Manchester*, was the funeral of my maternal grandfather which was held in a part of the northwest of England that borders north Wales. My journey back home from Singapore to Manchester airport was filled with sadness and

From World City to the World in One City: Liverpool through Malay Lives,
First Edition. Tim Bunnell.

regret at not having been able to see my grandfather before he died. Conversations that followed the funeral gave rise to further regrets. Especially for Welsh family members whom I had not seen since my early childhood, the fact that I was living and working in Southeast Asia emerged not only as a topic of conversation but also as a connection to my late grandfather's life. My great-uncle David recalled stories that he had heard from my grandfather about his time in Singapore. Had I not heard those stories before? Certainly I was aware that my grandfather had worked in the merchant navy, shipping out of Liverpool towards the end of the Second World War and into the immediate postwar period. This memory had been sustained by the painting of a Blue Funnel Line ship set against the Liverpool waterfront that was in the room where we always ate during childhood visits to my grandparents' home. But I had rarely asked my grandfather about the seafaring period of his life, blurring historically as it did into a topic that was off limits – the war. I never got to hear my grandfather's recollections of Singapore and a host of other places 'around there' (as my great-uncle David put it) which were overlapping points in our life geographies, many decades apart.

Back at work in Singapore, curiosity about the mid-twentieth-century maritime routes that had taken my grandfather from Liverpool to Singapore reminded me of the possibility of seafaring journeys in the opposite direction. To what extent was Mafiz's father in *Dari Jemapoh ke Manchester* merely a product of filmmaker Hishamuddin Rais's creative imagination? And, if Malay sailors really had sent postcards back to villages in Malaysia from ports such as Liverpool in the 1960s, were any of these men still living in England? Although the seemingly most straightforward way to answer the first of these questions was to ask Hishamuddin himself, unfortunately – for him even more than for me – he was in detention in 2002 under Malaysia's Internal Security Act. By the time that he was released in mid-2003, I had found the answer to the second question: newspaper articles written by the London-based Malaysian journalist Zaharah Othman confirmed that there were indeed Malay ex-seamen living in Liverpool and other former British maritime centres such as Cardiff and London. When I eventually met Hishamuddin in Kuala Lumpur in early 2004, I had already read about some of the ex-sailors whom he had encountered in London in the 1980s – most memorably Man Tokyo, whose knowledge of the Japanese language gained when working in shipyards in Japan during the Second World War had helped him to secure roles in British war films.

Another, more serendipitous, source of information about Malay ex-seamen in the city of Liverpool in particular came through a friend and former colleague at the National University of Singapore. Phil Kelly's family are from Liverpool and, in email correspondence in the period after my grandfather's funeral in May 2002, I asked Phil if he was aware of a Malay presence in his home town. He wrote back some weeks later to report that his Aunt Valerie ('just retired from many years as the telephone operator at the Liverpool School of Tropical Medicine') had kindly unearthed several leads for me. These included contact details for Liverpool's Al-Rahma mosque (a reasonable place to seek Malays who, in Malaysia at least, are constitutionally Muslim); the nursing home where a Mr Hassan ('an elderly chap with good English and very knowledgeable') was staying; and a 'Malaysia/Singapore Association' (the Malay Club) housed at 7 Jermyn Street. With this information and inspiration gained from reading Zaharah Othman's newspaper articles – which included mention of meeting Mr Hassan (Arsad Hassan) at 7 Jermyn Street in 1996 – I headed back to the northwest of England, to Liverpool, in December 2003.

During this initial pilot visit to Liverpool, a graduate student from Malaysia introduced me to an ex-seaman known as Dol. Born in Singapore in 1929, Dol had gained seafaring experience working on the

Figure 0.1 Malay deck crew of the MV *Charon*, circa 1947. Photograph courtesy of Fadzil Mohamed.

MV *Charon*, a Liverpool-owned Blue Funnel Line ship that had operated between Singapore and Western Australia in the 1940s. Moving on to work on oceangoing ships, he first arrived in Liverpool as a seafarer onboard the MV *Gladys Moller* on a very cold day in December 1950. At that time, Dol recalled, there were 'hundreds' of Malay men like him in Liverpool. By December 2003 only around 20 remained. The lives of these men and other people who met at the Malay Club on Jermyn Street – including descendants of ex-seamen as well as Malaysian student sojourners and their family members – provide a window into Liverpool's historically shifting urban social geographies.

1

Introduction
Locating Malay Liverpool

When Dol arrived in Liverpool in the winter of 1950, among the 'hundreds' of Malays already in the city were men who had left the *alam Melayu* (Malay world) before the Second World War.[1] In terms of British imperial history and geography, the very presence of such men in Liverpool in the first half of the twentieth century is significant. Seafarers from British Malaya, and from neighbouring territories that were not tinted pink on maps of British Empire territory,[2] settled in imperial port cities – Cardiff, Glasgow and London as well as Liverpool – prior to the New Commonwealth immigration which is conventionally understood to mark the advent of multiethnic Britain. Over the past three decades, scholars have done much to illuminate earlier histories of Asian and black people in Britain, implying or even asserting that it has always been an ethno-racially diverse society (e.g. Fryer, 1984; Visram, 1986, 2002; Muhammad Mumtaz, 1996). In contrast, there are those who believe that the importance of small communities prior to the 1950s has been overstated. Given their lack of visibility and influence, as well as their statistical insignificance at the national scale, Ian Spencer (1997: 2) asserts that Britain really has 'become a multi-racial society only very recently'. While this may be true at the national level, at smaller scales of analysis – at the level of cities or in particular dockside parts of cities – there are clearly places that have long been marked in profound ways by an Asian and/or black presence.[3]

From World City to the World in One City: Liverpool through Malay Lives,
First Edition. Tim Bunnell.

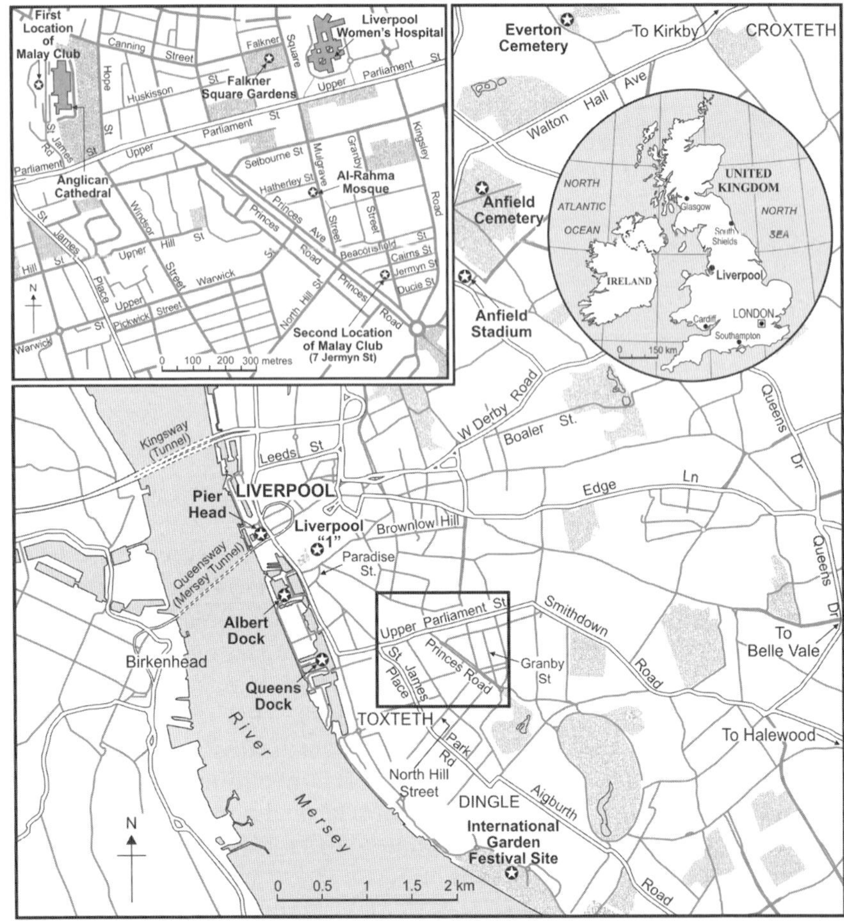

Figure 1.1 Liverpool and the two sites of the city's Malay Club. Produced by Lee Li Kheng.

Most Asian and black seamen arriving in Liverpool either side of the Second World War stayed and socialized in the south docks area of the city although, by the time Dol arrived, that had begun to change. Some of the prewar generation of Malays in Liverpool had formed families in and around the south docks, and several of their homes also provided lodging for visiting Malay seamen. Malay men met up in the basement of a house on St James Place (see Figure 1.1), which had a Yemeni-run cafe on the ground floor. Across Parliament Street from St James Place, towards the city centre, was where Liverpool's Malay Club was first located. Established by a Malacca-born man named Johan Awang who had moved to Liverpool from New York City after the war, the club occupied the first floor of a house which faced the Anglican Cathedral. The building and indeed most of the street on which the Malay Club was initially sited (St James Road) is long gone, existing today only in the memories of a dwindling number of people who frequented the club in the 1950s. Even among these men and women memories often merge into, or are conflated with, those of another place. With demolition imminent in the streets below the Anglican Cathedral, in the early 1960s a group of men from Malaya and Singapore pooled their resources to buy a house on one of the streets that run perpendicular to Granby Street in what is today known locally as the Liverpool 8 area of the city.[4] In line with a wider shift in population out of the south docks area, 7 Jermyn Street became the new home of the Malay Club from 1963.

The operation of the Malay Club in its successive locations spanned an era during which Liverpool experienced profound transformation, not only of its built environment and internal social geography, but also economically and in terms of external linkages. When the club was first established, the city still boasted a port of worldwide fame and importance. Back in the 1880s Liverpool had even been termed a 'world city'.[5] Although, in hindsight, Liverpool was well past its commercial peak long before the Second World War, the city to which Johan Awang moved from across the Atlantic remained a key maritime centre for ships, goods and people from around the world, and especially from far-flung territories of the British Empire (Lawton, 1964). As waves of demolition continued to hit the south docks and adjacent city centre streets, the Granby Street vicinity of the Malay Club's second home in Liverpool 8 became the area of the city most visibly marked by the demographic effects of imperial maritime connections. Granby Street is remembered as having been a thriving commercial thoroughfare in the 1960s.[6] However, the surrounding area subsequently became synonymous with 'inner-city' social and economic problems arising in part from Liverpool's diminished position in the national and international economy after empire. Number 7 is in the section of Jermyn Street that connects Granby Street to Princes Avenue, the site of infamous street disturbances in the early 1980s. Media coverage of these 'riots' popularized the toponym 'Toxteth' and marked it on national mental maps as the 'new Harlem of Liverpool' (Belchem, 2000: 29). The city of Liverpool more widely came to be seen as the epitome of British post-imperial and postindustrial urban decline (Lane, 1997). When I first visited in 2003, the Malay Club was one of only two buildings in the section of Jermyn Street between Princes Road and Granby Street that had not been abandoned and boarded up (see Figure 1.2).[7]

Figure 1.2 The section of Jermyn Street that includes the Malay Club (at number 7), December 2003. Photograph by the author.

The urban landscapes of the south docks and Liverpool 8 may be read as evidence of the changing commercial fortunes of the city in general, and in terms of even wider geoeconomic and geopolitical shifts. But the operation of the Malay Club across its two sites also allows – perhaps even demands – a more fine-grained, human-centred examination of urban and social change. From its inception, the club articulated social connections with other Atlantic maritime centres (particularly New York, which had a Malay Club of its own from 1954) and with British colonial territories, especially in the Malay world. There is no shortage of research which takes seriously the role of empire in shaping metropolitan spaces, but very little of that work has focused on the agency of colonial peoples in imperial cities.[8] Important exceptions such as Antoinette Burton's (1998) work on Indian visitors to late nineteenth-century London centre upon the experiences (and written records) of privileged colonial subjects. Tony Ballantyne's work on the Sikh diaspora, in contrast, highlights one way of beginning to recuperate the agency of subaltern seafaring sojourners and settlers. He distinguishes 'two interwoven, overlapping but occasionally independent sets of webs'

(Ballantyne, 2006: 81): on the one hand, those associated with formal imperial structures serving British merchants, missionaries and administrators; on the other, webs that were fashioned by Punjabis themselves. Following Ballantyne, it is possible to conceive of seafaring Malay social webs connecting imperial Liverpool to the *alam Melayu* in Southeast Asia and many other parts of the world within and beyond the British Empire. Extending beyond Ballantyne's conceptualization, my own interests also include urban places that both supported these webs and were transformed by them. Examination of the co-constitution of such urban places and Malay social webs (themselves intertwined with, yet exceeding, wider commercial linkages) allows for an historical analysis of world city Liverpool in relational and territorial terms (McCann and Ward, 2010).

In this book I trace some of Liverpool's shifting urban social geographies from the tail end of its time as an imperial maritime world city. The lives and long-distance social connections of young Malay men arriving as seafarers during that period extend across Liverpool's subsequent postimperial, postmaritime and post-world city transformations. Much has been written about how the city came to be dependent upon imperial trade and maritime-related commerce, as well as about the correspondingly devastating economic effects of postwar decolonization and the contraction of Liverpool's port functions (Lane, 1997; Wilks-Heeg, 2003; Murden, 2006). While Liverpool was labelled a world city in the late nineteenth century and remained an important metropolitan node in the colonial regime of accumulation in the mid-twentieth century, it has certainly not featured on the world city maps or rosters of late twentieth-century economic globalization (e.g. Friedmann, 1986; Beaverstock *et al.*, 1999). However, this should not be taken to mean that urban places and practices within the city ceased to be constituted through relations with far-flung 'elsewheres' (cf. Mbembe and Nuttall, 2004: 348).[9] To date, efforts that have been put into documenting Liverpool's diminished position in the new international division of labour and the contemporary global(izing) economy have not been matched by documentation of the more-than-economic worlds of connection through which the city continues to be imagined, inhabited and (re)made.

Shifting constitutive relations with the Malay world in Southeast Asia are significant in part because that region has been remapped into narratives of miraculous economic 'rise' that contrast sharply with those of Liverpool's 'demise'. Liverpool and Southeast Asia have not only been repositioned in very different ways in imaginings of the wider structural economic order of things, but also in relation to each other. In maritime terms, during the 1970s, a growing proportion of the ships coming to the city from territories of the former British Malaya flew the flags of the independent nation states of Malaysia or Singapore rather than the red ensign of British ships (shown in suitably frayed form but, unfortunately, also in black and white on the front cover), many of which had been registered in Liverpool during colonial times.[10] More widely, ethnic Malay citizens of Malaysia and (to a much lesser extent) Singapore increasingly came to and through Liverpool as students, skilled professionals, journalists and tourists rather than as seafarers. These Malay women and men spun new social webs that neither simply replaced nor reinvigorated older ones, but refashioned them – and Malay Liverpool. Meanwhile, the geopolitical territorial fact of Malaysia and Singapore as independent nation states recast the nature of extant transoceanic and transcontinental connections. From the 1990s political elites in Malaysia in particular became increasingly concerned that Malays should extend their worlds and commercial operations beyond the national economic context. As a site of historical Malay diasporic connection, Liverpool thus came to be imagined an as Atlantic outpost of Kuala Lumpur-centred 'worlding' aspirations (Ong, 2011). At the same time, both Liverpool and cities in Southeast Asia form part of globe-spanning circuits of capital and urban development expertise. Liverpool, like Kuala Lumpur and the city-state of Singapore, has been reimaged through investment in material infrastructure and the marketing of ethnocultural diversity. In the year before my pilot visit to the Malay Club, Liverpool was officially branded and marketed as 'the World in One City'. The worlds of connection that brought seamen such as Dol to this one-time imperial maritime centre, and the worlds that they in turn brought with them to the south docks and Liverpool 8 areas, have been drawn into efforts to reposition post-world city Liverpool in the global economy of the twenty-first century.

Worlds of Connection, Worlds in Cities

Examining Liverpool's urban geographies through Malay lives, I advance three key sets of arguments in this book concerning the relational and territorial dimensions of cities, and historically sensitive ways of studying them.

The first concerns Liverpool's long-distance social webs or networks, and the wider geographies of connection with which they have been intertwined. Malay social webs spun in late colonial times not only exceeded formal political economic linkages, but also *preceded* globalization and *outlived* imperial world city Liverpool. The former is significant because it is specifically late twentieth-century forms of long-distance social relations that have given rise to the scholarly subfields of transnationalism and transnational urbanism. Some of the leading proponents of transnationalism have warned against its 'spurious extension' (Portes *et al.*, 1999: 219) to cover practices, processes and experiences that are already captured by prior concepts such as migration and assimilation.[11] Alejandro Portes and his colleagues emphasize the intensity, complexity and regularity of social contacts across national borders. While this would seem to delimit transnationalism to an era of globalization enabled by late twentieth-century technologies of transportation and communications, Portes *et al.* do also recognize important historical antecedents such as various trade diasporas and overseas commercial representatives. I contend that mid-twentieth-century maritime work made possible regular and sustained social connections between Liverpool and the Malay world that may be considered as one such example of transnationalism before the current era of globalization. What is more, this is an antecedent associated with colonial seafaring labour rather than with merchant diasporas or imperial administrative elites – what might thus be considered an historical form of 'transnationalism from below' (Smith and Guarnizo, 1998) or subaltern transnationalism (Featherstone, 2007).

Although the subsequent decline of the city's port undoubtedly meant that Liverpool became less relation-rich in commercial terms than during its time as a maritime world city, I show that economic and social connections to wider worlds have continued, albeit in often highly modified ways. With regard to social connections, this is partly due to advances in technologies of communication which, in addition to facilitating economic globalization and expanding possibilities for transnationalism in general, have made transnationalism from below much less dependent upon work-related mobilities. However, as I have already suggested, there is also evidence of post-world city forms of economic connectivity that have variously extended and transformed historical social webs. The diversity and historical variability of Liverpool's economic connections are important to urban and regional studies given that existing research on the city–economic globalization nexus has overwhelmingly focused on a very limited subset of economic activities, namely advanced producer services and associated 'world city' networks. Even as somewhere that is not a key node for advanced producer services (like most other cities around the world), Liverpool has continued to be remade through wider economic and associated social worlds of connection. Casting Liverpool more specifically as a 'post-world city', I show how interconnections associated with different historical periods and human mobilities overlap and entangle, such as when students from postcolonial Malaysia became active members of the Malay Club that was initially established by and for colonial seamen. Examination of Liverpool in this way contributes to work that extends the city–economic globalization nexus beyond the existing preoccupation with contemporary 'world cities' or 'global cities'. More significantly, I argue, my work serves to diversify the range of social as well as economic connections through which cities are understood to be co-constituted and worlded, drawing attention to ways in which multiple strands of transnational urban 'connective tissue' (McCann, 2010: 109) intertwine over time.

A second set of arguments follows on from this and has to do with the territorial grounding of transnational social webs or networks. I have noted that Ballantyne's insights into colonial social 'webs' did not include explicit consideration of the sites or places from which those webs were suspended (and which they, in turn, remade). The tendency for transnational discourse to focus on cross-border sociospatial relations rather than on the sites from or to which nation-state borders are crossed has been identified and subjected to critical scrutiny by geographers (see Mitchell, 1997; Featherstone *et al.*, 2007). When transnationalized worlds have been conceptually territorialized at all, this has tended to concern the abstract 'city' rather than any grounded site of urban social interaction. Brenda Yeoh and colleagues (2000: 149) were among the first to point out that the city needs to be understood instead as a 'space of transnational people flows anchored in and articulated with specific local urban geographies'. Michael Peter Smith's influential work on transnational urbanism has developed similar ideas by locating transnational social relations in translocally connected places (Smith, 2001, 2005; see also Collins, 2012). I argue that Malay transnational urban networks in Liverpool were anchored or locally grounded in the successive sites of the city's Malay Club, which were themselves located in particular areas of the city. The anchoring metaphor, of course, is particularly apt for the first location of the club in the south docks area as well as for the early years of its operation at 7 Jermyn Street – a period during which Liverpool remained a major seaport and when seafaring Malay mobilities connected the club to other maritime centres including in Southeast Asia and across the Atlantic to New York. Yet I show that 7 Jermyn Street continued to anchor Malay worlds of connection in postmaritime Liverpool, long after men such as Dol stopped working at sea.

Changes to the social composition of the Malay Club as the translocal place of Malay Liverpool reflected both wider political economic shifts and the life course trajectories of (ex-)seamen who had first arrived in the city at the tail end of its maritime pre-eminence. Liverpool-born descendants and family members of Malay seafarers became increasingly prominent at the club. While their growing presence could be viewed as evidence of localization or unworlding, children of Malay seamen experienced the club as a place to 'be Malay' and as a site of connection to Malay worlds. In later life, it was also where they could share stories about trips to *the* Malay world region (*alam Melayu*), not only with each other and with ex-seafaring men but also with non-seafaring Malay students and professionals who had travelled in the opposite direction. For the latter group, the Malay Club became a home away from their (independent nation-state) homes in Southeast Asia and a conduit for cultural, religious and political ideas from Malaysia. For a Malay-dominated Malaysian state that looked with envy at the economic successes of ethnic Indian and especially Chinese transnational communities, 7 Jermyn Street located a Malay diaspora in Liverpool. In addition, as city authorities in Liverpool sought to capitalize on post-maritime demographic diversity, Malaysian sojourners were well placed to mark the Malay community – sited/sighted at 7 Jermyn Street – on the map of the World in One City. In all these ways, and others explored in this book, I argue that the Malay Club was the site of Malay-ness in Liverpool and also anchored (diverse and historically shifting) translocal connections, particularly to the Malay world in Southeast Asia.

The third and final set of arguments has to do with what the lives of people who met at sites such as 7 Jermyn Street in Liverpool reveal about the relational (re)making of cities. Life histories and geographies can tell us not only about connections to other worlds and the urban territorial anchoring of those worldly connections, but also about multiple *worlds in cities*. Much has been made in urban studies over the past decade of a need to expand and diversify the range of cities that are drawn upon in urban theorization (Robinson, 2006; Roy, 2009). I argue that it is also time to diversify the range of lives and experiences drawn into relational studies of cities and the ways in which they are worlded (Simone, 2001). The recent burgeoning of work on how cities are remade through the circulation and mutation of urban policies in an era of neoliberal globalization has included examination of the human mobilities of policy experts (such as consultants, planners, architects and local government officials) as well as flows of policy discourses, imagery and plans. There have also been important calls to expand the range of 'policy actors' beyond expert professionals to include activists and even city residents in consideration of how policies are variously formulated, mobilized and territorialized (McCann and Ward, 2010: 175). Examination of ordinary people's often extraordinary life geographies extends relational urban worlds beyond policy domains altogether, and beyond consideration of *contemporary* connections. While a range of existing work unsettles notions of the novelty of neoliberal era policy mobilities, this is itself largely expert-centred, considering the worldly connections of municipal government figures, architects, planners, engineers and other professional actors (Saunier, 2002; King, 2004; Clarke, 2012). The memories and stories of 'non-expert' individuals, families and other social groupings constitute largely undocumented archives of everyday or subaltern forms of historical urban worlding. These are also *lived* archives of memory, not only yielding insights into connected geographies of a bygone era but also compelling consideration of how historical connections inhabit contemporary imaginings, practices and worlds in the city.

In a more explicitly methodological vein, I draw attention to the importance of insights into relational urban geographies that can be derived from *emplaced* lives, or from the lives of people in places. At first, this sounds counter-intuitive. One of the methodological mantras of recent relational urban scholarship, especially on policy mobilities, has been the importance of following things that (re)make cities across space. To the extent that this has mostly meant tracing 'back stories' of existing policy effects, the methodological next step appears to entail ethnographic presence in moments of relational urban remaking (Jacobs, 2012). Either way, there is a presumption that mobile and multi-sited methods are those most appropriate for, or equal to, the study of constitutively interconnected urban worlds. While I do not doubt the value of such methodological diversification, there is a danger that the current emphasis on mobile methods occludes continued possibilities for also examining 'cities in relation' (Söderström, 2014) from specific sites or places. In this book, the Malay Club forms an entry point to world-spanning historical urban interrelations and circulations. I demonstrate how examination of urban lives in and through places can open windows into unexpected constitutive connections across time as well as space. My grounded analysis exemplifies the historical openness of seemingly ordinary urban places to wider worlds (Massey, 1993), although 7 Jermyn Street, in turn, opened up worlds of multi-sited or at least 'distended' (Peck and Theodore, 2012) research possibility.

Sites and Routes of Fieldwork

I did not initially intend to focus my field research upon a particular urban locality. The original objective of the Malay Routes research project was to examine historically shifting connections between Liverpool and the *alam Melayu* through life histories and geographies of Malay ex-seamen. This was intended as a corrective to work in which imperial linkages are either evacuated of their human content (as merely lines on maritime maps, for example) or else narrated through the experiences of more privileged officer classes. The plan was to make contact with the 20 or so remaining Liverpool-based Malay ex-seamen during the lunch meetings that I knew were held at the Malay Club at 7 Jermyn Street on Wednesdays, and then to follow up with in-depth life story interviews elsewhere – possibly at their homes or even in a café or pub. Things did not work out that way, partly for the simple reason that few of the men whom I got to know during fieldwork in 2004 were interested or willing to meet with me beyond the club. Most of the interviews and conversations that I had with ex-seamen in this initial period of field-based research were limited to 7 Jermyn Street, either on Wednesday lunchtimes or during special events. As fieldwork in 2004 and over the subsequent three years remained more firmly anchored at 7 Jermyn Street than I had anticipated, so it soon became apparent that the Malay Club had long functioned – and continued to function – as a node in social networks extending to the *alam Melayu*. Research at 7 Jermyn Street came to include not only efforts to tap memories of colonial maritime routes and to trace associated historical 'lifepaths' (see Daniels and Nash, 2004), but also examination of varied forms of (re)connection with the *alam Melayu* and participant observation of unfolding local community dynamics.

The fact that much of my fieldwork took place at 7 Jermyn Street during Wednesday lunchtimes has shaped this book in other important ways. The first and most straightforward concerned the fact that only a handful of the ex-seafarers in and around Liverpool actually made it to Wednesday lunches on a regular basis, and some never attended at all. In addition to issues of age and frailty, personal disagreements and enmities kept some men away, except during social gatherings that followed funerals.[12] Of those who did attend Wednesday lunches on a regular basis, some were much more energetic and articulate than others, and it was their voices that tended to dominate public story-telling. Another significant point is that the majority of people who attended the lunchtime gatherings between 2004 and 2007 were not ex-seafarers at all, but either their British descendants or student sojourners from Southeast Asia (particularly Malaysia). Some of these men and women became much more important to my research than I anticipated, both as sources of knowledge about ex-seamen and as translocal subjects in their own right. If during the maritime era the Malay Club had been a place of social interaction among locally based and visiting Malay seamen, by 2004 their non-seafaring descendants and Malaysian students interconnected Liverpool and Southeast Asia in a more diverse range of material and affective ways. Their very presence at the club also had implications for the stories told there by ex-seamen.

Given that most Malay seafarers who stayed in Liverpool married local women, and few children or grandchildren of Liverpool-based ex-seafarers are Malay-language speakers, public narration was often left to those men who were most comfortable conversing in English. Meanwhile, the presence of mostly ethnic Malay students – women as well as men – meant that lunchtime conversation tended to avoid topics sensitive to contemporary performances and expectations of Malay-ness in Malaysia.[13]

In the early stages of my research, I made a point of trying to interview ex-seamen at the club before or after lunchtime when fewer students and family members were present. For the most part, this meant joining or initiating conversations – either in English or in Malay, or a mixture of the two languages – rather than conducting more formal, one-to-one life history interviewing of the kind that I had originally envisaged. Nonetheless, these moments opened up a range of topics of conversation that would not have been aired in the less staunchly masculinist lunchtime setting. My gender positionality, as much as my knowledge of Southeast Asia and Britain, shaped the extent to which I was able to join conversations and to steer them towards preferred topics or specific details. Often, detailed questions were spurred by findings from archival or other documentary sources, while conversation at the Malay Club in turn prompted further archival forays in search of verification or elaboration.[14] As my research progressed, however, I became less concerned with attempting to direct conversation and correspondingly more content to collect fragments of life histories and geographies that emerged from the regular flow of chatting and storytelling at the Malay Club. Of course, notes taken from conversations and observation of storytelling at the club raise important wider issues of privacy and confidentiality that would not have arisen had my methods been limited to formal interviews and archival research. Although everyone at the club knew why I was there, and I was never deliberately covert in taking notes or photographs, over time I blended in and, in the flow of conversation, it is entirely possible that people forgot about my documenting presence. In cases where there was any ambiguity about informed consent to use information concerning specific individuals in my work - whether that information was obtained from the club or elsewhere - I have referred to them only by their nicknames.[15]

The club featured in my research not only as a means of tapping into individual historical experience but also as a site in and through which: (1) memories and life stories were actively produced and reproduced; and (2) individual and collective memory intertwined. Memories are at once personal and social. Social collectivities such as the people who gathered at the Malay Club variously structure, mediate, censor or silence memories (Chamberlain and Leydesdorff, 2004). Prevailing forms of social interaction thus shaped fragments of life stories narrated at the club. It is partly because 7 Jermyn Street was a social space in this way that the site can be understood as having played a constitutive role in (re)producing individual and collective memory. Not only did the presence of particular faces direct individual recollections to collective experiences ('remember that time when we …'), but assembled audiences often played a more active part in variously disputing or elaborating others' stories. In one case, a Singapore-born man whose supposedly faulty recollection of his time at sea in the 1960s was publicly corrected in the club narrated a suitably updated 'memory' to me later the same day.[16] In other cases, it was not voices or other human stimuli that appeared to be at work. Smells or aromas, especially from the kitchen, often prompted recollections, while artefacts and even the decor were enrolled into stories and conversation.[17] In other words, through the co-presence of ex-seafarers with overlapping life geographies, the expectations of Malaysian students and family members who came to lunch, and even through the role of non-human stimuli – not to mention my own inquisitive presence – 7 Jermyn Street (re)shaped memories and gave rise to particular performances of self and collective identification. In the words of Dolores Hayden (1995: 43), 'places make memories cohere in complex ways.'

The Malay Club was a place that sustained a *community*, though some qualification is required concerning my use of that term in this book. What has emerged from my research at 7 Jermyn Street cannot in any straightforward sense be cast as the history of Liverpool's 'Malay community'. As I have already described, not all Malay ex-seamen living in or around Liverpool attended the club. In addition, I met a handful of people at the club – ex-seamen as well as people with no direct connection to seafaring – who did not include 'Malay' among their range of self-identifications. It is perhaps more accurate to conceptualize the Malay Club as a place which assembled people with various overlapping identity traits (most notably material and imagined ties to the *alam Melayu*) into a 'polythetic' (Clifford, 1997: 44) grouping[18] than it is to envisage 7 Jermyn Street – as I initially did – as a way 'into' a pre-existing ethnic Malay community.[19] Even among the ex-seafaring generation who met up at 7 Jermyn Street, what might conventionally be assumed to be ethnic (i.e. Malay) social networks may be examined more precisely in terms of spatial practices of friendship (Bunnell *et al.*, 2012).[20] Just as friendships sustained over many decades brought Malay men to the Malay Club, long-held animosities kept others away. Jermyn Street-centred friendship networks included 'mates' who would not ordinarily identify as Malay, as well as *kawan* (lit. friends) who would. Even allowing for the historical porosity and mutability of the boundaries of Malayness,[21] the 'community' assembled through 7 Jermyn Street was clearly more-than-Malay.

Particularly significant for my research was recognition that the Malay Club was bound up with the *ongoing* (re)making of a 'community', both as part of urban and social transformations in Liverpool and through transnational linkages. The pilot visit to 7 Jermyn Street during which I first met Dol coincided with a meeting concerning a community funding application that had been submitted to a local charitable organization. At the time, my interest in attending the meeting was primarily as an opportunity to talk with a Malay ex-seaman as well as to glean historical information about what was referred to as the 'Malaysian and Singapore community' from the funding application material. I soon came to see such material more critically, as active components of discursive processes of urban community making. The role of Malaysian students, in particular, in these processes gave them clear transnational and postcolonial dimensions. Students from Malaysia drew upon modes of presenting ethnocultural difference that are a taken-for-granted part of the sociopolitical landscape of Malaysia. In the context of contemporary Liverpool, however, it was also important that in applications for various forms of social funding – from local government agencies looking to work through community groups, as well as from charitable organizations – explicit mention was made of 7 Jermyn Street. This located the community in the neighbourhood of Granby Toxteth (as the surrounding electoral ward was officially known in 2003), conferring eligibility for forms of social funding, even though the residential addresses of its diverse members were much more spatially dispersed. In my research, the Malay Club was thus not only the *site* of social events that could be examined ethnographically, but also came to feature as somewhere that *sighted* and was *cited* as a locus of community – a visible spatial reference point that itself performed something in the discursive construction of a fundable, neighbourhood-based community.

Individual subjectivities were also much more 'in-the-making' than I initially appreciated. In part, this had to do with the kinds of performances of cultural identity that were necessary to secure and justify funding (the other side of which was marginalization from community events of ex-seamen who were unable or unwilling to realize themselves in such ways). More generally, however, subjectivities continue to be (re)made throughout the life course. One of the misjudgements that I made in the original planning of my research was to imagine elderly ex-seamen as occupying settled subject positions, offering fixed vantage points from which to look back upon and narrate their historical seafaring lifepaths. Of course, as long as life goes on, one's own past appears and is remembered in shifting ways. Some of the men whom I met at the Malay Club were also more eager to talk about their most recent bus trips around the northwest of England or journeys 'back' to Malaysia or Singapore than they were to try to dredge up faded details of maritime routes and experiences from half a century ago.[22] At first I treated this as part of a frustrating layer of conversation that had to be worked through in order to reach memories of world city Malay routes and historical connections. Yet this is an attitude that I came to see as incompatible with the spirit of my wider research intentions. In a project conceived to foreground the lives of Malay seafarers as part of Liverpool's constitutive connections, I was ignoring the ongoing life geographies of these men (and of other women as well as men who attended the club). Extension of the project beyond mid-twentieth-century maritime networks was thus bound up with restoration of ex-seamen's contemporary agency and my awareness of their ongoing subjectification as part of both transnational and highly localized urban social worlds.

My growing interest in the continuing lives of elderly ex-seamen in Liverpool and the development of strong social ties with a range of Malay Club attendees – Malaysian students and British descendants of Malay seafarers, as well as a handful of the ex-seamen – gave rise to ethnographic engagements 'back' in Southeast Asia as well as elsewhere in the city. Although multi-sited research can be expensive and time-consuming, for me, living and working Singapore, it was invariably easier and cheaper to meet with ex-seamen and their visiting family members in sites in Singapore or Malaysia, or even in Indonesia, than it was to conduct further fieldwork in Liverpool. I knew from interviews and conversations at the club that return trips to Southeast Asia had been highly transformative for Malay men who had lived or been based in Liverpool since the 1950s or 1960s.[23] Joining family reunions in Malacca (Melaka), Kuala Lumpur and Singapore gave me access to sites of subjectification and memory production that I had previously only been able to infer from a distance. Just as the Malay Club in Liverpool gave rise to certain individual and collective memories, so alternative surroundings, and the presence of different people, fomented other kinds of memories. In particular, as might be expected, I learned much more about pre-departure periods in the lives of ex-seamen. This enlivened my understanding of histories and geographies of Liverpool's maritime world city linkages with colonial Southeast Asia, which had previously been much more reliant upon secondary and (documentary) archival sources, and allowed me to read aspects of those archives in new ways. Meeting up with ex-seamen, their family members and even Malaysian (ex-)students in Malaysia also allowed me to catch up on developments in Liverpool, especially on news about the position of the club and 'community' in urban regeneration processes.

Finally, the position of the Malay Club in my increasingly distended research also changed because of developments in Liverpool. During field research up to 2007 the club was the key site for me to join conversations about ex-seafarers' forthcoming trips to Southeast Asia – sometimes planned with assistance and advice from Malaysian students who were familiar with the route from Liverpool to Kuala Lumpur or Singapore via Manchester airport – as well as about experiences of recently completed trips. I shuttled between diverse archival sources and 7 Jermyn Street, bringing documents and photographs as well as lots of questions to the club. However, a combination of dwindling numbers of first-generation ex-seafarers, uncertainty over the future of the housing stock in and around Jermyn Street, and the handover of leadership of the club to a Malaysian man with little time to devote to its day-to-day running, meant that 7 Jermyn Street opened less frequently from 2006. When I began six months of sabbatical leave in Liverpool in 2008 the club had closed down altogether. My research, which had previously been sited in 7 Jermyn Street but not explicitly about it thus inverted, having become substantively about Liverpool's Malay Club (and the people who had met up there) but no longer conducted within its walls. By this time, I had a sufficiently wide network of friends and informants in the city to conduct further primary research beyond Jermyn Street, and other sites of research assumed prominence in my fieldwork.[24] Subsequent interviews and conversations with ex-seamen, their family members and (ex-)students included coverage of the club's historically shifting sociospatial position in Liverpool and as part of social networks extending to the *alam Melayu*: from the late colonial maritime period that had brought Malay seamen to one-time world city Liverpool through to a twenty-first-century era of culture-led urban regeneration.

Organization of the Book

Just as the journey of my fieldwork involved unexpected sites and routes, this is not the book that I expected to emerge from the Malay Routes project. While I planned to conduct fieldwork in Liverpool in order to uncover the city's historical maritime connections with Southeast Asia, my ethnographic research became at once more spatially confined (mostly to 7 Jermyn Street) and more geographically extensive (through meetings and participation in events in Malaysia, Singapore and Indonesia). Both the territorial and relational dimensions of the book are, in turn, different from what was planned or anticipated. In territorial terms, while the city of Liverpool remains a significant frame of analysis, neighbourhood and, of course, place or site are also very important. Meanwhile, examination of Malay Liverpool over a period of more than half a century brings into play imperial, transatlantic, national and even supranational framings. In relational terms, the book is, above all, less maritime oriented than I had anticipated in my original research proposal. The past decade has seen a blossoming of work which contests the 'terracentricity' of academic history and geography, bringing into view alternative interoceanic paradigms and 'seascapes' (e.g. Bentley *et al.*, 2007; Anderson and Peters, 2014). Life geographies of Malay men in Liverpool who worked at sea and who inhabited worlds along sea lanes and highways clearly speak to this field. However, my coverage of maritime linkages is concerned more with the territorial urban geographies and club sites that anchored Malay social networks than it is with 'watery worlds' (Wigen, 2007: 1) per se. In addition, equally prominent in the book are the non-seaborne travels and connections of ex-seamen, their family members and Malaysian students.

The seven main chapters that follow are organized in broadly chronological terms, beginning from the tail end of the era during which Liverpool was a prominent imperial maritime and commercial centre – a world city. The next chapter traces the shipping routes that connected the *alam Melayu* to Liverpool, positioning the city and seafaring Malay men in world-spanning commercial and social webs. In Chapter 3 I focus down onto the social geography of Liverpool as 'home port' to men from the *alam Melayu* with varying degrees of attachment to the city. This is followed by three chapters set in the context of Liverpool's repositioning in the new international division of labour and in relation to the concomitant political economic development of independent nation states in Southeast Asia. Chapter 4 examines changes to the social composition and transnational connections of the Malay Club on Jermyn Street associated with the post-independence remaking of territories of the former British Malaya and Liverpool's interrelated post-maritime economic transformation. In Chapter 5 I consider Liverpool as a destination for students, tourists and diaspora seekers from nation states in Southeast Asia as they became more affluent and, especially in the case of Malaysia, increasingly concerned with transnational Malayness. 'Return' journeys of Liverpool-based ex-seafarers to emergent centres of urban modernity in Southeast Asia form the focus of Chapter 6. Attention then turns to recent and ongoing culture-led urban regeneration strategies in Liverpool, particularly its rebranding as 'the World in One City'. I analyse opportunities for Liverpool-based Malaysian students to make Malay(sian)s visible and fundable in the context of community-led urban governance regimes (Chapter 7). Chapter 8 details local celebration of *Merdeka* (Malaysian independence) in two events intended to heighten community visibility in the lead up to Liverpool's year as European capital of culture.

I conclude the book by revisiting the main arguments and comparative contributions of the study. I also consider what Liverpool's status as the European capital of culture in 2008 implied for Malays based in the city and for the Liverpool 8 area in which the Malay Club was located. The year 2008 marks the end of a period of well over half a century across which I have sought to trace Liverpool's Malay worlds of connection. In that this period extends back to before the Second World War, the book may be said to contribute to work which unsettles conceptions of the war marking the beginning of multiethnic Britain. However, like official proponents of the world in one city, I am more concerned with Liverpool – or, in my case, particular parts of that city – and its constitutive connections than with national-scale imaginings or framings. It might even be suggested that this book contributes to the work of imag(in)ing Liverpool as 'the world in one city' by drawing attention to yet another of its ethnocultural groups and associated more-than-national connections. While I certainly hope that readers interested in the historical presence of Malays in Liverpool (and Britain more widely) will find informative material in the eight chapters that follow, 'the World in One City' is in fact among their objects of critical analysis. In Liverpool, as elsewhere, civic interest and investment in historical diasporic linkages have been skewed to what are perceived to be profitable pathways of (re)connection. In commercial terms, there is probably little to be gained from consideration of Liverpool's Malay world connections or of the sites that anchored them. But tracing them, as I do in this book, provides important insights into the often overlooked relational constitution of urban places and social lives.

Notes

1 Notes from conversation, 5 December 2003. It is impossible to establish precise numbers, not least because of the varying degrees of attachment of Malay men in Liverpool to the city or Britain more widely. When men such as Dol recall there having been 'hundreds' of Malay men in Liverpool in the 1950s, this certainly must have included men who were using the city as a seafaring base and men passing through the city on a regular basis (without necessarily ever subsequently settling in the city). The presence of many such men, of course, is unlikely to have been captured on electoral registers or census reports. The 1961 census for Lancashire records 63 males born in the Federation of Malaya and 66 born in Singapore, but these figures would have

included children of 'white' British parents who were based in those colonial territories (as perhaps evidenced by the fact that 34 and 24 females are recorded as having been born in those respective territories). If the difference between male and female numbers is taken as an indicator of non-white male migrants, the total is 71; and this is for the whole of Lancashire (which at that time included the city of Manchester). In the postwar period during which Dol arrived, it may have felt as though there were 'hundreds' of Malays in the city – and at particular moments, depending upon the timing of when ships with Malay crews arrived, there may well have been. As the number of ships and Malay crew diminished from the 1960s, however, the number of men rooted to Liverpool through citizenship choices (i.e. becoming a citizen of the UK rather than of what became the independent nation states of Malaysia or Singapore) and/or family commitments never reached three figures.

2 Formal colonies, protectorates and dominions that were coloured pink on maps of the British Empire (see Harley, 1988). I follow Haggerty *et al.* (2008) in considering 'imperial' connections that extended beyond such territories of formal control to include wider commercial reach or influence.

3 In work on Liverpool, Herson (2008: 68) notes, 'Liverpool's minority populations were highly visible in the localities they frequented, and their foreign compatriots who, as sailors, hit town in search of entertainment, drink and women accentuated their apparent presence'. However, 'in sheer numbers it was small in relation to the city as a whole'. As such, it is perhaps fair to suggest that experience of 'cosmopolitan' Liverpool was confined to specific parts of the city.

4 Neither geographical delimitation nor naming of the 'area' that I am referring to is straightforward. As is noted below, the 'riots' that took place on some of the adjacent streets in 1981 were located in 'Toxteth' in national media coverage. However, this toponym does not appear to have been widely used by people living in the locality concerned and, for some, denoted other nearby, and distinctly 'white' neighbourhoods (see Frost and Phillips, 2011: 68). One scholar has used the term 'Granby Toxteth' (Uduku, 2003) and I considered employing this toponym to denote a more spatially delimited area around Granby Street. The problem here is that 'Granby Toxteth' was the official name of a short-lived electoral ward which no longer exists and, even more so than 'Toxteth', was never adopted as a place name by people who actually live(d) there. 'Liverpool 8', taken originally from postal code demarcations of space, is a more established term and has also been employed by local black and minority ethnic group activists. I have decided to use the term Liverpool 8 in this book. As in its everyday usage, this does not imply strict adherence to postal code mappings, however, not least because that would include Dingle, a 'white, Protestant, close-knit community with the reputation of being racist' (Hall, 2003: 205). Parts of the south docks also have an L8 postcode so the dockside areas that I am distinguishing from Liverpool 8 are contiguous and have no clear or fixed limits. 'Liverpool 8' is an area with blurred boundaries and of shifting territorial scope, but one historically centred upon Granby Street, the main commercial thoroughfare for black and minority ethnic Liverpool after the Second World War.

5 'Liverpool: port, docks and city', *Illustrated London News*, 15 May 1886.

6 Interview with Joan and Kevin Higgins, Liverpool, 12 September 2004. The house on Upper Huskisson Street where Joan's father Youp bin Baba (Ben Youp) lived functioned informally as a boarding house for Malay seafarers (see Chapter 3).

7 It should be noted, however, that the large proportion of boarded-up houses in the vicinity had at least as much to do with city council housing policy as it was a reflection of wider urban or regional economic 'decline' (see Chapter 8).

8 The light that Edward Said (1993) casts upon empire's 'overlapping territories' and 'intertwined histories' illuminates connections between metropolis and periphery in terms of cultural production rather than through examination of the lived presence and experiences of colonial peoples. Historical geography scholarship on imperial cities, meanwhile, gives more attention to urban landscapes, form and design than it does to the lives and agency of colonial people in the 'cross-mappings between empire and the modern European city' (Driver and Gilbert, 1999: 3). In Anthony D. King's work on the emergence of London as global city, he notes that 'there were relatively few if any members of the peripheral, colonial population in the city' (1990: 64). Although he does identify some exceptions, and even makes mention of Malays in the city, these figures are marginal to his analysis of a colonial mode of production and division of labour that 'kept colonial peoples and institutions distanced from the core' (p. 38). Subsequent postcolonial urban scholarship, which does give more attention to the place of former colonial people in the making and marketing of London (Jacobs, 1996), assumes that their presence at this urban 'edge of empire' began with postwar migration.

9 The focus of Mbembe and Nuttall's own work is on African cities' 'embeddedness in multiple elsewheres' (p. 348).

10 Lawton (1964) notes that by some estimates Liverpool accounted for one-seventh of the world's registered shipping in 1913.

11 As these authors quite reasonably point out, 'if all or most things that immigrants do are defined as "transnationalism", then none is because the term becomes synonymous with the total set of experiences of this population' (Portes *et al.*, 1999: 219).

12 Funerals brought people together as a community but, with the passing of each ex-seafarer, the first-generation community members also dwindled further (see Chapter 8).

13 This was particularly the case for alcohol consumption and other 'un-Islamic' practices.

14 Key archival and documentary sources are listed at the end of the book. Full citation details are provided in endnotes.

15 This makes them identifiable to others 'within' the group that assembled at 7 Jermyn Street and associated social networks, but not to a wider public. Dol is one example. I expected the brief set of questions that I asked him when we met in December 2003 to be a prelude to a more

detailed, formal and voice-recorded interview which never transpired. This also raises the issue of what constitutes an interview as opposed to a conversation or a chat. Clearly the boundary is blurred, especially in contexts where there are third (sometimes fourth and fifth) parties in attendance and where it is difficult to plan formal meetings in advance. I use the term 'interview' to refer to that subset of my conversations that were largely dyadic, face-to-face and voice-recorded. I was able to interview eight *alam Melayu*-born ex-seamen in Liverpool, some on multiple occasions (in one case, five separate times), mostly at 7 Jermyn Street. A list of the *alam Melayu*-born men who feature most prominently in (and, in some cases, across) subsequent chapters, and a brief summary of their lifepaths, is provided at the end of the book. The list includes one man who did not attend the club during the time that I was in Liverpool (although he had done so in previous decades) and four men whom I never met in person at all as they had died before I started my fieldwork. In the latter cases, I have constructed their life geographies from the recollections of family members, friends and acquaintances and archival sources.

16 Hashim, who boasted that his memory is 'like a computer', was the man who contested the memory of another ex-seafarer from Singapore (fieldnotes from conversation at 7 Jermyn Street, 14 October 2006).

17 As Delores Hayden (1995: 18) writes: 'If place does provide an overload of possible meanings for the researcher, it is place's very same assault on all ways of knowing (sight, sound, smell, touch and taste) that makes it powerful as a source of memory, as a weave where one strand ties in another'.

18 The individuals concerned had many shared and overlapping characteristics but no one of those characteristics was necessary or sufficient for group membership.

19 I was certainly guilty at the outset of my research of looking through the kind of 'ethnic lens' that scholars such as Glick Schiller and Çağlar (2009: 184) have cautioned against: 'migrants from a particular nation-state or region are assumed to constitute an ethnic group before their identity, actions, social relations and beliefs are studied'. The danger of employing a term such as 'quasi-community', of course, is that it suggests the existence of other, more internally coherent and unified ('real') communities. As such, I continue to use the term 'community' albeit often in scare quotes.

20 On dangers of the 'ethnic lens' more generally, see Glick Schiller and Çağlar (2009). Glick Schiller and Çağlar have highlighted a tendency for diaspora or transnational migration studies to presume internal coherence and commonality among co-ethnics, thereby obscuring transethnic social relations and underspecifying a diverse range of intraethnic social relations (see also Glick Schiller *et al.*, 2006; Glick Schiller and Çağlar, 2011).

21 Even within the *alam Melayu*, Malay-ness is recognized as a historically 'contested and wandering identity' (Barnard and Maier, 2004: ix). The geographically dispersed origins of the men in my study – mostly from what

are today Malaysia and Singapore but, in a smaller number of cases, from coastal parts of Indonesia – means that even before leaving the *alam Melayu* they may be expected to have had diverse understandings of, and relations to, '*Melayu*' or 'Malay'.

22 Fadzil Mohamed, for example, said that he used to travel the world on ships, but had come to travel the world on buses, with his bus pass (notes from conversation, Liverpool, 25 July 2009). The use of scare quotes around 'back' (to Malaysia) is in acknowledgement of the geopolitical changes that took place during the period when men such as Fadzil were based in Liverpool. They could go 'back' to territories that had become the nation state of Malaysia, but that political entity did not exist when they 'left'.

23 Those who returned to what had become the nation state of Malaysia in particular were often immersed in Islamized contemporary expectations of what it means to be a 'good Malay' (Chapter 6) – expectations that were also in line with the Malay subject articulated by Malaysian students in Liverpool in their community-making discourse (Chapter 8).

24 Two such sites are worthy of note. First, 182 Boaler Street, home to the Malaysian graduate student Sharidah Sharif and her family, had become a hub for Malaysian visitors to Liverpool as well as for Malaysian students based in the city. A second, shifting set of sites were cafés in Liverpool city centre where Fadzil Mohamed met with members of his family for breakfast on Saturday mornings. Two of Fadzil's children, Farida and Paul, were as eager to learn about their father's life as I was. There emerged a collaborative process of assembling fragments of Fadzil's life stories, tapping our very different knowledge to draw out different strands of Fadzil's memory and experience.

2

From the Malay World to the Malay Atlantic

[T]he days of the far flung routes of Zamboanga and Moulmein, to Bangkok and Banjermassin are but a dream, and linger merely in the memories of old men.

K.G. Tregonning, circa 1960[1]

The city of Liverpool may be one of the capitals of a long Atlantic twentieth century, but it is not the only such city. There are several. London is one. New York is another.

Ian Baucom (2005: 35)

The seafaring labour of Malay men sustained shipping networks that connected world city Liverpool to coastal settlements across a dispersed and ethnically diverse Malay world region (*alam Melayu*) in Southeast Asia, as well as to a wider world of port towns and cities. I begin this chapter by tracing back the life geographies of Liverpool-based ex-seamen in order to examine Malay seafaring mobilities in British colonial Southeast Asia and the surrounding islands and seas of the *alam Melayu*. Singapore was the hub for shipping networks in the region and an interface with wider oceanic routes. It was here that the Ocean Steamship Company of Liverpool located its regional headquarters. Interoceanic trade connections from Singapore to port cities along the east coast of the United States, in particular, expanded from the last decades of the nineteenth century. In the second section of the chapter

From World City to the World in One City: Liverpool through Malay Lives,
First Edition. Tim Bunnell.

I show how Malays and other *lascars* (Indian Ocean seafarers) followed commodities such as rubber along associated networks of commerce. The founder of Liverpool's Malay Club moved to the city from New York, not directly from the *alam Melayu.* Seafaring work enabled Malay men to spin webs of social connection not only between the *alam Melayu* and Liverpool, but also between Liverpool and other major Atlantic port cities, especially New York.

World City Liverpool in the *Alam Melayu*

In 2004 Majid was the quiet man at Liverpool's Malay Club on Jermyn Street. I can still picture him in the brown armchair next to the window of the front room, gazing at snooker on television. My suspicion was that he was half-watching while half-listening to other, much more animated, ex-seamen recounting their colourful life stories. Unlike me, Majid had no doubt heard them all before. Well into his eighties, he did not talk much in either Malay or English, but I was gradually able to piece together Majid's life geography, including seafaring travels that extended back further than those of the more talkative septuagenarians at the club. Majid was born in 1917 in the village (*kampung* or *kampong*) of Serkam, Malacca.[2] By the time he was old enough to go to sea in the 1930s, there was a well-established tradition of young men from the village working for the Straits Steamship Company which was headquartered in Singapore. More than three-quarters of the Malay men in the company's service came from Serkam and 'other kampongs behind Malacca' (Tregonning, 1967: 88). According to K.G. Tregonning, in his official history of the Straits Steamship Company, *Home Port Singapore*, '[a]mong the Malays, in particular, a tradition of service built up from 1890 onwards. Son followed father, and generation succeeded generation of Straits Steamship Company men.' Majid's village, 'on the main trunk road to Singapore', is noted as 'one particular kampong where this family tradition of Straits service was maintained' (p. 88). Sadly, Tregonning does not tell us how the tradition began. It may well be that he was simply unable to find out. Most official documentation on the Straits Steamship Company was destroyed during the Japanese occupation of Singapore during the Second World War. As such, Tregonning's comment that 'far flung routes ... linger merely in the memories of old men'[3] was not only a statement about historical changes to regional transport linkages, but also an acknowledgement of the methodological difficulty of researching them.

What is not in doubt is that operations of the Straits Steamship Company formed part of a broader expansion of British commerce in Malaya from the late nineteenth century. The three British territories of

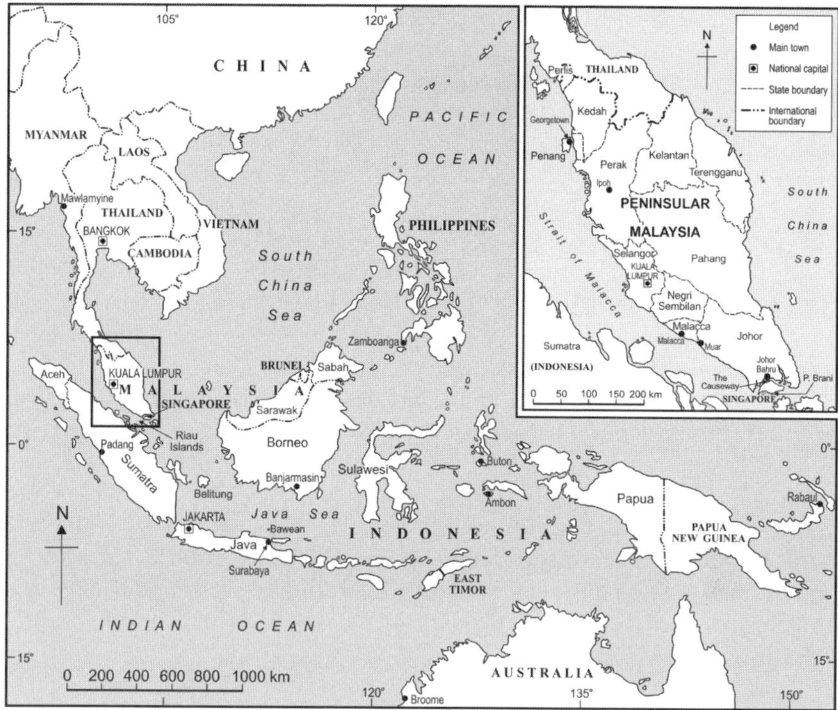

Figure 2.1 The Malay peninsula and the wider Malay world region (*alam Melayu*). Produced by Lee Li Kheng.

Penang, Singapore and Malacca (see Figure 2.1) were controlled by the East India Company and consolidated as the Straits Settlements in 1826. When the Straits Settlements became a Crown colony in 1867, control was transferred from Calcutta to the Colonial Office in London. This meant that the governor of the Straits Settlements in Singapore and leading merchants were able to press London more effectively for a 'new policy of intervention' (Federation of Malaya, 1956: 472). The Straits Settlements became administrative bases from which the tentacles of British colonial rule and commerce found their way into adjacent peninsular territories. The Malay states of Perak, Selangor, Negeri Sembilan and Pahang came under British 'protection' between 1874 and 1888. By 1895 they were conjoined administratively as the Federated Malay States (FMS). Singapore-based Straits Steamship Company vessels were among the so-called 'mosquito fleet' of small coastal ships taking tin ingots to the smelter on Pulau Brani (Brani Island), off Singapore. Malacca was not prominent in this trade, but continued to form part of the Straits Steamship Company's operations along the west coast of the Malay peninsula. The Straits Steamship Company opened an office in Malacca after the First World War (Jackson and Wurtzburg, 1952), and Malay deck crew and quartermasters from villages such as Serkam were prominent in networks of coastal commerce (Tomlinson, 1950).[4] By the time Majid came to work for the Straits Steamship Company, its ships operating out of Johnston's Pier in Singapore plied regular routes carrying hundreds of deck passengers on routes stretching '1000 miles in all directions'.[5] The Straits Steamship Company's fleet, and the seafaring labour of men such as Majid, 'had played a major part both in opening up the Malay States and in placing Singapore in a pre-eminent position as a regional trade centre'.

Through companies such as the Straits Steamship Company, British colonialism was accompanied not only by increased commercial activity but also by new possibilities for people to move across the region (Kahn, 2006: 37). This is certainly not to suggest that regional mobilities and networks started with late-nineteenth-century British colonial commerce. While the Straits Steamship Company may have afforded new opportunities for maritime employment, seafaring traditions were well established long before the company's formation in 1890. More widely, as Joel S. Kahn (2006: 37) puts it,

> before the advent of modern colonial rule, ordinary Malays inhabited a transborder world which encompassed dispersed territories in Singapore, British Malaya, parts of the Netherlands East Indies (Riau, Sumatra, parts of Borneo), the southern islands of the Philippines, southern Siam and parts of Indochina, across which large numbers of peoples who came to be classified as Malay moved relatively freely and more or less continuously.

The British 'forward movement' had three main regional implications. The first, referred to by Kahn, concerned the possibility for a diversity of 'archipelagic groups' coming to British Malaya – 'Acehnese, Minangkabau and Mandailing from Sumatra, Banjarese from Borneo, and Bugis from Sulawesi (The Celebes)' (p. 65) – to become 'Malays'. Under British rule and administrative practices during the twentieth century, the term came to signify an ethnic grouping of Muslim people, 'sufficiently homogeneous that they could be readily distinguished from the other two main races of colonial Malaya, namely the Chinese and the Indians' (p. 47). Second, long-established Malay world networks – social, cultural and religious as well as economic – became entwined with the routes and schedules of British commerce. The list of Straits Steamship Company ships departing from Johnston's Pier to 'ports of call with fascinating names' (Tomlinson, 1950: 29), for example, gave commercial regularity and colonial administrative legibility to routes across the *alam Melayu*. Third, colonial expansion served to centre Malay world networks more firmly upon British Malaya and, in particular, Singapore. Not only did the island flourish as a 'staple port' with the expansion of tin and rubber production in the Malay peninsula (Huff, 1994) but, during the period between the 1920s and 1950s, Singapore became 'the commercial, political, religious and cultural/intellectual hub of the modern Malay World' (Kahn, 2006: xvi).

Cultural and especially religious motivations for travelling along routes to or through Singapore often had important commercial dimensions. Perhaps the clearest example concerns Muslim pilgrimage. In an era prior to the take-off of commercial jet travel in the 1960s, Muslims from across the region came to Singapore to take ships to Jeddah. Singapore was the 'pilgrim hub'. 'From [what became] Peninsular Malaysia they came from towns and villages in Johore; from as far north as the state of Selangor, and as far away as Kelantan in the north-east. But there would also be others from different parts of Indonesia, and from Sabah and Sarawak, drawn often by the reputations of a particular *sheikh haji* who was known to their community' (Green, 2006: 21). Many would-be pilgrims did not get any further than Singapore, becoming merely *Haji Singapura* (and perhaps 'Malay' in the process). In the case of Boyanese (from the island of Bawean in the Java Sea), who were 'not traditionally a seafaring people', the first migrants to Singapore were said to have been pilgrims who stayed in Singapore on their way to Mecca. The intention was to work in Singapore 'for enough money to enable them to continue their voyage to the holy land' (Vredenbregt, 1964: 117).[6] Of those who did board ships to Jeddah, many never made it back to Singapore. Jaafar Mohamad, a self-described 'Singapore Malay' of Boyanese ancestry, worked as a cook on board a pilgrim ship called the *Tyndareus* in the 1950s. Most of the pilgrims during that time were elderly and they took white burial clothes (*kain kafan*) with them (Green, 2006). Jaafar recalled the large numbers of elderly pilgrims who died on board each day.[7] Yet despite the high mortality rate, tens of thousands of pilgrims from the *alam Melayu* passed through Singapore twice – that is, during outward and return journeys – as part of their once-in-a-lifetime religious voyages (see Tagliacozzo, 2013). For the shipping companies concerned, these religious journeys were big business.

The carriage of *hajj* passengers to the port of Jeddah provides an example of Liverpool's commercial involvement in the *alam Melayu*. The *Tyndareus* on which Jaafar worked in the 1950s followed a long list of Liverpool-registered ships involved in the pilgrim trade from

Singapore (and Penang). Perhaps the most famous pilgrim ship to have operated on this route was the fictional SS *Patna* in Joseph Conrad's novel *Lord Jim* which was based around actual events on board the SS *Jeddah*. After a large leak was sprung in bad weather, the British captain and officers abandoned hundreds of pilgrim passengers, only for the ship to be towed to safety. Although the *Jeddah* was not a Liverpool-owned ship (Sherry, 1966), during the period when it set sail from Singapore to Jeddah via Penang in July 1880, Blue Funnel Line ships of Liverpool's Alfred Holt and Company were already operating pilgrim ship services on this route (Hyde, 1957). The 'pilgrim trade' was of course seasonal, but the distinctive Blue Funnel Line vessels would have been a familiar sight among the diverse ships in the harbour at Singapore throughout the year. One visitor in 1879 described Singapore as the 'Liverpool of the East' (Burbidge, 1880: 14). However, merely to liken the two ports is perhaps to obscure the role that Liverpool shipping companies and merchants played in Malay world commerce centred on Singapore – and, by extension, in the commercial development of Singapore itself.

Liverpool merchants played a prominent role in inserting Singapore into regular steamship services to Europe and beyond. Agency houses with links in Liverpool had been attracted to Singapore from the 1820s when growing trade between China and India first established the island as a significant transshipment centre (Falkus, 1990: 89). Singapore's position as the main regional port of call for oceangoing ships owed much to its gateway location between the Indian Ocean and the South China Sea. While the Sunda Straits had the same geographical advantage, the development of steamships in the mid-nineteenth century favoured the route through the Straits of Malacca to Singapore; steamships required coal and so needed to stay close to shore (Huff, 1994: 8). The Peninsular and Oriental Steam Navigation Company (P&O) steamship the *Hindustan*, which entered into service between India and Suez in 1842, had its route extended to Singapore two years later (Lawson, 1927). According to one shipping history, however, as far as direct metropolitan routes were concerned, 'the credit for the first regular steamship service to the Far East is due to one Liverpool man alone – Alfred Holt' (Chandler, 1960: 212). Holt's three pioneer vessels in the China trade, *Agamemnon*, *Ajax* and *Achilles*, travelled from Liverpool round the Cape to Mauritius (8,500 miles or 13,680 km non-stop), then to Penang, Singapore, Hong Kong and Shanghai. The opening of the Suez Canal in 1869 made the eastern trade more attractive to steamships and 'enabled the sea journey from England to be completed in 42 days instead of 116' (Federation of Malaya, 1956). By the mid-1870s, 14 of Holt's Blue Funnel Line vessels carried goods right through to Penang, Singapore and beyond (Falkus, 1990: 28).

Singapore's regional prominence as a staple port owed much to the access provided to world markets through Liverpool-based shipping services. As Huff (1994: 10) puts it, 'the ready availability of shipping helped to draw regional exports to the port'. In 1914 more Blue Funnel Line ships passed through the Suez Canal than of any other line and 'the great harbours in Singapore and Hong Kong were forested with familiar blue funnels' (Falkus, 1990: 4). Through its involvement in shipping 'conference' agreements, between 1919 and 1941 the Blue Funnel Line acquired a virtual monopoly on sailings to the Straits, China and Japan from the west coast of Britain (p. 129). Blue Funnel Line ships also came to operate other important routes from Singapore. During the First World War acquisition of the Indra Line gave the Ocean Steamship Company (which owned and operated most of Alfred Holt and Company's Blue Funnel Line vessels) a seat at the New York conference (p. 161), resulting in the establishment of regular services between the Far East and the east coast of the United States. By this time, the corner of Collyer Quay and Finlayson Green in Singapore was popularly known as 'Blue Funnel Corner' (Jackson and Wurtzburg, 1952: 6). Mansfield and Company (aka 'Mansfields'), agents to the Ocean Steamship Company, had moved to this site in 1901. Two years later, 'the link between Liverpool and Singapore became closer, and formal' when Mansfields became a limited liability company with nearly all the shares owned by the Ocean Steamship Company (Falkus, 1990: 71). It is important to emphasize that the Mersey remained the 'hub' of the Blue Funnel Line's operations (p. 29) – and 'much rested on the shoulders of the small group of Managers in Liverpool' (p. 7). The city of Liverpool was perhaps at its commercial zenith in 1914 (Lawton, 1964: 358) and clearly 'the success of Singapore was of material benefit to Liverpool.'[8] Equally, however, Liverpool, and especially the Ocean Steamship Company founded by Holt, had contributed to turning Singapore into 'the greatest transshipment port of the Orient'.[9]

While the metropolitan routes operated by Blue Funnel Line ships contributed to Singapore's development as a centre for regional exports, Alfred Holt and Company had a more direct involvement in trade within the *alam Melayu.* The company's initial move into regional services based on Singapore began on a small scale in 1879 with an incursion into the Sumatran tobacco trade (Falkus, 1990: 40). In 1882 the company entered the Bangkok–Singapore rice trade and by the end of the decade owned either wholly or in part small vessels trading regularly between Singapore and Borneo and beyond (p. 40). During the First World War, German firms were liquidated and Alfred Holt and Company played a key role in replacing the services of the German shipping line, Norddeutscher Lloyd, through an agreement by which 'the Liverpool firm provided new ships for the SSC to expand its operations and in exchange acquired the ownership of just under a third of that company' (Huff, 1994: 146). Through this piece of wartime expediency, Alfred Holt and Company effectively acquired a 'local fleet to serve their main line steamers in South-east Asia' (Falkus, 1990: 51). During the following decade, the 'the link with Liverpool was strengthened when Mansfield and Company, controlled and principally owned by Holts [Alfred Holt and Company], became managers of the SSC' (Huff, 1994: 147). The Straits Steamship Company itself expanded in the interwar period, either absorbing or taking control of seven regional shipping lines between 1922 and 1934 (p. 146). By the latter date, the Straits Steamship Company's fleet accounted for 55 of the 81 local steamers based on Singapore. These were the small ships that brought commodities to 'the great gathering ground' (Falkus, 1990: 31) of Singapore, from where oceangoing Blue Funnel Line ships 'took tin ingots and rubber to the markets of the world' (Jennings, 1973: 24). Malay men such as Majid and Jaafar were thus working on maritime networks controlled ultimately from world city Liverpool even while they were employed on the Straits Steamship Company's regional services.

Some of the men whom I met at the Malay Club in Liverpool between 2004 and 2007 gained their first experience of routes beyond the *alam Melayu* on Blue Funnel Line ships after the Second World War. Jaafar was one of them. Another was Fadzil Mohamed who worked the night shift (7 p.m. to 7 a.m.) on the diesel-powered MV *Charon* with around 30 Malay deck crew, having gained regional seafaring experience on the Straits Steamship Company's *Empire Pacific*.[10] The sister ships *Charon* and *Gorgon* ran on the Western Australia route which dated back to 1891, initially bringing wool and fruit to Singapore (Hyde, 1956). The ships were 'designed for the highly individual carriage of people, animals, and refrigerated products which the trade served' (Falkus, 1990: 218) and had specially strengthened bottoms for use in northwest Australian ports where they had to lie in mud berths at low water (Clarkson *et al.*, 1998). Crew agreements included specific scales of food provision for 'Malay and Indian seamen' or 'Asiatic crews'.[11] Fadzil recalled '*lascar*' work on board the *Charon* in the 1940s as being particularly hard in that it included much of the loading and unloading in ports such as Broome and Carnarvon which did not have dedicated stevedores.[12] The Western Australia trade at that time included mother-of-pearl shell from Shark Bay and Broome, passengers from Koepang (Timor) and the Cocos Islands who worked in this industry, and other migrants heading for Australia's gold fields (Falkus, 1990: 46). When Fadzil got to Broome, one of the pearl divers he met working there was a Boyanese from Singapore.[13]

A passenger heading in the opposite direction during this period was a New Zealander who took the *Charon* on the Fremantle–Singapore run to begin colonial service in Malaya. T.K. Taylor recalls of the *Charon* and its sister ship: 'These vessels had accommodation for sixty passengers, and lower decks were adapted to carry sheep "on the hoof" from the north-west Australian ports to Singapore, and on the return journey, cattle from these ports to Fremantle.' Feeding the cattle was among the tasks of Malay crewmen such as Fadzil.[14] Taylor notes that cargo also included 'food products for the Singapore market – cases of oranges and apples were carried in the open on the decks' (Taylor, 2006: 35). The photograph of Malay crew aboard the *Charon* that is in the prologue of this book (Figure 0.1) includes Fadzil (back row, second from the left) as well as Dol and at least one other man who ended up living in Liverpool.[15] The faint writing on the life belt attests that the *Charon* was a Liverpool ship. As one company history of Mansfields notes, however, for the *Charon* and *Gorgon* – and, indeed, for the *Centaur* which eventually replaced them in the 1960s – Singapore was 'perhaps really their home port' (Jennings, 1973: 34). Yet that fact is itself evidence of the maritime commercial linkages between world city Liverpool and Singapore established by Alfred Holt, and maintained by the Ocean Steamship Company.

The Ocean Steamship Company's material presence in Singapore both reflected the influence of Liverpool and revealed something of the nature of that city's own commercial aspirations. Work on a new company office building on the Blue Funnel Corner site began in 1919 with initial engagement of the Liverpool architects Briggs and Thornley.[16] It was in 1922 that Mansfield and Company was appointed as agent for the Straits Steamship Company and both companies moved into the new Ocean Building when it was completed a year later (see Figure 2.2). A British businessman arriving in Singapore on a Blue Funnel Line ship recalls seeking the 'settled coolness and calm' of the Ocean Building and meeting the principal director:

> His wide office table was by a wide window commanding the anchorage, and it might have been in Liverpool except that its paper-weights were massive and opalescent sea-shells, and he was in white linen so neat that I was conscious of the defects in my own new raiment. (Tomlinson, 1950: 26)

Passengers arriving from the east coast of the United States might equally have wondered if they were back in New York. The Ocean Building in Singapore was modelled on New York's Flatiron Building (Jennings, 1973). Just as over half a century earlier, Singapore had been

Figure 2.2 The Ocean Building, Singapore, in 1947. Courtesy of National Archives of Singapore.

described as the 'Liverpool of the East', so Liverpool had itself long been likened to New York. The *Illustrated London News* in 1886 described Liverpool as 'the New York of Europe, a world city rather than merely British provincial'.[17] By the 1890s, in Graeme Milne's (2006: 278) words, 'to be American was to be modern, and Liverpool made much of its association.' If this association was manifested in the 'showy modernity of the Liverpool waterfront', then perhaps the Ocean Building brought a piece of 'Manhattan on the Mersey' to Singapore (p. 279). Liverpool's commercial presence in turn strengthened Singapore's connections to the wider Atlantic-centred world economy of the early twentieth century.

The allure of modern New York filtered through to would-be seafaring young men in Singapore. JJ, another of the ex-seafaring men who regularly attended the Malay Club in Liverpool in 2004, had been born in the state of Negeri Sembilan, Malaya but moved to Singapore during the Second World War with his mother, who worked as a nurse there.[18] Although JJ's mother was of Portuguese ancestry and his father was Ceylonese, JJ converted to Islam in later life (another way in which *alam Melayu*-born Malay speakers can come to be seen as 'Malay'). JJ served on Japanese boats with Malay crew during the war and, when it ended, found himself stranded in Rabaul, New Guinea. When he finally returned to Singapore, JJ began to train as a wireless operator while most of his Malay friends continued to work at sea. Some months later JJ recalled:

> I met some of my friends from, from New Guinea, Rabaul. You know seamen. All in flashy gear, and all that like, you know. I say, 'Hey! Where you guys been, man?' He says, 'What are you doing here?' I said, 'I'm learning to be a wireless operator.' 'Ah', he says, 'I've been to America, Australia, all over the world, man.'... Yeah ... all my mates, like you know, all the flashy gear. 'Ah' I say, 'so that's where you got them.' 'Yeah! I got it from New York, man' and all that like, you know? So my heart started to beat, I said, 'Oh, blimey. What the hell am I doing here?'

JJ socialized with his friends while they were back in Singapore: 'I used to see them everyday, like, you know, night time I used to go and ah, we used to have a few drinks, and all that. And ... and ... and, go to the dance hall. You know, the Malaysian, the Malaysian way of dancing.' It was at the end of their period of leave that JJ faced the big decision: 'So anyway, when the time came, they say, "Ok, come on, you want to go?" I say "Yeah." So they brought me to this agent.'[19] In this immediate postwar period, there was no shortage of companies willing to take young men with some seafaring experience as crew. Prince Line, Castle Line and Silver Line as well as Blue Funnel Line all employed Malays on oceangoing routes. Figure 2.3 shows young Malay men in Singapore back from Australia looking ready for adventures along mainline routes to Europe and the United States.[20]

While New York may have become the 'flashy' aspirational destination for young Malay men after the war, the role of Liverpool in Singapore's commercial life endured. Indeed, the return of Blue Funnel Line ships to Singapore was seen as something of a barometer for the postwar recovery of the economic climate. The chairman of Mansfield and Company, A. McLellan, recalled how at the end of 1947,

> a senior Government official, after one of his visits to the Singapore Harbour Board wharves, remarked to one of his friends: 'It is a most cheering sight to see so many Blue Funnel vessels alongside the wharves – it is just like pre-war days and extremely encouraging to realise how rapidly the Blue Funnel Line and British shipping generally is again getting into its stride.' (McLellan, 1953: 10)

Although the smaller coastal ships of the Straits Steamship Company that Majid worked on before the war never fully regained their stride given competition from road and rail, the Blue Funnel Line – and British shipping more generally – benefited from an uninterrupted period of high demand for shipping services that lasted until the late 1950s (Falkus, 1990: 294). By this time, 'there were around 3,000 Asian seamen serving on Holt [Alfred Holt and Company] vessels, roughly 300 being Malays recruited in Singapore' (p. 310).

Figure 2.3 Crew of the MV *Charon* in Singapore, circa 1947. Photograph courtesy of Fadzil Mohamed.

Boom time for Alfred Holt and Company provided further opportunities for Malay men to work in the Western Australia and pilgrim trades, and beyond. Jaafar Mohamad served with the Sarawak Steamship Company before securing work on the *Charon* in the early 1950s.[21] It was following this experience that he subsequently worked on the pilgrim ship *Tyndareus* and other Blue Funnel Line ships which took him to Liverpool and New York, among a host of other major seaports around the world. So through Liverpool-controlled shipping operations, this man of Boyanese ancestry who identified as a 'Singapore Malay' had travelled on routes around the *alam Melayu* out of home port Singapore; from the 'Liverpool of the East' to Liverpool; and from the 'New York of Europe' to New York (where many of his friends jumped ship). Jaafar eventually settled in Liverpool after the Blue Funnel Line ship he was

Figure 2.4 Blue Funnel Line advertisement, circa 1960. Reproduced by permission of Exel Limited.

working on was dry-docked there for seven months in 1960 following a collision in the Suez Canal. Having travelled 'up and down, up and down' over the years on Blue Funnel Line ships (see Figure 2.4), he was already familiar with the city and its diverse 'Malay' population – not only Malacca men such as Johan Awang (who ran the Malay Club on St James Road), Majid and Fadzil, but also Butonese, Acehnese, Javanese, Bugis, Ambonese and fellow Boyanese. Liverpool's commercial reach had resulted in the transfer of Malay world regional demographic diversity to this Atlantic world city, and helped to sustain world-spanning 'Malay' social webs.

Malays in the 'New York of Europe' … and in New York

Indian Ocean seafarers, including Malays, had experienced life in the docklands of British port cities for at least a century before Jaafar began to travel 'up and down' from Singapore. As trade expanded in the first half of the nineteenth century, and India became increasingly central to Britain's global trade and economy, so-called *lascars* 'became the mainstay of the labour force in British-registered ships bound for Europe' (Visram, 2002: 16). While technically connoting Indian sailors, '[i]n

Figure 2.5 A Malay seaman and other *lascars*. From Salter (1873).

actual use the term was applied to all indigenous sailors of the Indian Ocean region' (Ghosh, 2008: 57).[22] *Lascars* were, in Amitav Ghosh's words, 'a richly cosmopolitan group'. Figure 2.5, first printed in Joseph Salter's (1873) recollections of work as 'Missionary to the Asiatics in England', illustrates the diversity of Indian Ocean men who were labelled *lascars*. Among the *lascar* crew observed on board a ship called the *Irrawaddy* in Liverpool in around 1840 were 'Malays, Mahrattas, Burmese, Siamese, and Cingalese' (Melville, 1983: 187). This is recorded in

Herman Melville's 1849 autobiographical novel, *Redburn: His First Voyage*, which is based on a journey Melville had made to Liverpool a decade earlier. By this mid-nineteenth-century period, a range of often overlapping Oriental characters – including 'Malays' and 'Asiatics' as well as the more general term, *lascars* – had 'become familiar to the British imagination' (Barrell, 1991: 7). While these characters 'circulated by newspapers, by engravings, and by melodramas, pantomimes and plays', they were also to be found in dockland areas of Liverpool and other major imperial port cities, particularly London (see Fisher, 2004).

An account of work at the Strangers' Home for Asiatics, which opened in West India Dock Road in London in 1857, includes many references to 'Malays' and 'Javanese' among other 'Mohammedans' (Salter, 1873). Salter also makes reference to Malays in Liverpool. It is noted that the London Home became the 'centre of attraction to the stranger coming from the East', even those arriving in Britain at other ports: 'Asiatic seamen who have landed at Liverpool, and even Glasgow, have arrived by rail, if they could afford it, and many have tramped all the way, if destitute' (p. 88). As part of his London City Mission-funded role as missionary to the Asiatics in England, Salter decided to travel in the opposite direction. 'In Liverpool', he wrote, 'the natives of the distant East have been visited frequently, and found in larger numbers than in any other provincial town' (p. 230). During a visit to Liverpool, '[a]bout one hundred strangers heard the Gospel – Arabs, Malays, East Indians, and Chinese'; and an unidentified lodging house was said to have been 'filled with Manillas and Malays' (pp. 158–9).[23] Other sympathetic Christian listeners are reported by Salter to have had their 'purse strings' repeatedly liberated by the 'touching but deceptive appeal of the stranger in half-broken English' requesting 'expenses from Liverpool or elsewhere to the Asiatic Home, that he might obtain a ship' (p. 222). The alleged strategy of seeking wealthy benefactors at the seaside and other holiday retreats casts new light on Thomas De Quincey's famous literary encounter with the 'Malay' in his book *Confessions of an English Opium-Eater*. Perhaps this account was based on a face-to-face meeting in either the Lake District or in Liverpool[24] rather than on Orientalist writing or representation (cf. Barrell, 1991). In a later book about his missionary work, published in 1896, Salter describes 'Orientals' leading a 'vagrant life' between 'colonies' in London – 'in each of which, opium was dispensed to Arabs, Malays and East Indians' – and 'some rendezvous or other in nearly every considerable town in England' (Salter, 1896: 25).[25]

By the late nineteenth century, seafarers were not the only Malays to have travelled to and within Britain. During his last day on 'Malay soil' on 4 December 1883, a British traveller to Singapore learned that the 'Maharaja of Johore' (Sultan Abu Bakar) had visited Liverpool and other 'big towns' in England. D. Ker had the pleasure of meeting the maharaja at his palace in Johore Bahru and wrote about his experiences in one of a series of letters that were published in The *New York Times*.[26] Having travelled by carriage across Singapore to the Johore Strait, Ker and his wife met Incheh Abdul Rahman, 'a young man in European dress, but with unmistakably Malay features, who greets us in excellent English'. Educated in England and 'now so far Europeanized as to be a very agreeable companion', Abdul Rahman escorted the Kers across the Tebrau Strait in a steam launch crewed by Malays to a small pier where the maharaja awaited. Once settled inside the palace, the Kers learned of the maharaja's own European travels: 'our host talks so familiarly of Paris boulevards and London theatres, Scottish mountains, and Italian lakes that it is difficult enough while listening to his fluent English to realize that we are conversing with the Mussulman sovereign of a Malay principality.' The maharaja is reported to have recalled Liverpool as 'terribly smoky':

> Do you know what one of my people said the first time he saw Liverpool? He pointed to the masts standing up all along the river, and said the place looked just like the dead trees standing in a burned jungle.

After 'a few words about his recent Japanese tour', the maharaja is reported to have expressed a desire to visit America next. 'It will be a change after Japan, and there must be a great deal to see in New York.' Already familiar with the 'New York of Malacca' (as Ker had described Singapore in an earlier letter),[27] and having experienced the smoky 'New York of Europe' for himself, the maharaja aspired to see the real thing.

Just as London, Liverpool and Glasgow formed part of maritime networks extending to the Malay world via Singapore, so New York was familiar to Malay seafarers before Sultan Abu Bakar had an opportunity to visit. As in Liverpool, some of the earliest records of Malays in New York come from missionary-related activities. The Marine Temperance Society of the Port of New-York [*sic*] is said to have listed names of seamen 'not only of every Christian nation but those of Chinese, Malays, and other pagans' among its 28,000 members. Celebrating its twenty-first anniversary in 1854, the society reported ongoing weekly meetings at the Sailors' Home on Thursday evenings and regretted not being able to reach out to more of the 100,000 seamen visiting 'the commercial metropolis of the Western World' every year.[28] Giovanni Arrighi (1996) has detailed the emergence of an American cycle of accumulation from around 1860, with New York as its main world city. Ironically, it was an event in rival Chicago – the World's Columbian Exposition which began in May 1893 – that finally gave Sultan Abu Bakar the chance to see America. While visitors gazed at the sultan's model Malay house (with 'real' Malay people!) at the exhibition, *lascars* observed a rather different spectacle in New York. Firemen battled with a blaze at a warehouse on the northeast corner of South and Clinton Streets on 11 June 1893. The *New York Times* reported: 'The British steamer Macduff is lying at the wharf at the foot of Clinton Street. Her crew, consisting of Chinese, Malays, and East Indians, gathered at the bows of the steamship and watched the operations of the firemen with great interest.'[29]

Trade connections from Singapore to the east coast of the United States, and New York in particular, expanded from the last decades of the nineteenth century. Shipping companies formed the Straits-New York Conference in 1905 to agree the allocation of services, and there was a massive expansion in cargo between 1912/13 and 1938/39 (Huff, 1994), the period during which US economic hegemony was fully realized (Arrighi, 1996). Pacific shipping routes expanded during the First World War when rubber and tin were sent directly to the US. Huff (1994: 120) notes three main streams of shipping from the west which converged on Singapore: 'one using the Suez Canal, a second taking the Cape route and joining the Suez stream in the area of the Indian subcontinent, and a third beginning in the Indian area'. However, in the interwar period, rubber and petroleum provided important exceptions to this picture: 'Rubber was carried mainly by eight shipping lines on a "round the world" route which started from the Atlantic coast of the United States and went westward by the Panama and Suez Canals. Although this "round the world" service brought few goods to Singapore, rubber provided a large cargo for its "homeward leg" to New York' (p. 121). Malay seafarers and other *lascars* followed these commodities along maritime world city networks.

Brief accounts from New York suggest that a small group of Malays had settled there before the First World War. An article published in the Malaysian magazine *Dewan Budaya* in 1983 describes how young men from various states in *tanah Melayu* (the Malay peninsula or what is today peninsular Malaysia) arrived on merchant ships going backwards and forwards from Malaya (Mansor, 1983). These men were reportedly employed to clean rust from the floors and engines of the ships. In New York at that time, so the story goes, new factories were being built and Malay sailors were tempted to jump ship by the prospect of better-paying work.[30] They swam during the night to the shore where factory agents were waiting to give jobs to the sailors. While the wages were said to have been relatively good, the threat of deportation meant that these men only went out into town during the night. The First World War gave rise to a more open immigration policy with the result that young

Malay men were able to become American citizens.[31] Another larger group is said to have come to the city in the interwar period. Some of them served in the US military during the Second World War with the result that they, like the generation before them, were able to secure citizenship. It was this group that formed the Malay Club of America in Brooklyn in 1954.[32] The club reportedly had around 100 members at that time, but many more seamen from Southeast Asia visited this site on their travels. Some of these visiting seafarers, in turn, came to live and work in the city. Among the men who were interviewed for the *Dewan Budaya* article, some had reportedly returned to their villages in the *alam Melayu* but had been unable to fit in and so had gone back to New York.

The maritime connections of the Malay Club of America meant that Malay social networks reached beyond the *alam Melayu* into what had become the world's pre-eminent metropolitan centre. In his research on Minangkabau migration, or *merantau*, in the early 1970s Mokhtar Naim recalls meeting seamen 'following merchant ships under various flags sailing to many corners of the world' in the Geylang section of Singapore: 'Interestingly, they all set out as sailor-apprentices from Singapore when they were young, and in their respective communities they keep using Singapore Malay as their medium of communication, though they ethnically came from various parts of Indonesia and Malaya' (Mokhtar, 1973: 219–20). Hashim, who was born in another 'Malay' section of Singapore, Kampong Glam, and whose father had moved to Singapore from Ambon, became very familiar with New York City as a result of his seafaring travels. During his first trip, on the advice of his mother in Singapore, Hashim went to find his uncle Gir Ali, who was working as a barber in Brooklyn.[33] The family ate seafood together and Hashim was given money by his uncle to go to the movies. Hashim was so mesmerized by Times Square that he stayed out all night. While working mostly on Prince Line's 'round the world' service, Hashim visited New York 16 times in total, and clearly became very familiar with certain sites in and transects through New York City. During some of his later trips, fellow crew called him 'Hashim pilot' on account of his ability to guide first-time visitors to the best cinemas and places to buy much-prized Arrow brand shirts – which cost $3.99 in the shops but could be bought on Orchard Street, New York, for just a dollar. Hashim and other Malay seamen took boxes of them to resell in Hong Kong.[34]

Hashim also piloted Malays to seafarers' clubs. There was an Indonesian club on Allen Street – conveniently close to the bargains of Orchard Street – but Hashim preferred to go to the Malay Club of America in Brooklyn. This preference was in part reflective of his Malayization in Singapore as well as from serving with Malay crew on board

Prince Line and Silver Line ships. However, it also had to do with hostility between Ambonese and other 'Indonesians' associated with the Ambonese rebellion against the Indonesian government in the early 1950s.[35] The Malay Club of America in Brooklyn, Hashim recalled, was run by a man called Brian Sorong who was from Malacca. During one trip, Hashim was invited to Brian's house and Hashim came away with a huge stack of old, unwanted clothes. At the time when I interviewed him at Liverpool's Malay Club in 2006, Hashim was still in possession of the hat of an Ambonese man who had served as a sergeant in the US Army. It is important to note that Hashim – and, no doubt, some of his fellow Malay crew who became regular visitors to New York City and Brooklyn – also transported goods the other way. Hashim took bundles of newspapers from Singapore thus helping to keep Malays in, and passing through, this Atlantic world city plugged into events in the *alam Melayu*. The club run by Brian Sorong was among the social spaces through which not just newspapers but also diverse artefacts, personal news and gossip circulated.

The Malay Atlantic

Sites that brought together locally based and mobile seafaring Malay men in Atlantic world cities were socially connected not only back to the *alam Melayu* (via Singapore) but also to each other. Many of the men who eventually settled in Liverpool in the middle decades of the twentieth century had passed through New York and/or London (and vice versa). Some, such as Johan Awang, the man who established Liverpool's Malay Club, had lived and worked onshore in New York before settling in Liverpool.[36] However, as suggested from the composition of the crew of the *Macduff* who watched the 1893 warehouse fire, transatlantic Malay maritime mobilities extend even further back in time. Ex-seafarers in Liverpool traced the origins of a settled Malay presence in the city to men arriving on sailboats from New York in the 1920s. Like fragments of many of the stories assembled in this book, it has proven impossible to establish the veracity of this foundation story. None of the remaining former seafarers in Liverpool during my fieldwork (between 2004 and 2008) was among the men said to have sailed into Liverpool from New York. Yet, despite my initial suspicions, people such as Mohamed Nor Hamid (Mat Nor) – the first of several men to tell me the story – were not just 'pulling my leg'.[37] The New York foundation story had become part of collective social memory. Whether it is objectively 'true' or not, this memory provides a useful way into Malay seafaring routes that interconnected two of 'the capitals of a long Atlantic twentieth century'

(Baucom, 2005: 35). I use the term 'Malay Atlantic' to denote social exchanges and criss-crossings that are about Malays as more than seafaring labour, and to map men who came to be based in Liverpool in worlds beyond homeland and eventual migrant destination.[38]

Indirect evidence of Malay transatlantic sailing in the late nineteenth century emerges from the infamous Jack the Ripper case. One elaborate 'theory' in Britain suggested from the timing of the killings in London that they must be 'the work of a Malay serving in some sailing vessel sailing and returning to port for the latter end and first part of the month'. This implied that the Malay might be employed 'on board some vessel engaged on short trips out of the port of London'.[39] However, on the other side of the Atlantic, news reports suggested that the geographical range of the Malay seafaring 'assassin' extended beyond short coastal trips. Three years prior to the murders in the East End of London, Austin in Texas had experienced an apparently similar spate of 'bloody butchery' in which eight women had been killed. During that period in 1885, a Malay cook 'calling himself Maurice' was said to have been employed at Pearl House hotel, near to where most of the killings occurred. [40] Having been strongly suspected by detectives at the time, it was reported that the Malay cook 'suddenly disappeared and has not been seen or heard of since'.[41] The subsequent murders in London gave rise to the theory that 'Maurice' had 'drifted to Europe as the "Ripper"'.[42] However far-fetched and fuelled by racist stereotypes of Malay barbarism and butchery these theories are,[43] they are founded on contemporary acceptance of the plausibility of 'Malay' transatlantic mobilities.

In the subsequent two decades, 'Liverpool shipping increased in importance to reach its zenith by the First World War' (Lawton, 1964: 358).[44] It was war itself that expanded opportunities for Malay men to work on Atlantic seafaring routes. With thousands of British merchant seamen joining the army, ships became 'tied up for days in London and Liverpool awaiting crews'.[45] Not only was recruitment increased in the British colonies but also 'colonial seamen who had previously been confined to well defined routes and trades were transferred to other routes by the exigencies of war' (Evans, 1980: 8). Malays were among additional men signed up in April 1917, though several hundred Chinese were specifically 'imported' from Hong Kong because 'the Captains, officers and chief engineers prefer them to any other Orientals.'[46] A month later, the *New York Times* reported a 'mutiny' by Chinese and Malays on a British freighter.[47] The crew was not allowed onshore at Hoboken for immigration reasons but they reportedly thought that they were merely being denied shore leave. As noted already, this was also around the time when Malay men were being tempted onshore to work in factories (Mansor, 1983). Similar kinds of shore job possibilities expanded for 'Eastern crews' in Liverpool (Visram, 2002: 197). In other words, during the First World War there were Malays working on either side of the Atlantic as well as on the ocean itself.

When the labour shortage ended in the economic downturn after the war, Malays and other 'coloured' men became objects of hostility for demobilized British troops. In the summer of 1919 racial violence erupted in many British ports, including Liverpool. Major trouble in early June began with a fracas between black and Scandinavian sailors and culminated in the drowning of a Bermudian seaman, Charles Wooten, in the Queen's Dock. Yet attacks by white mobs affected all 'coloured' people as evidenced by a plea from a Filipino (in a letter to the *Liverpool Echo*) for people not to 'vent their spite on any darker skin' (cited in May and Cohen, 1974: 115). The disturbances in Liverpool had a 'demonstration effect' on south Wales, and Malays appeared prominently in the events in the port city of Cardiff (Evans, 1980: 13). The headline on the front page of the *South Wales Echo* on Saturday 14 June 1919 read 'Terrified Malays'.[48] A mob had gathered outside the house of L. Hassan at 8 Bute Terrace where 'a number of Malays' were lodging, and 'the crashing of glass was the first intimation that trouble was brewing.' The report continued:

> More glass was broken, and the Malays in the house took alarm and rushed upstairs, then up to the attic and on to the roof. The crowd, which by this time had swelled considerably, espied their dark sinewy bodies against the skyline, and a hoarse cry of anger was followed by a volley of stones aimed at the Malays as they clambered through the skylight of the house and dragged themselves on their hands and knees over the top of the roof to seek shelter on the other side.

What the *South Wales News* described as 'a dashing baton charge' by the police to disperse the mob saved the 'Malays on the roof' from more serious assault.[49] Nonetheless, the terror of this rooftop episode – as part of wider disturbances that left three men dead and many more injured – would have resonated throughout Malay Atlantic networks. In interviews with the prewar generation of Malay seafarers in New York in the 1980s, it was Cardiff, rather than London or Liverpool, which was most frequently recalled as the site of Malay settlement in Britain (Mansor, 1983).[50]

One Malay seaman who shipped out of Cardiff during the riots of 1919 was Mohamed Ben Ibram. One of his discharge books begins with service on a ship called the *Mildred Powell* which left Cardiff on 15 July 1919, two days after the headline events in Bute Terrace.[51] Mohamed

Ben Ibram first arrived in Liverpool in October of the following year (1920) on board the *A.E. McKinstry* having been on that ship for nine months, originally taking it from Port Talbot in south Wales. The home address listed for Mohamed on that ship's agreement is in Cardiff, at 263 Bute Street.[52] He later shipped out of Manchester and Liverpool on boats of the Larrinaga Line – widely remembered for hiring Malay crew – including on the *Mercedes de Larrinaga* which left Garston docks in Liverpool on 15 November 1922 for New York. After returning to Britain on another Larrinaga boat, the *Telesfora*, which had been to South America (in April 1930), Mohamed Ben Ibram worked continuously for the next five years on the *Manchester Hero*. This took him to Canada and the United States, 21 journeys in all, the last one (which filled his last surviving log book) returning to Manchester on 4 October 1935.

For other Malay men during the interwar period, Atlantic seafaring was not such plain sailing. In October 1929 the Colonial Office in London informed the Home Office that 'attention has recently been drawn to the fact that cases not infrequently occur [the draft read: 'are constantly arising'] in which Malay [the draft read: 'Malayan'] seamen on being discharged from their ships in Great Britain are treated as aliens because they are not in possession of proper documents to prove their British nationality to the satisfaction of the immigration officers.'[53] The specific case that had directed official attention to this wider issue was that of Adam bin Ma'Sah (also referred to as Adam Bacha). Adam had arrived in Liverpool on 28 April as a seaman on the Ellerman Hall Line's SS *City of Tokio* after originally signing on at New York. His documents were detained by the aliens officer in Liverpool who said that Adam would be sent back to New York. But when Adam returned to his ship, he was refused passage as he did not have his papers. Adam then made his way to the London head office of the Ellerman Hall shipping company who sent him to the police. After two days in detention, Adam was transferred to Brixton Prison where he developed pneumonia. It was in St George's Hospital that a member of the Malayan Information Agency found Adam and took up his case. A clearly exasperated Mr Ellerton wrote on 28 October:

> I gather that the Home Office are still not satisfied that the man is Malacca born and therefore a British subject, although I should have thought that a statutory declaration signed before a Magistrate and duly stamped was sufficient proof. Perhaps the Home Office is not yet satisfied that Malacca is a British Colony.

By this time, the Home Office had at least directed Adam's release from Brixton Prison and into the care of the Home for Asiatics in West India

Dock Road. The Malayan Information Agency arranged for Adam to get a free passage from Gravesend to Rotterdam and then on Ellerman Hall Line's SS *City of Durham* leaving Rotterdam on 2 November for Singapore. Adam bin Ma'Sah was thus repatriated from the Malay Atlantic prior to the period when wartime labour shortages made the British government much more welcoming to 'coloured' British seamen.

Malays based on both sides of the Atlantic contributed to the Allied effort during the Second World War. It will be recalled that Malays in New York were granted citizenship after serving in the US military. However, the Atlantic Ocean itself was a prominent theatre of conflict involving roles beyond formal military service. From an Allied point of view, the Battle of the Atlantic was ultimately about providing Britain with supplies of food, munitions and raw materials from the United States and Canada.[54] Requisitioning of ships began with the outbreak of war, and even before the Essential Work Order of May 1941 introduced 'conscription in all but name' for seafarers, the merchant marine had become 'a "civilian" occupation with a death rate already exceeding that of any of the armed services'. Nearly 30,000 seamen died on British merchant ships as a direct result of enemy actions (Marsh and Almond, 1993: 54). Among them was Mohamed Ben Ibram. This Singapore-born man who had survived the 1919 riots in Cardiff and worked on transatlantic routes for much of the subsequent two decades was on board the SS *Manchester Brigade* when it was torpedoed in 1940 and went down with all hands. Documents on Mohamed Ben Ibram held in the archives at the Liverpool Maritime Museum include pictures of him and the ship, a telegram of sympathy from King George VI, and a scroll of honour as someone who 'gave his life to save mankind from tyranny'.[55] There is also a box of medals, including the Atlantic Star, sent from the registrar general of shipping and seamen in Cardiff to Mohamed Ben Ibram's widow, Mrs Doris Irene Ibram, in Manchester. Born in 1894, Mohamed Ben Ibram had first served on the *Manchester Brigade* 16 years before it was sunk, on a round trip from Manchester to Canada.

Other Malay men survived the Battle of the Atlantic with dramatic stories to tell. Among those interviewed by the Malaysian journalist Zaharah Othman in the 1990s was London-based Pak Hamid, whose ship was torpedoed in the 'Bay of Beski' (Bay of Biscay). Evidence of a considerable Malay presence in the Battle of the Atlantic is provided by Pak Hamid's recollection that a Malay sailor aboard another merchant navy ship rescued him.[56] A Malay seaman from Singapore by the name of Omar bin Hitam was stranded in Liverpool when the city was bombed.[57] Yet wartime also enabled and motivated new Malay mobilities. The official log book of the *Telesfora de Larrinaga* on which Mohamed Ben Ibram had served in the interwar period continued to include Malay crew during the war. In March 1943 the ship was at Victoria Dock, London, waiting to leave for another transatlantic voyage. During the evening of 19 March a member of the crew was killed by an explosion in the engine room during an air raid. The explosion injured Ben Ali, the Cardiff-based ship's carpenter, and he was removed to the Seaman's Hospital before the ship set sail.[58] After spending six months under repair (Eccles, 2005), the vessel finally arrived in New York on 4 August. When it came to depart again 11 days later, Said bin Bakar, from Kebang, Malacca, had not returned to the ship and so presumably added to the existing Malay population on the New York side of the Malay Atlantic.[59] *Telesfora de Larrinaga* was one of only three out of twelve members of the original Larrinaga Line fleet to survive the war (Eccles, 2005).[60]

For roughly two decades following the end of the Second World War, Liverpool became the unrivalled capital of the Malay Atlantic. Ships returned to what had been the headquarters of the wartime Western Approaches Command, many requiring repairs at the Cammell Laird shipyard in Birkenhead (on the other side of the River Mersey and very much part of greater Liverpool).[61] The postwar boom in British shipping provided opportunities for men discharged in Liverpool to use the city as a seafaring base. Some even came over from across the Atlantic – perhaps surprising given the undisputed US commercial leadership in the postwar period and the fact that Liverpool had long been the port sending emigrants in the opposite direction (Herson, 2008). As has been noted, among the men who travelled from New York after the war was Johan Awang, from Telok Mas, Malacca. It has not been possible to ascertain whether the club that he formed on St James Road preceded the Malay Club of America, but there were clearly important transatlantic social connections between them (and with London, where another Malay Club operated at 100 Cricketfield Road in East London).[62]

Among Johan Awang's fellow Malacca men in Liverpool during the period in the mid-1950s when he established the Malay Club was Majid. Having first visited Liverpool before the Second World War, Majid had returned to his home village of Serkam, from where so many Malay men had been hired to work for the Straits Steamship Company. He shipped out of Singapore with another company in early 1942, just before the Japanese invasion, and jumped ship in Australia, eventually finding work with three other Malay men cutting sugar cane in Cairns.[63] Majid was able to leave Australia in 1946, but only through taking on the notoriously tough job as a fireman on board one of Larrinaga Line's few steamships that had survived the war. He arrived back in Liverpool in the summer of 1947 and, with the exception of a three-month period in Cardiff in the mid-1950s, was based thereafter in Liverpool.

Majid attended Malay clubs on both sides of the Atlantic.[64] Among his few recollections of the club sites that anchored Malay social networks in Liverpool during tail end of its pre-eminence as a maritime world city was that 'before it was really crowded here'.[65] Although Majid himself had apparently always been a taciturn man, many of the life geographies and world city routes narrated by other men at 7 Jermyn Street in 2004 followed in his historical wake. Everyone accepted that Majid had earned his place in that comfortable brown armchair by the window.

Notes

1 OA 879, K.G. Tregonning, 'The Mosquito Fleet', circa 1960.
2 Notes from conversation with Majid, 10 September 2004.
3 OA 879, K.G. Tregonning, 'The Mosquito Fleet', circa 1960.
4 H.M. Tomlinson who travelled on Straits Steamship Company ships in the interwar period, noted of the SSC's 'little ships': 'Their officers are from the home country, with Malays on deck and Chinese in the engine-room.' But Malays also worked as quartermasters, and had a reputation for competence: 'I should like to say that the European who fancies his superiority to a seasoned Malay sailor, or a Chinese craftsman, has yet to learn his place in life. I found it a select and cheerful community, the crew of a little ship, in which a man's only worth was his fitness for his task. A Chinese in the engine-room knew where he was, and could be left to it, whatever happened; and the bearing of a Malay quartermaster gave not the slightest impression that he thought you the better man. One could face adversity at sea in the company of those fellows' (Tomlinson, 1950: 10–11).
5 OA 879, K.G. Tregonning, 'The Mosquito Fleet', circa 1960.
6 This was certainly not unique to Boyanese. According to Jacob Vredenbregt (1962: 118), 'many inhabitants of the Indonesian archipelago emigrated temporarily to Malaya and Singapore to work on the plantations or find some other job, and thus to save the necessary money for the pilgrimage to Mecca.'
7 Interview, Liverpool, 9 May 2008. Despite the poor conditions described by Jaafar, they represented a great improvement when compared to earlier periods. Before the First World War, pilgrims were said to have been 'carried in what must have been very primitive conditions' (Falkus, 1990: 37), though these in turn were said to have been 'certainly an improvement on the notorious local sailing craft used hitherto' (p. 38).
8 OA 879, K.G. Tregonning, 'The Mosquito Fleet', circa 1960.
9 OA 7.A.2. 154, 'British Malaya and Adjoining Territories: Notes for Exporters', 1936.
10 Fadzil Mohamed was born in Muar in Johor state, moved to Malacca during the war, then on to Kuala Lumpur, where he worked briefly as a *peon* (servant boy) for a British family, and finally back to Johor. He eventually

walked over the causeway to Singapore, where he stayed with his brother-in-law who was working as a policeman before beginning seafaring work with the SSC. Fadzil recalled receiving wages of 66 Malayan dollars per month in 1946 and that, at the time, there were 8.5 dollars to 1 pound sterling. Notes from conversation with Fadzil, Liverpool, 3 May 2008.

11 BT 381/3931, Agreement and Account of Crew, 3 January 1946; Agreement and List of Crew, 8 March 1946.

12 The term *lascar* refers to indigenous sailors of the Indian Ocean region who worked on British ships for wages and other conditions that would have been unacceptable to British seafarers. The term *lascar* is dealt with in much more detail later in this chapter. However, relating more specifically to Fadzil's recollection, it is worth noting that one of the additional clauses listed in a crew agreement for the *Charon* from March 1946 was that 'the Malay deck crew agree to work cargo at any time and at any port of call as required by the Master,' BT 380/3931, Agreement and List of Crew, 8 March 1946.

13 Notes from conversation, 12 April 2008. The Boyanese man, Abdullah, later became a seafarer himself and eventually died in Manchester. His presence in Broome is further evidence of long-standing 'Malay' economic mobility. A special correspondent for *The Age* who visited Broome in 1899 remarked that Malays (as well as Japanese and Manila men) working in the pearling industry had brought with them 'all the diseases and vices of the Orient' (cited in Reynolds, 2003). In 1901 around half the Asian workforce in Broome were said to have been Malays.

14 Notes from conversation with Fadzil, 3 May 2008.

15 Ngah Musa (Musa) is the man at the far left of the front row, holding a broom.

16 Construction of the building is credited to the Singapore-based firm, Swan and McClaren (Seet, 2011).

17 'Liverpool: port, docks and city', *Illustrated London News*, 15 May 1886.

18 Interview, Liverpool, 23 September 2004.

19 The prevailing practice at that time was for local crews to be engaged through intermediary agents or brokers who became authorized crew suppliers. For Malay seamen, this intermediary was known as the *ghaut serang*. Recruiting agents were officially entitled to collect 10 per cent of the seamen's first month wages as commission (see Nathan, 2005).

20 JJ is not pictured, but Dol is at the far left and Fadzil is second from the right in the top row.

21 Interview, Liverpool, 9 May 2008.

22 Visram (2002: 365n45) notes how while the term *lascar* came to mean Indian sailor in Britain, *khalasi* is the preferred term for seamen in various Indian languages. *Kelasi* is also the Malay-language term for seafarer. *Laskar* is 'soldier' in Malay; *lashkar* is 'army' or 'camp' in Urdu; and *lashkari* is 'soldier' in Portuguese.

23 Salter specifically mentions a Filipino boarding house owner, Josef Filipe (p. 159). The presence of Filipino lodgings around Frederick Street in the 1880s has led one researcher to dub this area 'the Little Manila of

Liverpool'. See Nestor P. Enriquez, 'Filipinos in Liverpool: Little Manila on Frederick St', available online at:. http://filipinohome.com/02_10_15 liverpool.html# (accessed on 31 July 2008).

24 De Quincey stayed in Liverpool in 1801, albeit in the Everton area of the city rather than in the south docks (Murray, 2008).

25 Even if De Quincey's writing was based on an encounter with one of these 'dusky wanderers', this does not necessarily mean that he would be considered a 'Malay' by today's definitions (see Krishnan, 2006).

26 'A potentate of Malacca', *New York Times*, 3 March 1894. Sultan Abu Bakar had 'laid the foundations for the modern state of Johore' after succeeding his father in 1862 (Hanna, 1966: 17). In 1864 he used money gained from the British for the sale of land at Telok Blangah in Singapore to fund 'a splendid palace in Johore Bahru' (p. 19). One historical account noted of Abu Bakar: 'In his palace, he lived and entertained in a style which won the approbation even of visiting British gentry' (Hanna, 1966: 19). D. Ker's description of the 'Maharajah' as a 'Potentate of Malacca' rather than Johore is a legacy of an historical tendency among Europeans to refer to the whole Malay Peninsula as 'Malacca'.

27 'Off the coast of Siam', *New York Times*, 20 November 1893.

28 'New-York seamen', *New York Times*, 10 April 1854.

29 'Hard fight for firemen', *New York Times*, 12 June 1893.

30 According to Vivek Bald (2013: 6), hundreds of Indian seamen working on British steamships did likewise, 'in search of less brutal and captive work and better wages onshore'.

31 Bald (2013: 117) notes a 'brief window of time after US factories had shifted into wartime production and before the restrictions of the 1917 Immigration Act tightened the reins on Asian immigrants and "alien seamen"'.

32 Mansor Puteh's (1983) magazine article shows photographs of *Merdeka* (independence) celebrations in 1957 as well as other pictures of gatherings for Hari Raya Puasa (to mark the end of the Muslim fasting month) and the like.

33 Interview with Hashim, Liverpool, 1 August 2006. The rest of this paragraph and the subsequent one are also based on the interview.

34 This is an example of the wider phenomenon '"buying cheap" in one location and "selling dear" in another' that is noted in Vivek Bald's (2013: 106) work on Indian seamen in the USA.

35 Hashim identified primarily as 'Ambonese'. There were said to have been 10 or 15 of his (Ambonese) 'countrymen' settled in New York during the time when he first visited in 1959.

36 See Chapter 1.

37 Making a joke by tricking me. Conversation with Mat Nor, 3 September 2004.

38 Clearly this resonates with and is indebted to Paul Gilroy's brilliant work on the 'Black Atlantic' (Gilroy, 1993).

39 'Is the murderer a Malay? A new theory of the murderer', *Pall Mall Gazette*, 10 November 1888.

40 'The Malay cook', *Atchison Daily Globe* (Kansas), 19 November 1888.
41 'Is the "ripper" a Malay cook?', *Evening Star* (Washington, DC), 20 November 1888.
42 'Is the "ripper" a Malay cook?', *Evening Star* (Washington, DC), 20 November 1888.
43 An anonymous letter sent from Manchester to the *Pall Mall Gazette* is replete with racist stereotypes of Malay-ness. Malays are said to be known by 'authorities' to be 'extremely vindictive, treacherous, and ferocious, implacable in their revenge, and on the slightest provocation, or imaginary insult, will commit murder'. These 'vicious attributes' and the propensity to 'run a-muck' are 'hereditary and apparently ineradicable' (10 November 1888).
44 Lawton (1964: 359) notes that '[i]n 1913 Liverpool handled 41 per cent of the export trade and 30 per cent of the import trade of the United Kingdom and was estimated to have one-seventh of the registered shipping in the world.'
45 'English shipping halted', *New York Times*, 15 April 1917.
46 'English shipping halted', *New York Times*, 15 April 1917.
47 'Sailors in mutiny routed by police', *New York Times*, 21 May 1917.
48 *South Wales Echo*, 14 June 1919.
49 'Renewed riots at Cardiff: badgered Malays seek refuge on roof of house', *South Wales News*, 14 June 1919.
50 Cardiff, the 'coal metropolis', was a major Atlantic port in its own right (Daunton, 1977). More importantly, as a result of its coal trade, Cardiff, like Liverpool, 'gathered in seamen from many parts of the globe' (Evans, 1980: 6). While news reports on the riots allow identification of L. Hassan's boarding house at 8 Bute Terrace in 1919, a post-Second World War study of the Bute Town district includes a single Malay boarding house (with seven beds) as part of a list of seamen's lodgings in the city; this also notes a steady decline in the number of Malays among the 'coloured "Alien" seamen' registered in Cardiff from 88 in 1934 down to 41 in 1938 (Little, 1948: 98). Nonetheless, as late as January 1932, more Malays were officially listed among 'coloured Alien seamen' in Cardiff than in Liverpool (132 compared to 73). IOR L/E/9/954, Home Office figures sent to the India Office.
51 Maritime Archives and Library, Merseyside Maritime Museum, DX/2010, Career Papers of Mohamed Ben Ibram.
52 BT 99/3504. Number 264 was an Arab restaurant and boarding house where a coloured man was killed after being badly beaten in an attack by youths, discharged soldiers and sailors on 12 June (Evans, 1980: 16).
53 CO 273/559/22, file on 'Adam Bacha nationality'.
54 According to one study, the battle 'had few moments of great drama. Rather, it was a five-year slog of attrition always played out against the foul weather of the North Atlantic.' Yet it was a campaign that Britain 'had to win for her very survival' (Kemp, 1989: 2).
55 Maritime Archives and Library, Merseyside Maritime Museum, DX/2010.

56 Zaharah Othman, 'In their element at sea', *New Straits Times*, 27 March 2000.
57 National Archives of Singapore, Oral History Interviews, accession number 003260, reel 1.
58 BT 381/1383, entry in official logbook on 19 March 1941.
59 BT 381/1383. He is reported as having 'taken his gear with him'.
60 Eccles notes that the ship was eventually sold in 1949. There is a picture of the *Telesfora* in his book on page 75.
61 I take the term 'greater Liverpool' from Haggerty *et al.* (2008: 3).
62 Zaharah Othman, 'In their element at sea', *New Straits Times*, 27 March 2000.
63 Notes from conversation with Majid, Liverpool, 10 September 2004.
64 Notes from conversation with Majid, Liverpool 6 October 2004.
65 Notes from conversation with Majid, Liverpool, 10 September 2004.

3

Home Port Liverpool and its Malay Places

Having traced maritime routes that brought Malay seamen to Liverpool, and sustained the city's commercial reach to the *alam Melayu* and a wider world of port cities, attention now turns to the social geography of Malay Liverpool. I begin this chapter by recalling the local social networks and intimate relations that made the city an attractive base for Malay men even during the interwar period when a shortage of seafaring work heightened official and everyday racism. This extends the study beyond Malay *men*, bringing into view the women and children of dockside urban communities. Despite the prevalence of racism in Liverpool in general, I show in the second section of the chapter how Chinatown and the south docks – those areas of the city most demographically marked by imperial maritime connections prior to the Second World War – are remembered by people who grew up there as spaces of everyday cosmopolitanism. In the third section, I consider changes in the family lives of the wives and children of Malay seamen associated with the rhythms of seafaring employment. While all families on 'ship street' (Kerr, 1958) experienced fluctuations according to whether or not husband/father was away at sea, children of Malay seafarers recall their lives shifting in and out of Malay-ness, especially with regard to food taboos and preparation rituals. As I show in the fourth and final section, Liverpool-based Malay seamen themselves experienced Malay-ness through specific urban sites: boarding houses, cafés and, of course, the two successive sites of the city's Malay Club. A series

From World City to the World in One City: Liverpool through Malay Lives,
First Edition. Tim Bunnell.

of 'places to be Malay' – places which brought together men with a diverse range of attachments to Liverpool as 'Malays' and anchored social networks extending to the *alam Melayu* and sailor towns around the world – culminated in the purchase of 7 Jermyn Street as the second home of the Malay Club in the early 1960s.

Somewhere Worth Staying?

When Mohamed Nor Hamid (Mat Nor) arrived in Liverpool in 1952, he was able to stay with the neighbour of his uncle, Youp bin Baba (Ben Youp). Mat Nor had followed the established Malay seafaring career path to Liverpool that was sketched in the previous chapter in relation to other men, serving on Straits Steamship Company and other 'mosquito fleet' boats around the *alam Melayu*,[1] then on Blue Funnel Line's Western Australia service. Before leaving Singapore for Colombo to begin his first oceangoing work, he returned home to Tanjung Keling outside Malacca. Mat Nor's mother consented to his plans saying that her brother was living in *Eropah.* While literally translating as 'Europe', this term, Mat Nor recalled, encompassed any lands where *orang puteh* (white people) lived and he was not even told which country his uncle was staying in, let alone provided with a specific address. Yet when Mat Nor's Prince Line ship arrived in Liverpool, he found out from other Malay seamen there that Ben Youp was living with his family in Upper Huskisson Street (see Figure 3.1). Ben Youp, it turned out, was away at

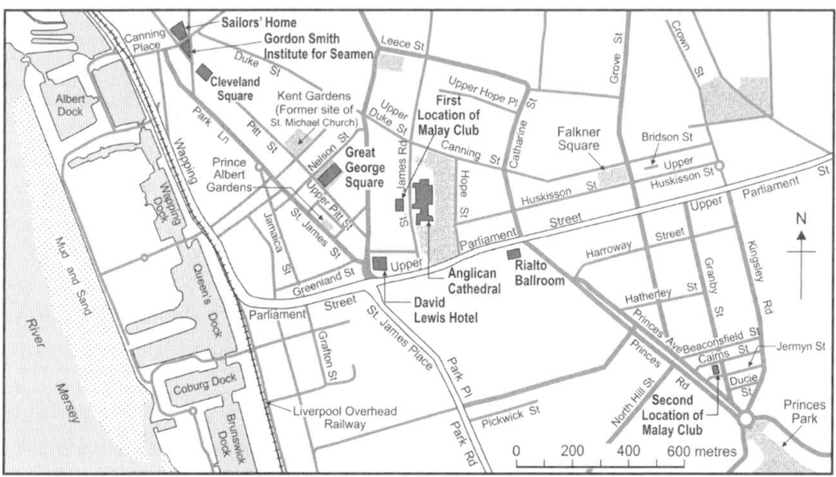

Figure 3.1 Malay Liverpool, circa 1960. Produced by Lee Li Kheng.

sea, and guest rooms in the house at number 144 where he had lived since before the war were fully occupied with other visiting Malay seamen.[2] Mat Nor was able to stay next door, at number 142, the home of another Malacca man.[3] The area around what was once Upper Huskisson Street is today Liverpool Women's Hospital, and so another part of mid-twentieth-century maritime Malay worlds now exists in the memories of diminishing numbers of people. It is important to note, however, that in this case such memories are not limited to elderly ex-seamen. Numbers 142 and 144 Upper Huskisson Street in Liverpool 8 among other Malay places are also remembered by the family members, friends and neighbours who helped to make Liverpool – or at least certain parts of the city – home for seafaring men from the *alam Melayu.*

It is not difficult to understand why Malay seamen decided to use Liverpool as their home port in the two decades after the Second World War. The family connections that Mat Nor enjoyed were not necessary for finding the way to Malay boarding houses. There was a well-established tradition of Malays who worked on the docks in Liverpool looking out for new arrivals. Even those who slipped through this net and ended up at the Seamen's Mission in Canning Place were often directed to 144 Upper Huskisson Street and other houses like it.[4] Staying at such Malay places meant that seamen quickly felt at home and plugged easily into local urban social networks. There was also no shortage of seafaring work during this period. The historian Jon Murden has described it as a postwar economic 'golden age' in which worldwide demand for Britain's manufactured goods soared and Liverpool's port and merchant marine served the rapidly expanding trade (Murden, 2006: 402). As Mat Nor put it:

> We forget about all the life in Singapore, you know. That's why most of the Malays stay here because it's a happy life in Liverpool, very happy, very easy to get a job. Any time you want a ship you can get. They send the telegram to the house you see … sometimes three or four telegram come in a day.

The telegrams invited men to the 'pool' where they were able to sign onto ships, subject to passing a medical examination. Given the high demand for seafaring labour during this period, even those Malay men who were not British subjects appear to have experienced little difficulty in securing work.

This rosy scenario contrasts sharply with the experiences of seamen in the prewar period whose motivations for staying in Liverpool (and other British seaports) are much more difficult to ascertain. Given inferior rates of pay for seamen signing on overseas – a legacy of the *lascar* and

Asiatic 'articles' considered in the previous chapter – foreign seamen settled in Britain 'in the hope of obtaining better pay and conditions' (May and Cohen, 1974: 118). However, a racially hierarchical labour market (at sea, as well as on land) left 'coloured' people extremely vulnerable during economic downturns. In the context of the growing competition for jobs after the First World War, which boiled over into racial violence in 1919, an Indian man who had been given 24 hours notice to quit his position as a river hopper on the Mersey complained that 'the white men must be re-instated first, the unions insist on it' (cited in Visram, 2002: 199). Scandinavians were given preference over non-whites even though the latter included British subjects like himself and most Malays.[5] Rozina Visram (2002: 202–3) notes:

> In March 1921, Raymond Oliver, the solicitor to the Islamic Society, on behalf of his Muslim clients, 'Arab, Malay, Somali and Indian seamen', complained to the India Office of their deliberate exclusion from jobs 'on account of their colour'. He argued that as 'British subjects' who had served 'most loyally' in the war, they were 'entitled to employment in British ships, in preference to seamen of alien nationality'.

Malay merchant marine war veterans are among the British subjects who appear in the Colonial Office's records of 'destitute coloured men'. Minutes from August 1919, for example, include the case of a seaman from Singapore who had had a foot amputated following an injury sustained when his ship was torpedoed. Usop bin Brahim, whose case for repatriation had been processed in June, visited the Colonial Office again two months later and reportedly created 'a most hideous uproar' when told that nothing further could be done for him.[6]

Even able-bodied men who were not repatriated faced difficulties securing work and so a high risk of destitution. In June 1921 the India Office received a letter from the Strangers' Home for Asiatics in London concerning the SS *Dabchick* whose captain had refused to take two 'Malay seamen'.[7] While the men had initially been offered work, the captain was concerned that he would be liable for their repatriation to Singapore after they were discharged in Bombay. During the same month, the India Office recognized the impoverishment of 'Indian and Arab seamen' and offered to pay a maintenance allowance of four shillings per day to unemployed seamen in Cardiff and London through the British and Foreign Sailors' Society.[8] One application from this society in London concerned five men from Singapore staying at the house of L. Nairoolla in High Street, Poplar.[9] More than a decade later, *The Keys*, the quarterly publication of the League of Coloured Peoples, mentioned the case of 'a Malay who had been unemployed for twelve years but had recently received employment as a result of the League's activities in Cardiff'.[10] By this time, as recognized by the League and organizations such as the Colonial Seamen's Association in London, a subsidy provided to 'tramp ships' (those with no fixed schedule or ports of call) on condition that they only employ British subjects, deepened the economic marginalization of many non-white seamen, irrespective of their nationality.[11]

For much of the interwar period Malay seafarers – including those born in parts of British Malaya which made them legally British subjects – experienced 'the various disabilities which attend to aliens in Great Britain'.[12] This phrase is taken from the Colonial Office file on Adam bin Ma'Sah, whose unhappy time in Britain was described in the previous chapter. It will be recalled that Adam arrived at Liverpool on board the SS *City of Tokio* in April 1929. Home Office correspondence in the file reports:

> He produced for the inspection of the Immigration Officer a declaration made by his father in Malacca to the effect that the son was born in Malacca but that no record of his birth could be traced. The Immigration Officer did not consider that this document sufficiently established the national status of the man and he was refused leave to land under Article 15(1) of the Aliens Order.[13]

This 1920 Aliens Order, together with the Special Restriction (Coloured Alien Seamen) Order five years later, the Colonial Office verified, served 'to place upon any coloured seaman desirous of landing for discharge at a port in Great Britain the onus of proof that he is of British nationality'.[14] What is more, the 1935 report in *The Keys* on coloured seamen in Cardiff notes that even men with apparently suitable documentary proof 'had been compelled for the last ten years to register as aliens through the threats and by the coercion of the police authorities'.[15] This scenario was not unique to Cardiff. Indeed, according to May and Cohen (1974: 119), it was a special registration system for 'aliens' introduced in Liverpool that was extended to other ports 'and later given administrative sanction in the Aliens Order of 1925'. Since 'the distinction between "coloured seamen" and "coloured" residents was fudged', all coloured British subjects in port cities without the appropriate documents were effectively de-nationalized (Visram, 2002: 206).[16]

While the actions of agencies and institutions varied and shifted over time,[17] non-white seamen in Britain appear in government records as a problematic if not outright undesirable presence. Such conceptions were bound up with broader racist fears about demographic contamination and miscegenation. As Jacqueline Nassy Brown (2005: 28) suggests in her research on Black Liverpool, the Order of 1925 'really should have been named appropriately the Coloured Alien Semen Order'. In more ways than one, then, officials were concerned that the discharge of coloured seamen should take place somewhere – anywhere – other than in Britain. It is revealing that the India Office's reply to the query about the captain of the SS *Babchick* made clear that there was no concern about his 'Malay' crew discharging in Bombay.[18] In addition, even after the Malayan Information Agency – through the Colonial Office – had secured Adam bin Ma'Sah's release from prison in October 1929, the Home Office was insistent that this Malacca-born British subject 'will not however be allowed to establish himself in the United Kingdom'.[19]

Despite these far from welcoming official attitudes and vulnerability to labour market fluctuations, 'coloured' seamen did establish themselves in Liverpool and other port cities in Britain. An article in the *Liverpool Echo* published in the aftermath of racial violence in June 1919 reported: 'Few of our ports can show such a tendency to the formation of distinct foreign colonies as Liverpool does. We have our Chinatown, Dark town and other alien quarters all in more or less distinct areas of the city.'[20] The numbers in 'dark town' in particular were said to have 'grown tremendously' during the First World War.[21] Demobilization of alien and British subjects who served in the army and navy increased the black population in Liverpool to about 5,000 (May and Cohen, 1974: 118). Malay se(a)men also contributed to Liverpool's 'precocious multicultural-demographic profile' (Belchem, 2000: xiii). A report on 'The Economic Status of Coloured Families in the Port of Liverpool' published in 1940, for example, includes a short profile of a 'Boy (16 and a half years old): Father a Malayan, working as an ordinary seaman' (Caradog Jones, 1940: 22).[22] The very different economic and political conditions in the south docks 'foreign colonies' in the 1920s and 1930s make it difficult to read back motivations for settlement then from the experiences of seamen who arrived after the Second World War. However, Mat Nor was adamant that economic factors had always been secondary at best: 'I don't care what the people say, all the Malay stay in Liverpool, England, through woman.'[23] While the heteronormativity of his statement might be questioned, along with the way that it downplays the importance of homosocial friendship networks, it would seem reasonable to suggest that intimate relationships and family formation were the main reason why Malay men made 'home port' into home.

After Mat Nor's uncle, Ben Youp, got married in Liverpool, his wife Priscilla was disowned by her white Protestant parents.[24] The social ostracism from friends and family endured by working-class English and Irish women who formed marital or other intimate relations with 'coloured' seamen has been well documented (e.g. Frost, 1999; Brown, 2005).

Diane Frost (2008: 161) notes that '[t]heir experiences were indicative of the continuing importance of "race" and the deep-seated racism that continued to prevail in post-war, post-imperial British society.' In this context, the decision to enter into 'interracial unions' with men from Malaya – as with the west African men who formed the focus of Frost's empirical work – 'tells us much about the persistence of human agency and the possibilities of resistance to dominant forms of ideology' (p. 161). For all the emphasis on Malay seamen's agency and mobilities in this book, it was to a considerable degree 'local' women's urban sociospatial journeys and contributions to cosmopolitan dockside communities that appear to have made Liverpool somewhere worth staying.[25] Given that such contributions extended back at least as far as the First World War, and included seafarers from many regions of the world, by the time that Malay men such as Mat Nor arrived in the 1950s, the locally born population of the south docks area of the city was already highly demographically diverse.

Remembering Cosmopolitanism and its Limits

The recollections of children of Malay seamen born before the Second World War help to picture the demographic diversity of the south docks area either side of the war. Ronnie Bujang, son of Amat bin Bujang from Malaya, was born in 1933 on Hurst Street, opposite Wapping Dock and in the shadow of the Liverpool Overhead Railway (the so-called dockers' umbrella) which ran along the dock road, southwest of the city centre (see Figure 3.1). After the war, Ronnie's mother, a Liverpool-born 'Spanish Filipina', moved 'up' – literally, in topographical terms – to what was then still the predominantly white Liverpool 8 area around Granby Street and ran a boarding house rather like the one operated by the Youps.[26] Ronnie later married Cathy Awang whose father was also a Malay seaman, but whose mother was Irish. Cathy had grown up in the Chinatown area 'below' the Anglican Cathedral, which was within the same city centre postal code area (Liverpool 1) as Ronnie's birthplace.[27] The conventional toponym 'Chinatown' is far from adequate in that the area which it denoted was home to people of varied ethnic and geographical origins, not only Chinese. Ronnie recalls:

> Where Cath was, there was every nation under God's earth there, you know: Japanese, Irish, Welsh, Chinese, Malay, African, Jamaican, everything, all getting brought up there.... So there was no such thing as a racist where she was living; and that was the beauty of it because I used to like going down to see her. You never used to get called names.

Cathy agreed: 'We didn't know what these bad [i.e. racist] names were 'cause we had every league of nations living in our tenement blocks.... We were all one big happy family.' This *in situ* 'league of nations' diversity runs against spatial imaginings of Liverpool's 'alien' or 'foreign' populations as having been parcelled into distinct racial quarters or colonies. Without denying the selectivity of Ronnie and Cathy's memories – not to mention their inflection with childhood nostalgia – historical forms of what might be termed 'ordinary cosmopolitanisms' (Lamont and Aksartova, 2002) clearly existed in parts of the city which were cast as socially problematic spaces in official narratives (when they appeared at all).[28]

The term 'cosmopolitanism' has a long history of varied connotations in the context of maritime Liverpool (Belchem, 2006). One late nineteenth-century Indian visitor to Britain was impressed with the 'world-embracing' commerce of Liverpool, London and Southampton. Amrit Lal Roy noted the presence of peoples of every nationality in these cities and considered them 'less provincial' especially in attitudes to people from non-Christian countries. However, it is doubtful whether Indian Ocean seafarers were embraced as warmly as Roy, the anglophile Edinburgh University-educated 'student turned tourist', especially beyond the south docks areas of Liverpool (Roy, 1888: 32–3 cited in Visram, 2002: 113).[29] Certainly, in Edwardian times, while '[c]osmopolitanism was a point of Merseypride, a factor that raised Liverpool above provincialism' (Belchem, 2000: xiii), this had to do with the city's commercial reach into far-flung corners of the British Empire (and beyond) rather than with acknowledgement of the demographic effects of population 'counterflows'.[30] As John Belchem (2000: xiii) suggests in his work on the pageant held as part of the city's 700th anniversary celebrations in 1907, 'in its history (as in its civic life) there was to be no place for settlers from overseas, "black scousers" – Kru, Lascar, Chinese and other sea-faring communities – drawn to Liverpool by the opening up of new markets and routes after abolition.'

It worth pointing out, however, that not only did the racial violence of June 1919 (mentioned above and considered in more detail in the previous chapter) draw attention to 'foreign' seafaring groups and associated spaces in the city, but these were termed 'cosmopolitan' in contemporary news reports.[31] In other words, even when coloured seafarers did find a place in civic imaginings of cosmopolitanism, it was through a trope of the 'cosmopolitan' as socially (and often also biologically) problematic.[32] To the extent that Liverpool's cosmopolitanism referred to social geographies within the city, this had less to do with hospitality to (or integration of) 'foreigners' than with their spatial containment in what were aptly referred to (and distanced) as 'colonies'.[33]

The childhood worlds of Cathy and Ronnie Bujang were highly spatially limited. Ronnie's positive memories of the immediate postwar Chinatown area are framed in contrast to other parts of Liverpool – indeed, to most of the rest of the city. It was in large part, of course, the absence of hospitality in the city as a whole that gave rise to dockside colonies in the first place. In distinguishing the area where Cathy lived in terms of the absence of racism and usage of 'bad names', Ronnie implies their ubiquity elsewhere. The sad variety of 'bad names' he endured in what was then still the overwhelmingly 'white' area around Granby Street was one of the reasons why he liked going back 'down' (the hill) to Chinatown. Ironically, in subsequent decades, it was precisely the Granby area – whether through the largely externally imposed toponym Toxteth or the more locally resonant Liverpool 8 – which became synonymous with black people. The territorial boundaries of what Brown (2005) refers to as 'Black Liverpool' shifted over time, but they did not simply go away. Brown's own informants in the 1990s sketched historical social cartographies of the racism that constrained them. For one, a pub aptly named The Boundary marked the limit of where he could travel without fear of either being beaten up by white youths or harassed by police. So hostile were some parts of the city that black people 'would not want or dare to go there' (Brown, 2005: 87). For generations of visiting Malay seamen too, there were clear spatial limits to Liverpool's appeal. Given the demographically heterogeneous composition of the city's limited zones of hospitality, and the fact that I met few people with Malay ancestry in the city who identified with 'black' politics, I prefer to term these areas as 'cosmopolitan Liverpool' or 'the other Liverpool' (Lane, 1997: 131) rather than as 'Black Liverpool'. Before and in the immediate aftermath of the Second World War, this referred to the south docks and Chinatown areas of Liverpool 1 where Cathy grew up, and only in subsequent decades did it come to refer to Liverpool 8 where Ronnie's mum's boarding house was located.[34]

The confined and largely self-contained nature of the south docks area during Cathy and Ronnie's childhoods is reflected in the ignorance of its demographic composition that prevailed in other parts of the city. Ronnie Bujang complained of having been subjected to a wide variety of racist names, none of which he considered appropriate for his geographical or ethnic origin.[35] 'Malay' was not a known category of either ethnic differentiation or racial abuse. This may have been fortunate given the stereotypical characterizations of 'Malays' that had circulated in other times and places. In the late nineteenth-century Jack the Ripper case which was considered in the previous chapter, notions of Malays as 'vindictive, treacherous and ferocious' were evident from newspaper reports on both sides of the Atlantic.[36] In literature too, from De Quincey to Dickens to Conan Doyle, the 'Malay' appears as a menacing eastern presence.[37] My interviews suggest that at least among Liverpool-born children of Malay seamen, Malay identity was not necessarily appreciated within Chinatown either. According to Cathy, she and her friends did not realize that they 'were anything', in terms of ethnic identity, until they were old enough to venture into other parts of the city. If Cathy here evokes a space of preracialized childhood innocence in Chinatown, in the city and national territory beyond, Malays, other non-whites and 'half-castes' were largely lumped together as less than Anglo-Saxons.

Unwelcoming attitudes to foreigners and even some specific racial stereotypes were bound up with geographies of colonialism. As Roy May and Robin Cohen (1974: 112) summarize it:

> The effect of the colonial experience on the growth of racism had a dual impact. On the one hand, racial theories which by the turn of the century had assumed a material force in their own right, were used to legitimize relationships of dominance and disability within the Empire. On the other hand, the very achievement of military superiority and administrative control over the colonized peoples fed back to the metropolis in the form of stereotypes, mythologies and ideologies which confirmed the supposed superiority of the Anglo-Saxon 'race'.

A letter on 'the Malay nature' published in the *Pall Mall Gazette* during the Jack the Ripper case is written with the kind of pompous authority brought back to the metropole by someone with experience of governing this particular colonial people.[38] Yet even the stereotype of the Malay 'running a-muck' which is mentioned in that Victorian era letter did not seem to filter down to interwar Liverpool. Perhaps this was due to the demise of popular imperialism after the First World War. More likely it is evidence that 'knowledge' of specific colonial peoples had always been largely restricted to those members of the metropole with direct military or administrative experience of the territories concerned. Popular imperial nationalism was very much alive in interwar Britain, and this reaffirmed senses of Anglo-Saxon superiority without necessarily conferring knowledge of specific territories or peoples (MacKenzie, 1986a). As John M. MacKenzie has shown, Empire Day, for example, was given great prominence in the 1920s and 1930s, including through radio (MacKenzie, 1986b). Also promoted through local education authorities, Empire Day was celebrated in schools across Britain (Mangan, 1986), including in Liverpool (Steele, 2008). At St Michael's School on Pitt Street in Chinatown, Empire Day celebrations in the 1930s included children dressing up in the costume of one of the colonies. Among those pictured in photographs in the Maritime Archives and Library at the Merseyside Maritime Museum are Ronnie Bujang's brother and at least one other friend with a Malay seafaring father.[39] In some of the photographs, it appears as if a child dressed as an Anglo-Saxon knight takes centre stage. Following the race-blind childhood that Cathy Bujang recalls of Chinatown, in the case of St Michael's School at least, this may have been simply to do with the aesthetic appeal of the knight costume rather than any colonial perception of the non-metropolitan 'others' as racially inferior.

Malay seafarers were well aware that they were treated as inferior to white people in Liverpool and elsewhere. Every Liverpool-based ex-seafarer had stories of racist experiences to tell, though not necessarily set in Liverpool. Mohamed Nor Hamid (Mat Nor) recalled how at a cinema in Australia the people who had happily been sitting next to him during the first half of a movie swiftly changed seats after the lights came on for the interval.[40] Ironically, it was trips to Australia on the MV *Charon* – and seeing *orang puteh* (white people) doing 'real work' for the first time – that had earlier disabused Mat Nor of any perception of the superiority of European colonial 'masters'. Yet on the MV *Cingalese Prince*, the oceangoing ship that first took him to Liverpool (see Figure 3.2), Mat Nor was employed on Asiatic articles. Even after the Second World War, therefore, long-standing lower rates of pay for *lascar*, Asiatic and other non-white seamen continued to provide a motivation to ship out of

Figure 3.2 Mohamed Nor Hamid (far left) on board the MV *Cingalese Prince*. Photograph courtesy of Mohamed Nor Hamid.

British ports such as Liverpool (see Tabili, 1994; Balachandran, 2007). In Liverpool itself, Mat Nor recalled one of his Malay friends, Osman ('Man Negro'), being refused entry to a dance hall on Williamson Square, in the city centre, in the mid-1950s.[41] One version of the story goes that this 'Malay' man had a father from Perak (a state in what is today Malaysia) and a mother from Abyssinia (Ethiopia); another suggests that Osman's parents had been from Ambon in Indonesia. Irrespective of the geography of his ancestry, Osman's nickname provides a useful reminder not only of the diverse origins and phenotypical features of people who had become 'Malay' (Chapter 2), but also that Malay seafarers themselves operated through racialized colonial registers. Yet the more immediate point here is that even in the 'happy times' of postwar Liverpool, Malay men were on the receiving end of racial discrimination in both their working and social lives – albeit to varying degrees depending on their precise phenotypical features.

While children of Malay seamen recall Chinatown as a space of cosmopolitan social interaction, it is difficult to identify anything internally specific to Liverpool that accounts for it having become *the* Atlantic home port for Malays either side of the Second World War. Among the immediate postwar generation of arrivals at least, there was little of the 'wow' factor that accompanied reminiscences of their initial encounters with New York City. When asked about their memories of 1950s Liverpool, the most common response concerned how smoky it was,[42] especially in winter when coal was burned to heat houses as well as to power factories and steamships, suggesting that little had changed in environmental terms since Sultan Abu Bakar's entourage had visited in the late nineteenth century.[43] In addition, as Paul Du Noyer (2007: 14) puts it, the port had already faded to become less the 'Gateway of Empire' that it had been in its glamorous Edwardian days, and more the 'Tradesman's Entrance'. A Singapore-based Malay journalist who visited Liverpool in 1952 was clearly not impressed with the city, describing it as dirty, full of bombed-out buildings from the Second World War and altogether 'not as beautiful as London' ('*tidak begitu chantek saperti London*') (Aminurrashid, 1961: 126).[44]

There is evidence that young Malay seamen arriving in Liverpool during this period embraced American popular cultural influences that are commonly said to have set the city apart from most of the rest of Britain. One man from Penang became known as Noor Elvis, for example, and another became a keen country and western singer[45] – but this is as likely to have stemmed from direct seafaring experiences across the (Malay) Atlantic as from having eventually settled in the 'Nashville of the North' (McManus, 1994).[46] Mat Nor recalled several dance halls that he and his friends could get into in Liverpool, but the fact that he also remembered having to endure listening to opera at the Seamen's Mission after the pubs closed in the afternoon suggests that young Malay men did not find the city's entertainment as exciting in the 1950s as is often mythologized.[47] In 1953 Lita Roza, who was said to have been 'part Malayan by birth' (Cohen, 2007: 30), became the first Liverpool musician to top the British charts. This feat was achieved with the 'rotten' American novelty song '(How Much) Is That Doggy in the Window' (Du Noyer, 2007: 63), although the local swing bands with which Lita Roza performed as a vocalist were evidence of a much more profound transatlantic musical influence (Cohen, 2007). Nonetheless, it was only in the 1960s that Liverpool's contribution to popular music really took off, with Merseybeat and, above all, the Beatles making the city 'a source of wonder to the world' (Du Noyer, 2007: 84).

When looking for reasons as to why Liverpool became the capital of the Malay Atlantic, therefore, it is necessary to move both upscale (to wider political economic relations and long-distance economic networks), and especially downscale (to personal relationships and places of associational life). If it was Liverpool's 'Main Street' (Dick and Rimmer, 2003) maritime commercial position that brought Malays to the city and gave them the chance to continue to work out of this port city, it was intimate social relations which usually led to more permanent anchorage. Sites such as 144 Upper Huskisson Street, where Malacca-born Ben Youp and his English wife lived and provided lodgings for visiting Malay seamen, played an important role in the social reproduction of maritime Malay Liverpool. Ben Youp is recalled by his daughter, Joan Higgins, as having agreed for her to be married to a visiting Malay seaman known as Freddie when Joan was 14 years old.[48] But for the intervention of Joan's mother, Priscilla, another one of the visiting Malay men who stayed on Upper Huskisson Street might have come to call Liverpool 'home'.

Home and Away

Those men who formed families but continued to work at sea spent more time away than in home port Liverpool. While I was often amazed at the ability of septuagenarian men to recall the names of ships they worked on half a century ago (and, in some cases, even details of their wages and the prices of goods they bought along the way), I heard relatively little about life on board ship. Periods away 'at sea' are narrated principally in terms of a series of portside places visited. No doubt this is at least in part because of the monotony of the ship as workplace. Given the conventional association of seafaring with (mostly male) mobility – and of mobility in turn with freedom – it is worth emphasizing that seamen spent much of their lives within highly spatially constrained, regulated and even factory-like working environments (Linebaugh and Rediker, 2012).[49] What is more, even when onshore, sailors tended to be confined, or to confine themselves, to portside areas. Stories of 'the sea', then, are often in fact about more or less exotic places bordering, though connected by, oceans and seas. For seafarers in many other ports around the world during the 150 years or so or up to the middle of the twentieth century, Liverpool was narrated as an infamous 'sailortown' – 'a world of sordid pleasure, unlimited vice, and lashings of booze' (Hugill, 1967). Yet the city features less prominently in the seafaring tales of Malay ex-seafarers who came to be based in Liverpool itself. Even the most exotic of places become ordinary or mundane over time; through familiarity, home port Liverpool became no longer part of the 'away'.

What did time away at sea mean for the families of Malay seamen back (at home) in Liverpool? This is clearly a very important question but also one to which I remain unable to provide fully satisfactory answers. In part, this inadequacy arises from the methodological siting of my research in a clubhouse frequented largely by male ex-seafarers. It proved very difficult to track down wives, ex-wives or widows of former seafarers, let alone to meet and talk with them. What follows here is based largely on recollections of family life from (both male and female) children of Malay ex-seamen. None of these informants had Malay mothers, but not all had mothers who identified as 'white' either. In every case, at least during the time when their fathers continued to work as seamen (as opposed to taking 'shore jobs' in Liverpool), 'away at sea' was the norm in family life. During these periods – that is, most of the time – it was mother who ruled the household. The 1958 sociological text *The People of Ship Street* provides details of seafaring family dynamics in Liverpool during that decade (Kerr, 1958). While Madeline Kerr's study focused on families of Irish descent, the 'tremendous power of the Mum' that she notes applies to wives of Malay men who worked at sea. Indeed, given the severing of friendship and family support networks which frequently followed the decision to enter 'interracial' unions (Frost, 2008: 155), wives and partners of Malay men required additional power, strength and resilience.[50]

Children in such family situations did not grow up with a strong sense of Malay identity or Malay-ness. For those who grew up in 'cosmopolitan' Chinatown, this may have been a good thing. By not thinking of themselves as 'anything' they did not suffer from anxieties over their place in some imagined racial hierarchy or as supposedly problematic 'half-castes'. This term was still in active circulation during my fieldwork in Liverpool and seems to have been more of a social burden for those who grew up in 'white' areas. Whether growing up in supposedly 'cosmopolitan' or white areas, both before and after the Second World War, there is a more general sense of regret at not having had the chance to learn more about 'dad's' culture, language or place of origin. Ronnie Bujang recalled feeling 'embarrassed' and even 'guilty' at not speaking Malay when he met 'old Malay fellers'. He lamented having been raised, as he put it, without his 'father's culture': 'someone should be there to say this is your culture, you must learn this, you must learn the language, but we had nobody.'[51] In the case of Teddy Lates, it was his own experience of working at sea in later life that provided the chance to visit Southeast Asia and so to learn more about his father's homeland.[52]

The adult children of Malay ex-seafarers whom I was able to interview recalled a sense of anticipation around the time when dad was due to return. Like many other families in the city, this was partly a matter of the prospect of receiving exciting gifts. Cathy Bujang remembered with obvious delight that she 'had everything' when her dad Eusop Awang was home from sea – 'it was like heaven.'[53] One might imagine that home was also a place where exotic stories were told. However, I found little evidence that children got to know much about the places their fathers (or husbands) visited or what they did there. Stan Hugill's book *Sailortown* reminds us of the danger of extending back modern 'sightseeing desires' onto earlier generations of seafarers. Writing primarily about European seamen, Hugill (1967: xx) notes: 'The first-tripper who was "going to see the world", soon learnt, in his first port, to follow the crowd to the pubs and brothels, and few were independent enough to break away from the mob'.[54] In the interwar period Hugill acknowledges 'the world of the sailor ashore' did extend: 'Some would get away from the dockside and the first and last pub … but only a few' (p. xxi). It may have been that some Malays differed from the stereotypical European seafarer who was the main subject of Hugill's writing. In addition, it is important to note the significance of the shift from sailing boats to steamships in general; steamship seafarers were recognized as 'family men' because of their more regular lifestyles (Kennerley, 1989). Nonetheless, it seems fair to generalize, as Hugill does: 'in the main, seafaring men kept to the waterfront' (Hugill, 1967: xxi; cf. Lee, 2013).

Whatever Malay seamen might have got up to 'away' in what remained of sailortown in the mid-twentieth century, many are remembered as strict fathers at home. Joan Higgins recalled how even when she had begun full-time work in her mid-teens, her father Ben Youp expected her to wear socks and long dresses so as not to show her legs in public. He also insisted that she had long hair and did not wear make-up. While associated tensions no doubt existed in many families in Liverpool during this period and were in part generational matters, Ben Youp is also said to have had a normative image of his daughter as 'a proper Malay girl'.[55]

Having eventually had her hair cut as she began to rebel, Joan was advised by her mother to tell a 'white lie' and say to her father that this cosmetic de-Malayization had been required for safety reasons at work (so that her hair would not get caught in machinery). Ben Youp's failing eyesight – he had cataracts in later life – also helped Joan's cause, especially as regards wearing make-up! Nonetheless, when she started to wear short skirts at home in the 1960s, Joan was expected by her mother to hide her legs with newspapers in the presence of Malay men. In other families, the strictness that accompanied dad's return home even offset the expectation of exciting gifts. The father's going away again could thus mean relief at the return of certain 'freedoms' at home.

The most frequently recounted shift between when dad was home and away was culinary. For Joan Higgins, eating Malay food was the most prominent part of the 'swing back' to 'dad's culture' when he was home. Like other Malay men during the period before the existence of halal butchers in Liverpool, Ben Youp kept and killed his own chickens. When he was home, the family ate rice with curries – mostly chicken but also rabbit – and did so with their hands. Food was also by far the most prominent cross-generational cultural legacy. Almost every descendant of Malay seafarers in Liverpool claimed to like to eat curry and spicy food; some, like one of Joan's brothers, were said to be able to cook it. Having the taste for spicy food became perhaps the common denominator marker of Malay-ness. So when Joan's daughter (Ben Youp's granddaughter) complained at the spiciness of one of her uncle's concoctions, her ancestral identity was brought into question: 'call yourself a Malay girl!?' Muslim food taboos rarely extended to 'second-generation' Malay girls and boys. In mid-twentieth-century Liverpool, Malay seamen – even those like Cathy's father Eusop Awang, who 'loved his Guinness' – steered clear of *babi* (pork). With very few exceptions, however, this did not apply to the rest of the family. Rather, a pork- and especially bacon-free household was one of the key distinguishing features of the time when 'dad' was home. The fact that the word *babi* was still remembered by descendants who knew very few other words of Malay is evidence of the significance of this shift. Some households even had separate sets of pots and pans for *babi*-free culinary interludes.

Most Liverpool-born descendants did not become Muslims. Both Ronnie Bujang and Teddy Lates were sent to a *zawiyah*, an Islamic religious school or an 'Arabic church' as they termed it, in the basement of a house on St James Road opposite the Anglican Cathedral.[56] More than half a century later, Ronnie Bujang could still recite some of the prayers that he learned, but had never considered himself to be Muslim. The only exceptions to this general rule were children of Liverpool-based seafarers – all daughters, as far as I am aware – who married later generations of Malay men from Malaysia who came to the city as students or cadets. Even as provision for Muslim worship expanded in the postwar period, the times when seafaring Malay men came home to maritime world city Liverpool were remembered in terms of trips to the Malay Club – in its two different locations – rather than to the mosque or to the earlier *zawiyah.*

Places to Be Malay

In 2004 Mohamed Nor Hamid (Mat Nor) recalled of his more than half a century in Liverpool, 'first time when I came here [in 1952], we got no place; Malay people got no place.'[57] Given that Mat Nor was able to make his way up to the house of his uncle Ben Youp on Upper Huskisson Street, and proceeded in interview to reel off a list of pubs and coffee shops that he and his friends once frequented, this seems like an odd recollection. What Mat Nor meant was that there was no specifically 'Malay place' in which he and his friends could socialize.[58] While an Arab Muslim shipowner provided space for Malays in the basement of his café on St James Place, this was primarily intended for religious activity.[59] As was noted in the previous chapter, it was in the 1950s that Johan Awang, one-time resident of the other side of the Malay Atlantic in New York, opened a Malay Club in Liverpool. Mat Nor first visited Liverpool on board the *Nordic* in 1952, so the club must have been established later than that, although I have not been able to establish a more precise formation date. What is clear is that Liverpool's Malay Club on St James Road and, subsequently, on Jermyn Street, became more than just places for Malays to meet. The club was a place in and through which seafarers, ex-seafarers and to a lesser extent their family members could be 'Malay'.

Prior to the formation of the Malay Club, Johan Awang's home on Greenland Street in the south docks area of Liverpool 1 was well known to visiting as well as Liverpool-based Malay seamen. The electoral register for 37 Greenland Street in 1950 records the presence at that address not only of Johan Awang and his wife Alice (known as Filipina Alice), but also two other Malacca-born men.[60] Malay ex-seamen, in Cardiff as well as Liverpool, recall visiting Johan Awang and Alice's house on Greenland Street during the early 1950s.[61] As has been noted, this was an economic golden age for postwar Liverpool, and British shipping in general, and it is reasonable to assume that the regular flow of seamen passing through the city during that time was an important motivation for establishing the club. As can be seen in Figure 3.1, Greenland Street is a short walk from St James Road. The Malay Club there is recalled as having had bunk beds for visiting seamen,[62] a big back yard and a games room with a dartboard.[63] There was also a prayer room upstairs although it seems that this was open to other Muslim men as the Malay Club itself was limited to the first floor of the building.[64] No cooking was allowed at the club during Ramadan (the Muslim fasting month), and this is cited by some as evidence that Johan Awang was quite a religious man. He worked in a halal butcher's shop on Granby Street and eventually became the first Malay man in the city to open a shop of his own, on North Hill Street.[65]

Food became central to memories of the St James Road club and of Malay Liverpool more broadly during that period. Recollections of the place never seemed to get very far before turning to food. The smell of rice from the kitchen pervaded the building (even though curry was cooked each day). The very mention of the smell of the place transported people back during interviews – 'I can just see it now' – but there are few other clues left today. It was at weekends that children and wives of seamen would be taken along to what was otherwise largely an adult male space. For some, it is not so much the club which is remembered from this period as the Hari Raya Aidilfitri and New Year parties which took place at the nearby David Lewis Hotel (see Figure 3.1). This was a tradition that continued after the club moved out of St James Road. Following the death of his wife Alice, Johan Awang returned to Malacca, and passed away there.

Demolition of buildings and indeed some entire streets 'below' the Anglican Cathedral formed part of processes of urban 'improvement' that extended back several decades. Before the Second World War, such efforts focused on the south docks area of the city. One report by the Ministry of Labour and the Ministry of Shipping in 1939 noted housing redevelopment carried out by the Liverpool Corporation while also suggesting the need for further work:

> Certain parts of the docks districts, mainly in the streets leading off Pitt Street and Great George Square, are the homes of a considerable number of Chinese, Indians and negroes.... The coloured community are generally well-behaved but the surroundings in which many of them live are not such as to encourage any attempt to reach a high moral standard.[66]

Air raids during the war accelerated processes of material environmental change, shifting the geographical locus of Chinatown and reducing the overall housing stock in the areas immediately south of the city centre (see Craggs and Loh Lynn, 1985; G.B. Lee, 1998). Much of what the Luftwaffe failed to destroy was demolished as 'slum clearance' in the postwar period. This was accompanied by further dispersal or 'decantation' of diverse members of the resident population to 'overspill' housing outside the city. But members of the 'other Liverpool', including some families of Malay seamen, also moved across and/or 'up' Parliament Street into the Liverpool 8 postal code area.

Liverpool 8 and Granby Street in particular emerged in the 1950s as the postwar centre of cosmopolitan Liverpool, just as Chinatown had been before the war. Ben Youp's daughter Joan recalls the street at that time as a 'buzzing place', full of exciting and exotic shops.[67] One of the Malay seafarers who stayed at the Youps' home on Upper Huskisson Street used to take Joan there to buy fruit whenever he came back from the sea:

> He used to come off every trip and he'd come home and he'd take me – 'cause I was the only girl, I've got three brothers – and himself and we'd go to Granby Street ... and there used to be a huge fruit stall there, a big fruit shop and we used to go in and he'd say to me, 'pick whichever fruit you want' – it was like going into wonderland!

It was not just fruit. Granby Street offered what was at that time a remarkable diversity of shops and products. As Joan's husband Kevin recalled from his own experiences of growing up in the area, 'Granby Street was very cosmopolitan, you had a real mixture of races down there and the shops were a mirror image of it really.' Granby Street was where spices and other ingredients for curries could be bought in an era before they were available in high street supermarkets; and where the young son of one Malay seaman got his comeuppance for munching on a stolen green chilli.[68] As already noted in connection with Johan Awang, Granby Street was also known as somewhere that halal meat could be purchased. It is perhaps not surprising, then, that the vicinity was selected as the site for a new mosque in the city. A foundation plaque for a planned £45,000 building with a 55-foot-high minaret was unveiled on 13 December 1965 on Mulgrave Street, which runs parallel to Granby Street.[69] Five years later, however, the mosque was still incomplete due to lack of funds and so religious Malays continued to congregate at converted premises on St James Road.[70]

The Malay Club itself made a much smoother shift up to the area of Liverpool 8 around Granby Street. Jermyn Street is one of the streets running perpendicular to Granby Street. It is on the much shorter western side that number 7 became the new home to the club. Surviving records show that an agreement was made on 4 June 1963 to purchase the building from Marjorie Josephine Steele for £1,500. A supplementary trust deed signed in 1974 names Abdul Salem and Bahazin Bin-Kassim as the trustees of the property. Born in Perak, Malaya in 1924, Bahazin became the first president of the club at its new location, and assumed the all-important role of cook.[71] A Malay man who began his undergraduate studies in Liverpool in 1970 remembered Bahazin as seeming 'different to the others', a distinction which was attributed to his aristocratic ancestry.[72] Under Bahazin's leadership, 7 Jermyn Street followed the former St James Road site of the club in becoming *the* Malay place in Liverpool. As had been the case at St James Road, the clubhouse on Jermyn Street included a prayer room. However, Bahazin is remembered as having been less strict than Johan Awang as regards the activities that could take place in the club. Food was available during Ramadan, for example, and Bahazin would say that it was 'between you and God' whether it was eaten or not.[73] Bahazin bought the house next to the club, living at number 5 with his English wife. With Malay lodgers staying at both numbers 5 and 7, Jermyn Street became a place in the city where it was always possible to find Malay-language conversation and food.[74] The daughter of one Malay ex-seaman recalled how most of the time as a child growing up on a 'white' housing estate outside the city in the 1960s, 'I felt like the odd one out', but during special occasions when she was taken with her sisters to Jermyn Street, 'I felt like I had a community.'[75] For children of seamen as well as (ex-)seamen themselves, 7 Jermyn Street was *the* place where they could be – at least partly – 'Malay'.

The Malay Club in its two locations played a part in making Liverpool 'home' to seamen from the *alam Melayu*. During the tail end of the period during which the city remained a key port in maritime routes to and from Southeast Asia, the social life of the club was a factor in Malay seafarers' selection of Liverpool as their seafaring base. Visiting seamen were able to insert themselves into the social networks of Malay Liverpool through number 7. While family-run lodging houses such as Ben Youp's home on Upper Huskisson Street allowed similar connections to be established in earlier years, the club (in both its locations) was a specifically 'Malay place' and contributed to making Liverpool somewhere worth staying. The Malay Club became the social focal point for men working at sea, those who had taken 'shore jobs' and even some who had retired. By the time the club was re-established on Jermyn Street in 1963, the ex-seamen who met and socialized there included retired 'elder statesmen' such as Ben Youp.[76] Ben Youp moved into Bahazin's house at 5 Jermyn Street and was a regular at the club next door in the early 1970s.[77] To the extent that the club continued to be a node in Malay seafaring social networks at that time, it was also a local place that facilitated an affective stretching of lives. It is doubtful that many men experienced 7 Jermyn Street in ways that would satisfy strict definitions of 'transnationalism', mainly because of the difficulty of attending the club itself on a regular basis (e.g. through being away at sea, through lack of time beyond onshore work and family commitments, or because of the physical distance of the club from the outer estates where the families of some Malay men were relocated) or simple lack of will (many men had deliberately left behind and sought to sever difficult familial or wider social relationships at 'home').[78] However, regulars at the club such as Ben Youp and of course Bahazin who ran it surely inhabited what might today be termed 'transnational social space' (Faist, 2000).

With extended maritime social connections came gifts, gossip and news from the *alam Melayu*, and exciting stories and artefacts from wider (Malay) worlds. Some children of Malay (ex-)seamen got a taste of maritime routes through visiting the club with their fathers. The worldly site of the Malay Club at one time included a parrot which had been taught to say '*makan*' (eat) and a range of rude words in English and Malay which thrilled Fadzil Mohamed's children.[79] However, in keeping with the lives of seafarers themselves, 7 Jermyn Street was also a site of what appeared to Liverpool-born children to be much less exotic activities. Paul Fadzil, who visited on Saturdays from the overspill housing area of Halewood when his dad was home from sea, recalled being told to sit quietly while the Malay men sat around watching horse racing – always horse racing! – on television, playing cards and chatting in what to young Paul was an incomprehensible language. It was frustrating for Paul that even the resident parrot seemed to understand and speak more Malay than he did.[80] Outside, men hung around, smoking and playing *sepak raga* (kick volleyball) in the street.

In contrast to when Mat Nor arrived in the early 1950s, Malays now had established their own place in the city. But Liverpool's commercial place in the world economy – as a maritime centre that sustained extended Malay social webs – was undergoing profound change. Although few people appreciated it at that moment, the shift in location of the Malay Club to Liverpool 8 in 1963 was made during a time when the postwar 'high watermark' for British shipping had already passed (Falkus, 1990: 302).[81] The 1950s had been a decade of shipping prosperity and it is unlikely that the club run by Bahazin on Jermyn Street ever received as many visiting seamen as had the earlier one on St James Road. Fewer ships came to Liverpool in subsequent decades, bringing fewer new Malay seafarers to sustain webs of maritime connection or to add to earlier generations who had come to call the city home.

Notes

1 He recalled the SS *Marudu*, SS *Surusa*, SS *Serdang* and MV *Rengan*. Notes from conversation, Liverpool, 6 September 2008.

2 There was once a guest book but this seems to have been lost when Ben Youp moved out of the house in the 1970s. Several men stayed there

including Majid and Fadzil. The electoral register for 1950 lists three men living at 144 Upper Huskisson Street besides Ben Youp and his wife, Priscilla. This included Yasan Mohamed who was from Sandakan, Borneo.

3 Nemit Bin Ayem, from Purukalam Tigi, Malacca, and his wife, Bridgit.

4 Interview with Joan Higgins, Liverpool, 12 September 2004. Frieda Gamill also recalls people knocking on the door of the house of her Indonesian father, Ahmat bin Gamill, at 50 Upper Hope Place, when ships with Malay crew had come in. Notes from conversation, Liverpool, 30 August 2008.

5 Most, though not all, Malay seamen were from Straits Settlements and therefore British subjects.

6 CO 323/810/7, 'Interviews with Destitute Coloured Men: minutes regarding and disturbances caused by colonial seamen awaiting repatriation', p. 78.

7 Ahmad bin Bucker and the distinctly Chinese-sounding Ah Wong. IOR L/E/7/1103. This raises a wider issue of whether men referred to in the historical records as 'Malay' were accurately labelled as such, even in terms of the racialized labour classifications of the time. In addition to ignorance on the part of employers and imperial authorities, individual seamen often attempted to 'crossover identity' in order to benefit from conditions afforded to other groups (Balachandran, 2007: 197). Balachandran notes, for example, reports from the 1930s of Indian seamen jumping ship in Singapore in order to acquire Malay certificates.

8 IOR L/E/7/1103, File 8231, 'Destitute seamen: maintenance and repatriation', p. 293.

9 IOR L/E/7/1103, File 8231, 'Destitute seamen: maintenance and repatriation', p. 294. All five names appear to have been highlighted on the original archival document suggesting perhaps that there may have been some doubt as to whether these men did indeed meet 'the conditions agreed with respect to Indian and Arab seamen'.

10 BL/025KEYS193510, P. Cecil Lewis, 'Cardiff Report – General Survey', in *The Keys*, volume 3, issue 2, p. 17. The League of Coloured Peoples was a civil rights organization founded in 1931 concerned with the promotion of racial equality.

11 According to the report, even those with apparently 'unquestionable evidence of nationality' were barred from work on subsidized ships 'and by a stroke of a pen hundreds of seamen were deprived of their only means of livelihood' (p. 16).

12 CO 273/559/22, file on 'Adam Bacha nationality', p. 14.

13 CO 273/559/22, file on 'Adam Bacha nationality', p. 16.

14 CO 273/559/22, file on 'Adam Bacha nationality', p. 13.

15 BL/025KEYS193510, P. Cecil Lewis, 'Cardiff Report – General Survey', in *The Keys*, volume 3, issue 2, p. 16.

16 According to Visram (2002: 210), 'Thousands of seamen born in India, Malaya, Africa, the Caribbean and the Middle East were re-classified as aliens, their British nationality and their rights of domicile snatched away – with bureaucratic logic.'

17 Apart from differences between agencies, May and Cohen point to the need to consider sheer 'bureaucratic muddle' (p. 121) and the 'inefficient or haphazard' (p. 120) nature of much government action.
18 IOR L/E/7/1103, File 8231, 'Destitute seamen: maintenance and repatriation'.
19 CO 273/559/22, file on 'Adam Bacha nationality', p. 11.
20 *Liverpool Echo*, 6 June 1919, p. 4.
21 It is likely that 'dark town' refers to the area around Upper Pitt Street where seamen from west Africa settled from the mid-nineteenth century (Frost, 1999; Uduku, 2003).
22 It is also noted of the unnamed boy: 'Visits the docks daily looking for a job as deck boy on a ship, but is handicapped by slight eye defect' (Caradog Jones, 1940: 22).
23 Interview, Liverpool, 29 September 2004.
24 Interview with Joan Higgins, Liverpool, 12 September 2004.
25 The term 'local' has to be used with particular caution here given the high proportion of migrants in the city, particularly from Ireland. During Liverpool's time as a world port city, the Irish were often considered racially distinct from 'whites' (Belchem, 2005) and this manifested in geographical segregation from 1871 (Pooley, 1977).
26 This was at 4 Bridson Street. Interview with Ronnie Bujang, Runcorn, 14 September 2004.
27 'Chinatown' originally denoted the area around Cleveland Square and Pitt Street in the south docks area of the city (Craggs and Loh Lynn, 1985), but a combination of clearance attempts – driven by fears of racial 'contamination' and stereotypes of opium as an inherently Chinese 'evil' – and the effects of bombing during the Second World War (see Lee, 1998) resulted in a shift to the area around Cornwallis Street and Great George Square (see Figure 3.1).
28 While Lamont and Aksartova (2002) focus on the negotiation of racial boundaries among working-class men, however, the 'ordinary cosmopolitanism' of Liverpool's prewar 'Chinatown' and other parts of Liverpool 1 clearly included working-class women who entered into relationships with foreign seafarers.
29 This speaks to contemporary debates about the class dimensions of cosmopolitanism and the extent to which the disposition is, or should be, limited to educated, mobile professionals (Hannerz, 1996; Smith and Guarnizo, 1998; Werbner, 1999).
30 The term 'counterflows' is taken from Michael H. Fisher's work on Indians in Britain (Fisher, 2004).
31 'The outbreak of passionate violence between black and white men in the city calls attention to a problem peculiar to Liverpool and other big ports. Seafaring communities are always of a *cosmopolitan* nature.' 'Liverpool's coloured colonies', *Liverpool Echo*, 6 June 1919, p. 4, emphasis added.
32 Ramsay Muir, the University of Liverpool professor tasked with writing the 700th anniversary history of Liverpool, notes that 'this amazingly polyglot and cosmopolitan population, consisting to a considerable extent of races

which are backward in many ways, and maintaining itself largely by unskilled labour, vastly increases the difficulty of securing and maintaining the decencies of life' (Muir, 1907: 305–6).

33 The formation of colonies or quarters was considered 'largely advantageous' in that it provided a 'check against the pollution of a healthy community by undesirables', *Liverpool Echo*, 6 June 1919, p. 4. The use of the term 'colonies' in particular denotes that the south dock and Chinatown areas of the city were 'imperial terrain' (Burton, 1998: 1), unsettling notions of colonial territories as being only 'out there' in worlds beyond the shores of the metropole.

34 Paul Du Noyer (2007: 99) captured the racialized geography in later decades as follows: 'Liverpool 8 claimed a unique place in the civic psyche. For most of white Liverpool this enclave up the hill, especially the central drag of Upper Parliament Street, was the dubious abode of coloured people. Liverpool is territorial at the best of times; add the extra complication of race and you had a virtual no-go zone.' See also note 4 in Chapter 1 above on the politics of naming and mapping this 'zone'.

35 'We'd be a paki one day and we'd be a chink the next.' Interview, Runcorn, 14 September 2004.

36 These particular adjectives are taken from an article in the *Pall Mall Gazette*, 10 November 1888 (entitled 'Is the murderer a Malay? A new theory of the murderer').

37 De Quincey's encounter with the Malay in *Confessions of an English Opium-Eater* was considered in Chapter 2 (De Quincey, 1985). In a series of articles first printed in the 1860s and posthumously published as *The Uncommercial Traveller* in 1875, Dickens writes of Liverpool: 'Down by the Docks, the shabby undertaker's shop will bury you for next to nothing, after the Malay or Chinaman has stabbed you for nothing at all: so you can hardly hope to make a cheaper end' (Dickens, 1911: 219). A similar depiction of Malays in London – as part of 'the dregs of the docks' – is found in Conan Doyle's short story 'The man with the twisted lip', set in 1889 (Conan Doyle, 1986: 166). Dr Watson visited 'a vile alley lurking behind the high wharves which line the north side of the river to the east of London Bridge' (p. 167) in search of an opium den frequented by his wife's missing friend: 'As I entered, a sallow Malay attendant had hurried up with a pipe for me and a supply of the drug, beckoning me to an empty berth.' Peter Fryer (1984: 189) has also noted references to 'Malay scums' in the schoolboy literature of E. Harcourt Burrage.

38 *Pall Mall Gazette*, 10 November 1888.

39 The photographs were part of an exhibition on Liverpool's Chinatown by Maria Lin Wong (see also Wong, 1989). I have been unable to secure permission to reproduce any of these images.

40 Interview, Liverpool, 10 September 2004.

41 Interview, Liverpool, 29 September 2004.

42 For example, interview with Mohamed Nor Hamid (Mat Nor), Liverpool, 29 September 2004; notes from conversation with Dol, Liverpool, 3 December 2003.

43 See Chapter 2.
44 Harun Aminurrashid also noted that the train station in Liverpool was big but not clean like the one in Singapore (p. 124).
45 Ali Kechil, interview, Liverpool, 27 September 2004. Ali referred to his singing as 'country and eastern'.
46 Ali said that his passion for 'country and eastern' had developed during visits to US port cities. Most seafarers with whom I spoke had visited ports in the US South. New Orleans was one of the cities of the American South in which Osman Negro was said to have experienced racist exclusion. Interview with Mohamed Nor Hamid (Mat Nor), Liverpool, 29 September 2004.
47 Mat Nor mentioned the Grafton, Rialto and Locarno ballrooms. Interview, Liverpool, 29 September 2004. More importantly, however, he noted that there were young Irish and Scottish women who were happy to go to the clubs with him and his friends.
48 Interview, Liverpool, 12 September 2004.
49 This raises the possibility that seafaring, along with plantation work examined by Zawawi Ibrahim (1998) was a way in which Malays were exposed to industrial capitalism prior to factory-based industrialization in Malaysia.
50 Frost (2008: 155) notes that women in such relationships 'devised coping strategies that were mutually supportive and beneficial'.
51 Interview, Runcorn, 14 September 2004.
52 Teddy's father served on board the *Fort Concord* during the Second World War and was one of the Malays who never returned from the Battle of the Atlantic (see Chapter 2).
53 Interview, Runcorn, 14 September 2004.
54 This view is shared by Herman Melville's character, Redburn, who not long after landing in Liverpool notes: 'I began to see that my prospects for seeing the world as a sailor were, after all, but very doubtful; for sailors only go round the world, without going into it; and their reminiscences of travel are only a dim recollection of a chain of tap-rooms surrounding the global, parallel with the Equator. They but touch the perimeter of the circle; hover about the edges of terra-firma; and only land upon wharves and pier-heads' (Melville, 1983 [1849]: 148).
55 Interview, Liverpool, 12 September 2004. The rest of this paragraph draws upon the same interview.
56 Interview with Ronnie Bujang, Runcorn, 14 September 2004.
57 Interview, Liverpool, 6 October 2004.
58 He went on to say, 'If you want to meet the Malay people, it's only two places: one, the pub; the other one, the coffee shop.' It is also worth noting, however, that not all of Mat Nor's circle of friends were or considered themselves to be 'Malays'.
59 Hoborby Cafe was owned by Ali A. Hoborby who employed Malay seamen on his ship, *Star of Aden*, and was said to have had 'a good heart for the Malays'. Conversation with Fadzil Mohamed, Liverpool, 2 August 2008.
60 Officially recorded as 'Bakar, Salel A.' and 'Salah, Eunos B.'.

61 Interview with Osman John Brahim, Cardiff, 13 August 2008. He visited Johan's house with another Cardiff-based Malay seaman who had previously lived in Liverpool.
62 Interview with Farida Chapman (daughter of Fadzil Mohamed), Liverpool, 6 September 2008.
63 Interview with Rosita Mohamed and her mother, Cheryl, Liverpool, 25 April 2008.
64 Notes from conversation with Mohamed Nor Hamid (Mat Nor), 1 July 2014.
65 Notes from conversation with Frieda Gamill (daughter of Amat bin Gamill), Liverpool, 30 August 2008.
66 IOR L/E/9/457. Report by B.R. Hunter, Appendix XI on Liverpool, 12–21 April 1939.
67 Interview, Liverpool, 12 September 2004.
68 Notes from conversation with Paul Fadzil, son of Fadzil Mohamed, Liverpool, 11 June 2008.
69 'Start to their new mosque', *Liverpool Daily Post*, 13 December 1965.
70 '£25,000 appeal for Liverpool's first mosque', *Liverpool Daily Post*, 21 December 1970.
71 Bahazin first appears in the Registry of Shipping and Seamen as 'Bahazim bin Said', but changed his name by deed poll in 1963. BT 372/1578/1.
72 Interview with Dr Abdul Rahim Daud, Kuala Lumpur, 5 November 2008. Rahim thought that Bahazin was descended from the Perak royal family.
73 Notes from conversation with Mohd Khusairi Bin Mohd Isa (a student in Liverpool in the early 1980s), Liverpool, 1 July 2008.
74 As such, it attracted not merely visiting Malay seamen and Malay (ex-)seamen based in Liverpool but also Malay visitors from elsewhere in Britain, including North Shields and South Shields, where other Malay ex-seamen had settled.
75 Interview with Rosita Mohamed (daughter of Jaafar Mohamad), Liverpool, 25 April 2008. There is further coverage of the 'overspill' housing estates, and particularly Kirkby where Rosita lived, in Chapter 4.
76 Interview with Kevin Higgins (son-in-law of Ben Youp, Liverpool), 12 September 2004.
77 Joan Higgins (daughter of Ben Youp), recalls that 'the Malays used to come from all over the place just to come and see him.' Interview, Liverpool, 12 September 2004.
78 Rather than citing cases of men who had sought to distance themselves for such reasons, the words of a man who explicitly denied that this was the case for himself are perhaps more revealing. When interviewed by a Malaysian journalist in Liverpool in 1989, Haji Talib Md Sin stressed that he had not run away to Liverpool because of any problems (*merajuk*) with his family, but simply to make a living. This suggests that Haji Talib thought that other Malays in Liverpool had been *merajuk* or, at least, that outsiders may have perceived them as such. Ahmad Rodzi Yaakob, 'Melayu Liverpool tidak pernah lupakan tanahair' [Liverpool Malays have never forgotten their homeland], *Berita Harian*, 12 July 1989. See also Chapter 5.

79 According to Fadzil, it was a seaman called Ahya Yaacob, from Singapore, who taught the parrot to speak 'bad words' in Malay. Notes from conversation, Liverpool, 12 July 2008.

80 Although he did also recall being given money to buy lots of sweets and chewing gum from a shop on Granby Street. Notes from conversation with Paul Fadzil, Liverpool, 11 June 2008.

81 Although Jon Murden (2006: 404) notes that 1964 saw what was then an all-time record tonnage of cargo passing through Liverpool.

4

Merseyside Malaise and the Unmaking of British Malaya

By the time agreement was reached with Mrs M.J. Steele for the purchase of 7 Jermyn Street – on 4 June 1963 – Singapore had voted by referendum for merger with the Federation of Malaya, which had gained independence from Britain six years earlier. Malaysia came into being on 16 September 1963, comprising the Borneo states of Sabah and Sarawak, as well as the Federation of Malaya and Singapore (see Figure 2.1). A supplementary agreement to the deeds for 7 Jermyn Street in 1974 held the property in trust for what was referred to as the Liverpool Malaysian Association. By then, however, Malaysia and Singapore were separate nation states (following the latter's expulsion from the Federation in 1965), so those trustees who were born on the island of Singapore originated from territories of the former British Malaya that were no longer part of Malaysia. In the first section of this chapter I consider the implications of Malaysian state formation and post-independence economic development both for the long-distance social networks of men who socialized at 7 Jermyn Street and for wider political economic relations between Liverpool and Southeast Asia. From the 1970s a growing proportion of visitors to the Malay Club on Jermyn Street were neither seafarers nor even ex-seafarers, but ethnic Malay students who attended British universities on Malaysian government scholarships. In the second section of the chapter, I trace a longer history of young men and women from (the territories that became) Malaysia pursuing their studies in and around Liverpool. Kirkby was home to

From World City to the World in One City: Liverpool through Malay Lives,
First Edition. Tim Bunnell.

a Malayan Teacher's Training College in the decade up to 1962 and, thereafter, a location of some of the 'outer estates' of Merseyside that were developed to rehouse people (including families of Malay seamen) 'decanted' from the city centre. Far from providing relief to pressures of growth and expansion, as I show in the third and final section, this so-called population 'overspill' further emptied out a city ravaged by its diminished economic position both nationally and in the new international division of labour. The citywide impact of the loss of waterfront employment was particularly hard for non-white people who had long faced racial discrimination in the labour market, and who were residentially concentrated in the Liverpool 8 vicinity of the Malay Club.

Transnationalization and Malaysianization

The making of Malaysia as part of the political map of Southeast Asia after the formal end of British colonialism transnationalized the long-distance social linkages of Liverpool-based Malay men. In ways that have been elaborated in the preceding chapters, in the quarter of a century or so after the end of the Second World War the regularity of maritime commercial linkages between Liverpool and the *alam Melayu* made transoceanic and interregional social webs of connection possible too. The subjects of transnational social spaces were not merely those working at sea – men such as Hashim going 'around the world' or Jaafar travelling 'up and down' – but also some of those Liverpool-based men who frequented Malay places in the city. Limits as to how far back such pre-globalization 'transnational' social connections can be traced concern not so much the regularity of interoceanic social connections as issues of political geography. To the extent that long-distance maritime connections did allow certain Liverpool-based men to engage in meaningful social and emotional involvement in two distinct contexts, this is not sufficient to satisfy the label 'transnational'. It is important also to consider at what juncture long-distance, intra-imperial connections came to extend across state boundaries. Liverpool-based Malays' long-distance maritime connections to the *alam Melayu* did not involve crossing the boundary of a sovereign nation state until the independence of the Federation of Malaya (on 31 August 1957) at the earliest. In other words, Malay transnationalization resulted not from new forms or technologies of social connection in a late twentieth-century era of globalization, but from the inscription of nation-state boundaries across *existing* social networks extending from 7 Jermyn Street to newly formed political territories in the former British Malaya (see also Bunnell, 2007).

Neither the formation of Malaysia nor Singapore's separation from it feature prominently in the recollections of ex-seamen in Liverpool. The same is true for the earlier independence of the Federation of Malaya in 1957. The latter is perhaps particularly surprising given that news of the date for independence (*Merdeka*) was first announced outside Liverpool, at the Malayan Teachers' Training College in Kirkby. The chief minister of the Federation of Malaya, Tunku Abdul Rahman, made the 'disclosure' and, in turn, the front page of the *Liverpool Daily Post* on 8 February 1956. Celebration of independence in Kuala Lumpur the following year was also reported in the press in Liverpool. Coverage from the Associated Press likened the independence celebrations to a 'scene from the Arabian nights' and (incorrectly) described Tunku Abdul Rahman as 'the first monarch of a free Malaya'.[1] On 5 September 1957 the *Liverpool Echo* reported that the Duke of Gloucester (who represented Queen Elizabeth II at the celebrations in Kuala Lumpur) had returned with a set of elephant tusks for her majesty.[2] While I met Malay men in Liverpool who expressed great pride at the achievement of *Merdeka*, few could recall what they were doing at this politically symbolic moment (or when they first heard about it) and I heard of no celebration at the club on St James Road. In many cases, of course, Liverpool-based Malay men were away at sea during the time when the news broke. In addition, although Johan Awang who ran the club at that time was from Malacca (which became part of the Federation of Malaya), many other seamen who attended it were from Singapore (which was not part of the Federation), or were Indonesians who had obtained work – and become 'Malay' – in Singapore. More widely, however, one is left with the impression that state formation at first meant little more than the redrawing of lines on maps as far as most Liverpool-based seamen from the *alam Melayu* were concerned.

The sight of Malaysian International Shipping Corporation vessels in Liverpool more than a decade later formed much more vivid memories for Malay ex-seamen in the city as well as for some of their family members. Mohamed Nor Hamid (Mat Nor), who had been on board a ship in Wellington, New Zealand at the time of *Merdeka*, was working at Liverpool's Gladstone Dock when the first Malaysian International Shipping Corporation *Bunga* ships – so-called because they all bore the name of a different tropical flower (*bunga*) – came to Liverpool. He recalled feeling pride at seeing the Malaysian flag for the first time.[3] The crew of the *Bunga Teratai* was invited to the club on Jermyn Street for a *kenduri* (feast). In 2004 Mat Nor could still recall the order in which the *Bunga* ships had first visited Liverpool. After the *Teratai* came the *Tanjong*, followed in turn by the *Melati*, *Saroja* and *Orkid*. One of Mat Nor's sons remembered a story from his childhood about the *Bunga*

Orkid having been haunted.[4] According to Mat Nor himself, this was because a woman had died in suspicious circumstances while cleaning the ship when it was still in the shipyard in Japan. Other children of ex-seamen had fonder memories of one or more of the ships. Paul Fadzil and his sisters, children of Fadzil Mohamed, were shown around the *Bunga Tanjong* by their father's distant 'uncle' from Malacca.[5] For Rosita Mohamed, daughter of Jaafar Mohamad, meanwhile, the key memory of a Malaysian International Shipping Corporation ship was having been treated to chocolate cake by the Malaysian crew.[6]

While it is feasts, ghost ships and chocolate cake that stick in the memories of different generations of people whom I interviewed in Liverpool, the formation of the Malaysian International Shipping Corporation was part of a heightened phase of Malaysian – and, more specifically, ethnic Malay – economic nationalism from the late 1960s. Although Tunku Abdul Rahman secured independence in 1957, his *laissez-faire* economic policy over the subsequent decade left British commercial interests largely intact. In addition, local ownership of the modern economy of the newly independent state that became Malaysia remained overwhelmingly in ethnic Chinese hands. Malay economic frustration resulted in low levels of support for Tunku Abdul Rahman's Alliance of ethnically based parties in the election of 10 May 1969 and electoral animosity escalated into riots in and around Kuala Lumpur on 13 May (Comber, 1983).[7] These events received extended editorial coverage in the *Liverpool Daily Post*, lamenting how, with the riots, Malaysia had 'lost the stability from which all of its prosperity stemmed'.[8] What is more, this came just as another perceived 'threat' to stability – communism – appeared to be receding. For a moment it seemed that John Hobhouse, Blue Funnel Line's expert on Southeast Asia, may finally have been proven correct in his earlier prediction of a bleak future for the region on account of 'communism and communalism' (Falkus, 1990: 325). Restoration of political stability after the riots – and replacement of Tunku Abdul Rahman with Abdul Razak Hussein as prime minister of Malaysia – was achieved through a more explicitly Malay nationalist political economy which presented its own difficulties to British business.

Singapore newspaper accounts of the maiden voyage of the Malaysian International Shipping Corporation's first ship, the *Bunga Raya*, in 1970 provide a sense of the emergent postindependence mood. The Malaysian minister of commerce and industry noted the 'prestige to our country to have her national flag flying in international waters' and described the maiden voyage as 'the beginning of the emergence of Malaysia as a maritime power'.[9] For the prime minister, it was more a case of *re*-emergence. Abdul Razak imaginatively connected new developments back to a 'golden age of the Malacca Sultanate' when 'our merchant ships roamed the seas far and wide'.[10] Rather more prosaically, the chairman of the Malaysian International Shipping Corporation noted how the sailing of the *Bunga Raya* marked the realization of the government's stated aim back in 1968 to participate in the Far Eastern Freight Conference by 1971.[11] Abdul Razak acknowledged that this was an objective set during the time of his predecessor, Tunku Abdul Rahman. While expressing 'our grateful thanks to our beloved and esteemed leader ... for his initiative and keen foresight in accelerating the formation of the Malaysian National Shipping Line', it is possible to detect from Abdul Razak's words in December 1970 a more assertive approach to realizing Malaysia's maritime and wider economic aspirations than that of his predecessor: 'As the leading producer of raw commodities which are essentially meant for overseas markets, we should no longer accept a situation where we are always at the mercy of outside forces.'[12] As Abdul Razak's minister of finance pointed out later that month, 'international shipping is dominated by the international shipping conferences which are virtually monopolies and which, in turn, are dominated by the major maritime powers of the world.'[13] *Bunga Raya* set sail from Port Swettenham on 10 December 1970 with a cargo of Malaysian rubber, timber, palm oil and canned pineapples and 'manned by an entire crew of 49 Malaysians',[14] but still as part of the Far Eastern Freight Conference agreement which dated back to colonial times.

The rise of national shipping companies such as the Malaysian International Shipping Corporation and Singapore's Neptune Orient Lines formed part of political economic processes that dismantled British imperial shipping privilege and contributed to Liverpool's decline as a maritime centre. So dependent were companies such as the Blue Funnel Line on the monopoly bestowed by the conference system – based on the so-called Lancashire and Yorkshire Agreement of 1911 – that its preservation 'became a principal object of policy' (Falkus, 1990: 135). However, as had long been recognized by Blue Funnel Line's regional experts, the political tide in Southeast Asia and elsewhere was running in the opposite direction, with newly independent governments demanding a share of trade for their own national lines as part of wider postindependence aspirations for 'economic indigenization' (White, 2008: 170). Moreover, in addition to facing growing competition for a share of shipping routes themselves, Blue Funnel and other British lines were 'wedded to a system built on a European-dominated world where Europe's manufactures were exchanged for colonial primary products' (Falkus, 1990: 252) – a world which was reconfigured by the entry of Asian nations into export-oriented manufacturing.[15] Conference developments which made the allocation of lines increasingly dependent upon the national origin of trades limited British shipping companies given that the United Kingdom experienced relatively little increase in overseas trade or manufacturing production after the initial post-Second World War resurgence in demand for British goods. With modified conference agreements in place, the absolute as well as relative volume of trade carried by British ships shrank after 1957 (Falkus, 1990: 302). In addition, at the end of the subsequent decade, as Abdul Razak and his finance minister implied, there still remained the prospect of the 'colonial' conference system being dismantled altogether.[16]

Ultimately, the end of the conference system was bound up with the technological shift to containerization in the 1970s as much as it was with economic nationalism. Both had profound impacts upon the fortunes of the Blue Funnel Line and Liverpool's economy more widely. For Blue Funnel, the brand which 'had epitomized British shipping and the port of Liverpool', containerization came 'like a hurricane' during the decade from 1965 (Falkus, 1990: 376, 361). It was in that year that Alfred Holt and Company made the decision to move to a 'co-operative container organization' with the result that 'by the beginning of the 1970s the traditional Far East liner trades had passed away from conventional Blue Funnel vessels to the huge container ships of the new consortium' (p. 256). Southampton, not Liverpool, was chosen as the British terminal for the container operations (Stammers, 1991). The larger group was renamed Ocean Transport and Trading Limited in 1973, reflecting the addition of a substantial land base to its marine interests. In the words of Malcolm Falkus (1990: 376) in his history of the Blue Funnel Line, 'As sea gave way to land, Liverpool gave way to London.' Liverpool never assumed the kind of centrality in land or air networks that it had once enjoyed in the maritime world, in part because the changing spatial division of labour in Britain pulled the locus of national economic activity away from the north and northwest towards the midlands and the southeast of the country (Meegan, 2003). Meanwhile, shifts in Britain's international trading patterns away from Commonwealth markets, including Malaysia (see White, 2004), and towards Europe further reduced the importance of Liverpool's port as the city became 'marooned on the wrong side of the country' (Lane, 1997: 23). Although Liverpool remained the largest exporting port in the Commonwealth as late as 1970 (Sykes *et al.*, 2013), the seaport and the wider economy of the city were undergoing steep decline by the time the first Malaysian International Shipping Corporation ships arrived, and the three-mile dock system south of the Pier Head closed in 1972 (Meegan, 1999).

At one stage in the 1970s, four *Bunga* ships each came to Liverpool every three months. They carried Malaysian – and mostly ethnic Malay – crew, at least two of whom settled in Liverpool.[17] Significantly, Malaysian International Shipping Corporation ships exported commodities from Southeast Asia which had previously been shipped by Liverpool-based lines such as Blue Funnel, and manufactured goods which had historically gone in the opposite direction. In addition, following containerization, these cargoes were often shipped to British and European ports other than Liverpool. The maiden journey of the container-ready *Bunga Raya*, for example, was to London, Hamburg, Bremen, Rotterdam and Amsterdam, but *not* to Liverpool. And since London continued to be the ship's main port of call in Britain, *Bunga Raya* was only the sixth Malaysian International Shipping Corporation ship to visit Liverpool (as recalled by Mat Nor) although other Liverpool-based Malay seamen had by then already seen the *Bunga Raya* in other ports around the world.[18] The Malaysian International Shipping Corporation ships and their Malaysian crew meant that the Malay Club continued to enjoy regular transnational social linkages with the *alam Melayu*, but their arrival in Liverpool also signalled wider technological, structural economic and geopolitical changes that undermined the pre-eminence of the one-time capital of the Malay Atlantic. During a time when decoration of the Malay Club on Jermyn Street included a picture of Abdul Razak (see Figure 4.1) – a man determined to undo the (neo)colonial shipping privileges that had

Figure 4.1 Hari Raya party at 7 Jermyn Street, circa 1970, showing Abdul Rahim Daud (foreground right) and Bahazin Bin-Kassim (foreground left). Photograph courtesy of Abdul Rahim Daud.

sustained Liverpool as a centre of maritime commerce – the arrival of the *Bunga* ships marked the end of an imperial world city era.

Student Connections: From Kirkby to the Inner City

As the number of ships coming to Liverpool declined in the 1970s, bringing fewer Malay seamen to the club on Jermyn Street, the number of Malaysian students began to increase. One aspect of the 'special position' of Malays in Malaysia was their preferential access to educational scholarships. This was stepped up during the 1970s as part of the Malay-centred economic development process overseen by Abdul Razak. Hundreds of young Malays were sent to Britain to study and Liverpool was among the cities which received undergraduate scholarship students, although the city was certainly never as central to the flows of Malay (and other Malaysian) students coming to Britain from the 1970s as it had been to the maritime routes of Malay seamen in previous decades.[19] Abdul Rahim Daud (Figure 4.1) was one of only two Malay students from Malaysia who began studies at Liverpool University in 1970, but he recalls that by his final year the numbers were much greater.[20] The Malay Club became a home from home for young Rahim:

> Last time there's no internet, phone also, no mobile so you say like as if total bye-bye to your parents, to your *kampong* [home village]. So you feel like homesick so that's why I used to go very often to the Malay Club so at least see them, meet them, at least I feel a reduced homesick a little bit.

In contrast, non-Malay students from Malaysia seldom visited the Malay Club and Rahim put this down to a matter of ethnic difference.[21] With the exception perhaps of pork consumption, however, there were few barriers to transethnic association. Some of Rahim's photographs of parties at the club in the early 1970s, for example, clearly show tables with bottles of alcoholic drinks. If young Rahim felt a little less homesick through connection with 7 Jermyn Street it was because of the Malay food and language. And if the club was a predominantly male, Malay space, this was a result of sheer numbers rather than the kind of pro-Malay ethnonationalism that Abdul Razak had accentuated in Malaysia.[22]

It is important to note an earlier wave of students in – or at least near to – Liverpool that preceded Malay-centred Malaysianization. In 1951 a Malayan Teachers' Training College was established in Kirkby, northeast of the city, to train Malayans who would return home to educate the first generation of independent citizens. By the time the college closed in

1962, around 2,000 Malayan teachers and teacher trainers had passed through Kirkby. Many seafarers recall meeting with these young Malayans, although for the most part social connections seem to have been much less significant than those with students from Malaysia (and the smaller number from Singapore) who attended the club on Jermyn Street in later decades. In part this was a matter of geography. Kirkby is located around 8 miles (12 km) outside the city centre and slightly further from the south docks area where most Malay (ex-)seamen and their families lived at that time. Zainal Arshad, a Kirkbyite who attended the college in the mid-1950s, exemplified this distancing through an account of the occasion when he and other Kirkbyites got roles as extras in the film *A Town Like Alice* at Pinewood studios: 'When we walked into the set [a replica Malay village] we saw all of these elderly gentlemen and we said, "Where did they come from? Did you bring them from Malaya?"' Zainal was told that the men were, in fact, retired sailors who had married in Britain and who had been brought from Liverpool to play the role of village elders in the movie.[23] Zainal claims to have been unaware of the existence of Malay sailors in the city until this encounter outside London.

Kirkby College was a significant site in the Malayan independence process. As already noted, Tunku Abdul Rahman announced the date for independence on 8 February 1956 at Kirkby College. The announcement followed constitutional talks in London and was made to more than 300 students at the college who reportedly greeted the news with 'resounding cheers and clapping'.[24] Along with another Malayan teacher training college at Brinsford, outside Wolverhampton, Kirkby had perhaps the single biggest concentration of Malayans in Britain at that time (although the decision to make the announcement at Kirkby may also have been influenced by the fact that Tunku Abdul Rahman's nephew happened to be studying there).[25] Kirkbyites saw themselves as an enlightened multiracial community that could serve as an example to less-educated Malayans back home. A powerful symbol of multiracial cooperation at Kirkby College around the time of independence was the erection of a Merdeka Arch, designed by an ethnic Malay student, Ahmad Khalid, but built mostly by Chinese Malayan students. The 1957 issue of the college's magazine, *The Panduan* (The Guide) notes that the Malayan government had given a grant of £120 to enable 'all Malayans at Kirkby and some from Liverpool and Manchester' to hold belated *Merdeka* celebrations on Friday 13 and Saturday 14 September.[26] Invitations were not extended to Malayan seamen or their families in Liverpool. As one Kirkbyite admitted in 2005, educated young men and women did not wish to associate with uneducated sailor 'drop outs'.[27] At least in some cases, therefore, the lack of connection with seafaring compatriots was a matter of social as well as geographical distance.

Despite being held apart by geography and consciousness of social status, inevitably there were encounters between Kirkbyites and Malay seamen in the city. Ex-seaman Mohamed Nor Hamid (Mat Nor) recalled meeting a group of five or six students from the college, including one who was *anak raja* (royalty), outside Lewis's department store in Liverpool city centre. After wandering round the store with them, Mat Nor invited the students to eat at a restaurant in Chinatown. Mat Nor recalled, 'I ordered everything, two fish, big prawns, vegetables, rice, everything', and the students seemed concerned that they may not be able to afford to pay.[28] When the bill came, Mat Nor, who had recently signed off a ship, paid for the whole meal with a £5 note. The delight that he took from this act of largesse was partly due to an earlier incident in Melbourne where Malayan students had made it clear that they did not wish to have anything to do with uneducated seamen types like Mat Nor. The irony, of course, is that Mat Nor and other Malayan seamen in port cities such as Liverpool were, in many ways, much more worldly-wise than the socially conscious young group which was being trained to educate citizens of the new nation state.

Although what one British Council officer referred to as 'Kampong Kirkby' largely stood apart from the city, one contribution made by the college to Liverpool 8 is worthy of note.[29] Permission to construct the mosque that was referred to in the previous chapter on the site of some bombed terraced houses on Hatherley Street was granted in 1958, and efforts to raise money for construction began. At that time, Muslims in Liverpool, including some Malays, congregated for prayers on Fridays at the house of Ali Hizzam, a Yemeni *imam* (Khan-Cheema, 1979; see also Muhammad Mumtaz, 1996). In addition to donations from locally based Muslims and visiting seamen, contributors to the new mosque fund included the Malayan government, which donated £500, and Baharuddin Marji, the resident Malayan staff member at Kirkby College, who donated £30 on behalf of the college in June 1960. Construction plans stalled until Liverpool's Muslim community was galvanized after 'a Malayan Muslim by the name of Osman Eusof died and had been buried as a non-Muslim' (Khan-Cheema, 1979: 48). What became known as the Al-Rahma mosque was finally completed in January 1975, 13 years after the last batch of students at Kirkby College had said *selamat tinggal* (goodbye) to Liverpool.[30]

While many Kirkbyites moved on to bigger and better things in newly independent Malaya and then Malaysia (which came into being in 1963), families of Malay seafarers were among the Liverpudlians moved out of Liverpool to residential estates in outlying areas of Merseyside, including Kirkby (Griffiths, 2006).[31] Kirkby had become part of the Merseyside Development Area in 1946, when the Liverpool

Corporation acquired a 99-year lease on a wartime Royal Ordinance factory.[32] The 1950s saw the development of an industrial estate and new housing estates as part of wider efforts to decentralize both industry and population to parts of Merseyside outside the boundaries of the city, as well as the opening of the Malayan Teachers' Training College. In a review of the college for the Liverpool Philomathic Society, Denis G. Rattle reflected that 'it has been disturbing to hear from so many students throughout the ten years how widespread and deep-rooted is the appalling ignorance about Malaya they met on every side from all types of homes.'[33] As a result of Kirkby College, however, '[m]any thousands of Merseyside homes at least know that not all Malayans are primitive naked savages living on roots in the jungle.' Nonetheless, during the subsequent decade, following the arrival of overspill populations from the city,[34] children of Malay seafarers in Kirkby recount stories of racism and of feeling as though they did not belong in this 'white area'. One of Jaafar Mohamad's daughters, Rosita, complained that 'I used to get called Nigger, Chink, Paki', while Rosita's mother recalled being involved in 'so many fights' to defend the children from racism. Rosita's recollections of racism echo Ronnie Bujang's complaints (in Chapter 3) about Liverpool 8 in the immediate post-Second World War period. But by the 1960s that area was no longer so 'white' and Rosita recalled the annual Christmas parties that were held in the Malay Club there as the one time when she felt that she 'had a community'.[35]

As (ex-)seamen and their families dispersed to housing estates outside the municipal boundaries of the city, students assumed greater prominence in the community that gathered at the Malay Club. Aside from Kirkby College, some of the earliest Malay students in Liverpool were seafaring cadets, and Blue Funnel Line's cadet training centre, Aulis, continued to operate until 1981 (Falkus, 1990). However, it was the arrival of Malay scholarship students from Malaysia in the 1970s that changed the composition of the Malay club most profoundly. Abdul Rahim Daud was a pioneer not only as one of the first batch of Malaysians to study at Liverpool University but also in seeking accommodation in Liverpool 8. After staying in university accommodation at Rathbone Hall during his first term as an undergraduate, Rahim moved out to rent a room from a Mr Carrim (a Malay ex-seaman who lived on Pickwick Street) for much of the next two years, before moving into 7 Jermyn Street itself.[36] The electoral register for 1972 shows five Malays living at the address, including Penang-born Saleh Chain who had moved to Liverpool from New York.[37] Next door at number 5, in addition to Bahazin Bin-Kassim and his family (see Chapter 3) were Ben Youp and a seafarer from Penang, Amat Rashid, who had previously lived in Glasgow.[38] Over the course of the next decade, it became increasingly common for Malay students to live at, or in the vicinity of, the club. One man who started his undergraduate studies in Liverpool in 1981 recalled that several of his Malay student friends rented rooms on Princes Road and that a group of around 10 Malay students regularly attended the club at that time.[39] This man, Mohd Khusairi, arrived in Liverpool only a matter of months after 'Toxteth' had achieved national and international notoriety as a site of inner-city rioting.

Urban Malaise

When Mohd Khusairi started his studies in September 1981, there was a police checkpoint at the entrance to Granby Street from Princes Road. Two months earlier, the area had been set ablaze during battles between young men and the police. Upper Parliament Street, the epicentre of these civil disturbances, was little more than a stone's throw from the Malay Club. The trouble started with a fracas which broke out when police attempted to question a black motorcyclist heading along Selbourne Street towards Granby Street (see Figure 1.1). However, this immediate trigger must be set in the context of much more widespread accumulated anger at police harassment of the Liverpool 8 black community. So-called 'sus' laws, which allowed the police to stop and search people whom they deemed suspicious, were directed disproportionately at black youths in Liverpool 8. The four nights of rioting that began on 3 July were described by the London-based national press as having taken place in 'Toxteth' even though local people referred to the area concerned as Liverpool 8 (see Frost and Philips, 2011: 68). Earlier in the year there had been riots in inner-city areas of other British cities as part of a 'national summer of discontent' (p. 6). Given these events and the international attention that they drew to economic deprivation as well as to police racism and violence in Liverpool, it is perhaps remarkable that young Malays such as Mohd Khusairi were allowed to begin their studies in the city at this time.

Liverpool and the surrounding Merseyside region had been particularly badly affected by more widespread economic malaise in Britain associated with deindustrialization and decolonization. The new international division of labour implied a 'global shift' of manufacturing industry to countries – including in Southeast Asia – with lower production costs than in the former imperial centre (Dicken, 2003). In a longer historical perspective, however, the problem was not Liverpool's own deindustrialization. The city and its surrounding urban region had not industrialized as much as most other British cities had in the first place. In contrast to Glasgow with its long-standing industrial base, for example, Liverpool's imperial economic pre-eminence was 'dependent on the trafficking and transit of empire goods' (Steele, 2008: 138), rather than on their manufacture. Although the need to 'try to create new employment opportunities to compensate for the already apparent decline of port and port-related activity' was recognized before the Second World War, and led to the city council becoming the 'first local authority in Britain to seek legal power to undertake local economic development' (Meegan, 2003: 56), even London, the centre of British imperial finance and trade, had done more to diversify its economic base in the 1920s and 1930s with the development of light engineering industries. The impact of deindustrialization on Liverpool, therefore, was to a large extent indirect in that the city functioned as a conduit for the import of raw materials feeding other industrial areas in Britain and for the export of their manufactured goods through companies such as Ocean Steamship and its iconic Blue Funnel Line. Not only were Liverpool's efforts at economic diversification too little too late, but changing patterns of national trade from Commonwealth countries to the European Economic Community (EEC, later simply the European Union (EU)) meant that the city 'ossified as a marooned imperial seaport in a post-colonial age' (White, 2008: 183). Nicholas J. White shows that into the 1970s, Liverpool's trading patterns 'remained orientated towards non-European markets' (p. 181) and to former colonial territories in Southeast Asia in particular.[40] The continued profitability of Liverpool companies such as Ocean Steamship during this period was increasingly achieved through diversification outside the city and, indeed, beyond the wider Merseyside region.[41] Abandonment of most of the city's docks by the 1980s was the most visible sign of Liverpool's dramatic commercial decline.

If Liverpool was badly affected by postimperial economic shifts, the Toxteth area in which the media located the city's 'riots' came to assume a symbolic centrality in imaginings of British urban malaise.[42] The urban, social and economic effects of deindustrialization only compounded what one scholar of race and racism in Britain refers to as a long-standing 'pervasive disrespect toward urban living' (Bhattacharyya, 2000: 165). In a country whose self-image had long been based on pastoral dreams, Gargi Bhattacharyya argues, the city connoted 'dirt and overcrowding' (p. 165). With authentic landscapes of national identity – and especially Englishness – considered to be rooted in the countryside, cities were imagined as containers for foreignness, especially in some sections of the national media. The social geographer Jacqueline Burgess (1985) shows that such negative views of the urban in Britain came together in the 1980s in the trope of the 'inner city'.[43] This imagined space encapsulated both historically specific effects of economic 'decay' and 'dereliction', and more long-standing postcolonial conceptions of racialized foreign-ness. The inner city was 'an alien place, separate and isolated, located outside white, middle-class values and environments' (Burgess, 1985: 193). In Liverpool, this meant Toxteth, 'the new Harlem of Liverpool' (Belchem, 2000: 29). Once home to white, middle-class professionals, the residential composition of this area had begun to change before the Second World War. By the 1980s the Liverpool 8 postal district included the ward with the highest proportion of 'racial minorities' in the city (National Dwelling and Housing Survey 1976, cited in Gifford *et al.*, 1989: 39). The street disturbances that took place there – like those in inner-city parts of London, Manchester and Bristol – were interpreted, framed and committed to public memory through the media as race 'riots', and are remembered by some as marking a time when 'black communities stood up against the police' (see Frost and Phillips, 2011: 30). Such imaginings do not tell the whole story – white youths joined battles against the police too – but nor are they purely imaginary.[44] More widely, there is no doubt that the impact of rising unemployment was particularly hard for people in Liverpool 8 who had long faced racial discrimination in the labour market, as well as racist policing.

The real and perceived problems of Liverpool 8 and of Liverpool more generally impacted in a variety of ways upon the composition of the people who socialized at the Malay Club on Jermyn Street. It has already been noted how the decline of British industry and merchant shipping, combined with containerization, resulted in fewer ships with Malay crew visiting Liverpool. Those who did come could still have a good time in Liverpool 8: 'There were shops and drinking clubs to cater for every race on earth. There was a sexy, disreputable atmosphere you did not encounter in ordinary Liverpool' (Du Noyer, 2007: 99). Malaysians were among the 'foreign seamen of various nationalities and colours' that John Cornelius (2001: 58) met at the exotic Lucky Bar on Upper Parliament Street. A reporter for the Singapore-based Malay-language newspaper *Berita Harian*, who visited the area in 1979, found that there was even a nightclub, the Matahari, playing Malay popular music.[45] However, chronic unemployment meant that, in contrast to the immediate postwar period, there were few job opportunities to encourage visitors to stay in the city, even if their immigration status allowed.[46] The same journalist who visited the Matahari nightclub reported that for every 10 Malay men whom he met during his time in Liverpool, 5 or 6 were unemployed.[47] Some of those who had settled in Liverpool in earlier decades moved elsewhere in search of new opportunities. One was Ronnie Musa who followed the changing national spatial division of labour and joined the 'Scouse diaspora' in moving south to London to work as a boilerman at Maudsley Hospital (Ramwell and Madge, 1992; and see Du Noyer, 2007: 173 on the Scouse diaspora). Unemployment or underemployment meant that those who remained in or around Liverpool had more time to socialize at the Malay Club, along with a growing number of Malaysian student sojourners.[48] The predominant trend among Malay (ex-)seamen and their families continued to be movement out of inner-city Liverpool 8, if not out of Liverpool altogether.

There was one maritime event that brought Liverpool-based Malay families together during this period. Tragically, this was the sinking of the MV *Derbyshire*. Owned by the Liverpool-based Bibby Line, and originally named the *Liverpool Bridge*, the *Derbyshire* had been laid up during a shipping slump in 1978/79 before undergoing repairs in Japan in early 1980 (Ramwell and Madge, 1992). Members of the crew were flown from Liverpool to join the ship in Marseille from where it set sail to Canada. Loaded with iron ore, the *Derbyshire* began what would be its last voyage on 11 July 1980. On 10 September the ship sank in waves 200 miles (320 km) off the coast of Japan during a typhoon. Among the 44 crew who perished were 4 Malay men. They included 56-year-old Ronnie Musa who, having 'swallowed the anchor' (given up seafaring work), had been miserable in his shore job at Maudsley Hospital and so had returned to Liverpool, and to the sea. A second Malay member of the crew was Badarun bin Sekah (aged 44), a Malaysian citizen from Temerloh, Pahang, whose death on the ship meant that the tragedy had transnational ripples extending from Liverpool to Southeast Asia (Bibby Line, 1981). The two other Malays who perished on board the *Derbyshire* were Liverpool-based men, Ali bin Bujang (aged 58) and Ali bin Haji Musa (aged 55).

The eldest of Ali Musa's four children, Charles Musa, recalled in interview that his father had secured a position on the *Derbyshire* through his friend Ali Bujang, who had been with Bibby Line since 1978.[49] Ali Musa himself was not a company man, but had continued work as a seafarer after arriving in Liverpool in 1956.[50] He married a woman of Irish ancestry and the family was 'shipped out' (as Charles Musa put it) from Princes Park to Kirkby in 1968. Charles's mother passed away in 1979. This bereavement, as well as the increasing difficulty that Ali Musa experienced in finding work, had made him determined to move back 'home' – in his case, to Singapore – with his family. His plan was to sign off the ship in Japan and to return from there to Singapore:

> He fully intended to go back to Singapore. He'd made enquiries with Shell to work at the oil refinery there through his brother, and for us to

> go back there. He was going to spend the rest of his days there – but he didn't it make, obviously.

Charles first received news that the *Derbyshire* was missing through an aunt who had heard about the ship's disappearance on local radio. Within an hour, Charles recalls, journalists from Radio City were knocking at the door. Among other things, they asked if Ali Musa was related to the other Musa on board – Ronnie. They were not related and, in fact, Charles and his siblings only got to know Ronnie Musa's family through the sinking of the *Derbyshire* and its aftermath, such that new community bonds were forged in tragedy.

The men on board were not insured, with the result that their families only received one year's salary as compensation. Ronnie Musa's widow, Cathy, left to raise six children, apparently 'took it really badly'.[51] In interview material from 1987 at the Merseyside Maritime Museum, she said:

> Losing my husband this way has shattered my whole life. It gives me nightmares. I could scream not knowing what happened.... I remember seeing Ronnie off when he flew from Speke (airport) to join the ship in Japan. There were young boys there on their first trip and they were so excited at the adventure. It was Ronnie's second trip with Bibbys. He was a really good worker, a workaholic. But when he was at home he loved to stay in and do all the cooking. I lived for the kids and Ronnie, and now that he has gone I'm on my own with no-one. I feel very bitter at living on social security to help out my widow's pension. We used to be quite comfortable, but now I have to watch every penny.[52]

Glasgow-born Cathy Musa was one of the small group of wives who, as part of the Derbyshire Families Association, pressured the British government to open an official inquiry into the incident. When the inquiry was eventually held in 1987, it concluded that the loss was due to human error and so brought 'not peace but anger' (Ramwell and Madge 1992: 13).[53] Dave Ramwell and Tim Madge's book *A Ship Too Far* narrated the story of the *Derbyshire* up to 1992 and added pressure on the government to reopen the inquiry. A search funded by the International Transport Federation found the wreckage in 1994, after which the British government took action to organize a second expedition in 1997/98.[54] The conclusion of the resulting report was that the ship had sunk because the lid to a store hatch had been left unsecured, implying serious negligence on the part of the crew, which again was upsetting to their bereaved families. It was only in June 2000, almost two decades after the ship had gone down, that another formal inquiry attributed the sinking to damaged air pipes on the foredeck, clearing the crew of blame.

Just as there were grievances against the national government for its handling of the sinking of the *Derbyshire*, there was frustration at official responses – local as well as national – to the 'riots' of 1981. Political responses initially sidestepped the racialized nature of Liverpool's socio-economic problems. The Conservative national government focused its attention on private sector-led urban regeneration initiatives through the existing Merseyside Development Corporation and the Merseyside Task Force (which was set up after the riots by Michael Heseltine in his capacity as a special minister for Merseyside). Meanwhile, the Labour council, then under the leadership of the Trotskyite Militant Tendency, was antagonistic to affirmative action for non-white groups (Ben-Tovim, 1988; Merrifield, 1996).[55] Gideon Ben-Tovim (1988: 142) blames the 'colour-blind approaches' of both sides for the fact that post-1981 urban regeneration policies 'ensured practically zero impact on entrenched patterns of racial discrimination and disadvantage'. The inquiry into 'policies and community relations in Liverpool 8' initiated by Liverpool City Council confirmed Ben-Tovim's assessment: 'Black people in Liverpool have not, by and large, achieved even the limited advances in jobs, housing and equal treatment, that had been gained by more recently arrived Black communities in other major cities of Britain' (Gifford *et al.*, 1989: 21). What became known as the Gifford Report revealed the 'uniquely horrific' conditions of racism in the city at both institutional and everyday levels (p. 23).

Neither post-1981 urban regeneration policies nor the contribution of the Gifford Report to increased awareness of 'the need to combat racism and to take account of ethnic minorities in policy making' (Couch, 2003: 115) were recalled as having benefited Malay men or members of their families who lived through the riots. Among their number were Charles Musa and his siblings who had a 'grandstand view' of the street battles having moved back to the area from Kirkby two years before losing their father on board the *Derbyshire*.[56] Also in the vicinity during this period was ex-seaman Mohamed Nor Hamid (Mat Nor), who complained in interview that Malays did not receive even 'one penny' in the aftermath of the riots.[57] In his view, black and Somali community groups were the chief beneficiaries of new social funds, while Malays were overlooked.[58] Thus, while the 1980s may have witnessed 'a great political awakening for black and minority groups in Toxteth' (Merrifield, 1996: 215), this was experienced in highly differentiated ways, even if the groups concerned were 'united in the sense that they all experience racism' (p. 207). Racism and discrimination, of course, were experienced in variegated ways and to different degrees.[59] It was specifically black youths that suffered at the hands the police in the lead-up to the riots, and it is understandable that the Gifford Report focused largely on 'Liverpool Black people' (Gifford *et al.*, 1989). However, it may also have been significant that in the context of what became a highly competitive and complex 'race relations industry' (Brown, 2005: 247), counter-racist action worked more effectively for numerically larger and more visible minority groups than it did for Malays.

Mat Nor's recollections of institutional responses to the riots and the Gifford Report reflect logics of competition associated with the race relations industry. Yet they also serve as a reminder that Liverpool 8 after the riots was, and had long been, home to people who identified neither as white, nor black, nor 'Liverpool-born Black' (Brown, 2005).[60] In this regard, it is worth noting an historical Malay connection to the Liverpool Women's Hospital, one of the few tangible signs of post-1980s regeneration efforts that otherwise 'on the whole bypassed Liverpool 8' (Ben-Tovim, cited in Frost and Phillips, 2011: 119). Opened in 1995, the hospital was built on a site that included the part of the street where Mat Nor's uncle, Ben Youp, lived in the 1950s (Figure 1.1; and see Chapter 3). Ben and Priscilla Youp's daughter, Joan Higgins, recalled in interview the racial composition of the households at 'their' end of Upper Huskisson Street during her childhood: at the corner was a black family, then a white family, then her own family (the Youps), next to whom lived another Malay family, then 'Chinese, Chinese, white, white, white, black'. Just as Chinatown before the Second World War had been home to a variety of people with no Chinese ancestry (Chapter 3), so Liverpool 8 after the war was always more than 'Black Liverpool'.

Some of the families of Malay seamen associated with Liverpool 8 faced challenges similar to those of Liverpool-born black people, in terms of both dispersal and in-place experiences. As is reported to have been the case for black people who moved, or were forced to move, out of Liverpool 8 after the riots (see Michael Simon, cited in Frost and Phillips, 2011), for example, I have shown that Malays and Liverpool-born children of Malay seafarers experienced relocation to white estates such as Kirkby in earlier decades in terms of new forms of racial vulnerability rather than as upward mobility. These people often became disconnected from Liverpool 8 – and, in the case of Liverpool-born children of Malay seamen, from the Malay Club in particular – as a space of potential collective identity formation.[61] In addition, like Liverpool-born blacks, those people of Malay ancestry who remained in Liverpool 8 faced diminished possibilities for strengthening Malay community bonds and social organization, and forms of discrimination that were spatial as well as racial. Apart from impacts of wider economic decline and unemployment, the Granby area in particular became synonymous with drug dealing and crime with even the Granby Street post office closing down in 1994 following successive hold-ups (Merrifield, 1996).

Even well-meaning government and media efforts to identify and find solutions to problems arguably served to compound them. The very portrayal of Liverpool 8 as a problematic 'no-go' area was 'bad for business', not to mention insulting to its residents, irrespective of their ethnic identification (Frost and Phillips, 2011: 80).

Despite the difficulties that manifested at multiple scales – from the postimperial decline of British shipping which had sustained world city Liverpool, to the dispersal of the families of Malay seamen to the outer estates of Merseyside, and to social unrest in the 'inner-city' area where the Malay Club was located – in the 1980s and 1990s 7 Jermyn Street continued to bring together people with diverse connections to the territories that had become the nation states of Malaysia and Singapore. These people ranged from Malaysian students to descendants of Malay seamen who, in some cases, had never set foot in the *alam Melayu.* They also included, of course, the remaining first generation of (ex-)seamen themselves, a growing proportion of whom had more time to socialize at the club either because of the scarcity of regular employment or through having reached retirement age.[62] Part of the difficulty of organizing this diversity of 'Malays', and rendering them visible as a community, had to do with finding a name which related the geographical origins of its members to the postindependence political map of the former British Malaya. As was noted at the beginning of this chapter, a supplementary agreement to the deeds for 7 Jermyn Street in 1974 held the property in trust for what was referred to as the Liverpool Malaysian Association.[63] However, the majority of the founding contributors to the funds used to purchase the property originated from Singapore, not what had (in 1965) become the separate nation state of Malaysia. It was only in the 1990s that the Malay Club was officially registered as a charity with the more accurate, albeit cumbersome, title of Merseyside Malaysian and Singapore Community Association (or MSA for short). Community members such as Mat Nor, who had by then become president of the club, hoped that its official registration as the MSA would make the place of Malay Liverpool visible to local government and institutions that fund community development, as well as to a growing number of non-seafaring visitors from increasingly affluent, industrializing Southeast Asia.

Notes

1 'Malaysia's King takes the oath', *Liverpool Daily Post,* 3 September 1957.

2 'Back from Malaya: Duke and Duchess of Gloucester and gifts', *Liverpool Echo,* 5 September 1957.

3 Notes from conversation with Mat Nor, Liverpool, 3 September 2004.
4 Notes from conversation with Paul Hamid, Liverpool, 3 September 2004.
5 Interview with Fadzil Mohamed, Liverpool, 14 June 2008.
6 Interview, Liverpool, 25 April 2008.
7 The political implications of the 1969 riots for Malaysia are considered in Chapter 6.
8 'Editorial: the malaise of Malaya', *Liverpool Daily Post*, 19 May 1969.
9 'Change in patterns of transport', *Straits Times*, 9 December 1970.
10 'Important break-through for the country', *Straits Times*, 9 December 1970.
11 'Flagship is to carry container cargo, too', *Straits Times*, 9 December 1970.
12 'Important break-through for the country', *Straits Times*, 9 December 1970.
13 'Cargo rates: Govt may step in', *Straits Times*, 23 December 1970. The importance of 'conference' arrangements to Liverpool-based Alfred Holt and Company was considered in Chapter 2.
14 Though the captain and three officers were reported to have been Dutch. 'Malaysia launches shipping service', *Straits Times*, 10 December 1970.
15 This began in the mid-1960s in Singapore where, by 1973, the value of manufactured exports exceeded commodities for the first time (Studwell, 2007: 38). The first round of export-oriented industrialization in Malaysia began in 1970 (Drabble, 2000: 187).
16 The point was also made in late 1970 by Tan Eng Joo, the head of the Singapore delegation at a meeting of the Asian Shippers' Organization. The *Straits Times* cites Tan as suggesting that, 'though Singapore and Malaysia were politically independent, they were still "economic serfs", and were exploited by British shipping tycoons.' It was not enough to be part of the Far Eastern Freight Conference, Tan urged. Rather, Asian governments should 'pool together' their national shipping lines to 'break the stranglehold' of the 'colonial' system. 'Shippers urged to break the big hold', *Straits Times*, 6 December 1970.
17 Interview with Mohamed Nor Hamid (Mat Nor), 29 September 2004.
18 Fadzil Mohamed recalls seeing the *Bunga Raya* in Bilbao – and being shocked at how hard drinking its Malay crew members were.
19 As far as Malay(sian) students were concerned, the 'centre' was London and, more specifically, 44 Bryanston Square, headquarters of the Malaysian Students Department and home to Malaysia Hall (Abu Hasan, 2000).
20 Interview with Abdul Rahim Daud, Kuala Lumpur, 6 November 2008.
21 Rahim's Chinese Malaysian contemporary in Liverpool, Tan Chian Khai, agreed, putting the fact that he never visited the club down to his perception that it was 'for Malays and sailors'. Interview, Kuala Lumpur, 25 February 2008.
22 At least one Liverpool-based non-Malay ex-seaman frequented the club at that time in the 1970s, Benny Wee, an ethnic Chinese man from East Malaysia.
23 Interview with Zainal Arshad, London, 17 June 2005. Zainal was himself chosen to be a musician for a *ronggeng* (Malay dance) scene. One of the female dancers, Kelsombee Hashim, is pictured alongside the British star of the film, Virginia McKenna, in an article in the Singapore *Straits Times*

('Kirkby teachers star in a film', *Straits Times*, 19 October 1955). Among the ex-seamen who had roles in *A Town Like Alice* was Sunny bin Hassan who had arrived in England during the First World War when his ship was torpedoed '100 miles off the Irish coast'. He continued to work at sea after the war, before settling down in Liverpool, where he married in 1931. Sunny subsequently played the role of Haji Amyan in *Windom's Way*, which was also shot at Pinewood studios. 'Sunny bin Hassan gets film role', *Straits Times*, 19 August 1957.

24 'Malaya's independence day out: disclosure at Kirkby', *Liverpool Echo*, 7 February 1956.

25 Interview with Zainal Arshad, London, 18 June 2005.

26 Liverpool Record Office, H370.73MAL, *The Panduan: The Magazine of the Malayan College, Kirkby*, no. 6, 1957.

27 Interview with Yunus Rais, London, 17 June 2005.

28 Interview, Liverpool, 10 September 2004.

29 'Kampong Kirkby – 1951–1962' by Frank G. Smith, deputy area officer, British Council, Liverpool, in *Selamat Tinggal* (a special farewell number of The Magazine of Kirkby College Student Teacher-Trainers' Union), 1962, p. 34. Liverpool Record Office, H370.73MAL.

30 'Selamat Tinggal' was also the title of a special 'farewell' edition of the Kirkby College magazine in 1962. Liverpool Record Office, H370.73MAL.

31 Griffiths' book includes a photograph of the then new high-rise flats which came to be almost universally despised and have now mostly been demolished (p. 105). He notes that 'the great experiment of the outer estates' began in the 1930s following recognition that Liverpool needed to 'diversify, expand and industrialise' (p. 8).

32 With subsequent additions, by 1953, the Kirkby estate had 1,165 acres (471 ha) zoned for industry. 'The Merseyside Development Area', in *A Scientific Survey of Merseyside*, p. 182. Merseyside Maritime Museum, Maritime Archives and Library, 710 SMI.

33 'Strangers in a strange land', *Proceedings of Liverpool Philomathic Society 1961–1965*, p. 12. Liverpool Record Office, H370.73MAL.

34 Until the 1930s the city's population growth meant that it was possible to conceive of 'overspill' to surrounding areas of Merseyside such as Kirkby to relieve the often poor and cramped housing conditions in the city itself (Griffiths, 2006). However, for every decade after 1931, the population of the city declined. Outward relocation was thus not so much overspill as dispersal, and resulted in the city being turned 'inside out' (Meegan, 2003: 57).

35 Interview with Rosita Mohamed and her mother, Cheryl, Liverpool, 25 April 2008.

36 Interview with Abdul Rahim Daud, Kuala Lumpur, 6 November 2008.

37 Notes from conversation with Mohamed Nor Hamid (Mat Nor), Liverpool, 6 September 2008.

38 Notes from conversation with Mohamed Nor Hamid (Mat Nor), Liverpool, 6 September 2008.

39 Notes from conversation with Mohd Khusairi Bin Mohd Isa, Liverpool, 1 July 2008.

40 White (2008: 175) notes that even in 1957, the year in which the Federation of Malaya gained independence, that country plus Singapore accounted for at least 50 per cent of the total trade of the Ocean Steamship Company, 'both outward and inward'.

41 The decision of Ocean Container Lines to use Southampton, not Liverpool, as their British terminal was noted earlier in this chapter.

42 Interviewees in a volume on 'Remembering the riots' 30 years after the events of 1981 note that local people had previously referred to the area concerned as 'Liverpool 8' not 'Toxteth' (Frost and Phillips, 2011).

43 There was growing recognition of the socioeconomic problems of inner-city areas in Britain well before the notoriety afforded to areas such as Toxteth in the 1980s. Nationally, the government's first major urban policy initiative was the Urban Programme, which started in 1968 (Couch, 2003).

44 Andy Merrifield (1996: 214) notes from the 1991 census for Liverpool that even in Granby more than 70 per cent of the resident population was classified as 'white'. Although 'black poverty is often generated by a whole set of different structural and ideological forces than white poverty', whites in Granby, as Merrifield puts it, 'are fellow-sufferers and hence potential allies for blacks and other oppressed groups in their fight for justice'.

45 The Matahari nightclub was reportedly owned by a Malay ex-seaman from Singapore, Encik Hussein. 'Mereka masih berpeluang menikmati lagu2 Melayu berkumandang di disko2' [They still get the chance to enjoy Malay songs in discos], *Berita Harian*, 28 October 1979.

46 People from Malaysia or Singapore were not British subjects as had been the case for seafarers arriving from these territories before their independence from Britain.

47 'Kampung Melayu di Bandar Liverpool' [The Malay village in the city of Liverpool], *Berita Harian*, 21 October 1979. Richard Meegan (1999) notes that 1966 was the peak of postwar employment growth, and by 1981 the county as a whole had lost 183,000 jobs.

48 The subdivision of townhouses into flats and bedsits in Liverpool 8 meant affordable accommodation for Malay student sojourners in the immediate vicinity of Liverpool University. Some students, as well as (ex-)seamen, may even have been attracted to Liverpool 8's counter-cultural 'separation from English respectability' (Du Noyer, 2007: 99).

49 Interview with Charles Musa, Liverpool, 22 March 2010. Unless otherwise stated, the remainder of this paragraph is based on this interview.

50 Originally from Singapore, Ali Musa had jumped ship in San Francisco and was later deported (as a British subject) to Middlesbrough in 1952, before moving to Liverpool.

51 Interview with Charles Musa, Liverpool, 22 March 2010.

52 Merseyside Maritime Museum, 'Crew members and their families', available at: http://www.liverpoolmuseums.org.uk/maritime/exhibitions/derbyshire/crew_families.aspx (accessed 23 December 2011).

53 Ramwell and Madge (1992) believe that there were structural design flaws, in particular, catastrophic failure at 'frame 65' that caused the *Derbyshire* to 'snap like a twig' and plunge two miles.

54 Merseyside Maritime Museum, 'Crew members and their families', available at: http://www.liverpoolmuseums.org.uk/maritime/exhibitions/derbyshire/crew_families.aspx (accessed 23 December 2011).

55 As Murray Steele (2008: 138) puts it, the Labour Party seemed to be unaware of 'the conditions experienced by that legacy of empire located on their very doorstep, the black community of Liverpool 8'.

56 Interview with Charles Musa, Liverpool, 22 March 2010.

57 Interview, Liverpool, 6 October 2004.

58 In part, this had simply to do with numbers. Even when the minority ethnic population is broken down into subcategories – as was the case in the Gifford Report – what might be understood as minority minorities, like Malays, remain statistically invisible. The Gifford Report draws upon categories from previous survey and census data with a generalized 'Asian' category (Gifford *et al.*, 1989).

59 This variegation applies within as well as between ethnic groupings. In Chapter 4, for example, it was noted that in an earlier decade a Malay seaman nicknamed 'Man Negro' was refused entry to a dance hall in the city centre while his fellow Malay friends would have been allowed to enter. More widely, the work of Tariq Modood (2007) highlights the risk that generalized ethnic categories obscure a diversity of lived experiences and identifications.

60 As is examined in Jacqueline Nassy Brown's anthropological work, Liverpool-born black is a category which enabled people with black fathers and white mothers to become particular kinds of 'blacks' rather than 'half-castes' (Brown, 2005). Importantly, the category involves a genealogy that is spatial as much as it is racial, articulating a powerful case for belonging through being particular kinds of 'locals' rather than immigrants.

61 Children of Malay (ex-)seamen who grew up in predominantly 'white' areas of Merseyside outside the city of Liverpool visited or returned to Jermyn Street only during special occasions (if at all), precluding the development of either strong senses of Malay-ness or connection to Liverpool 8. In the words of Charles Musa: 'In the 60s, they were shipping people out to new estates, so we got spread all over Merseyside. When I was a child we all lived in or around Liverpool 8 and then our houses got knocked down. We ended up in Kirkby for a while.... The club, Jermyn Street, became less prominent in our lives' (Interview, Liverpool, 22 March 2010). There was no equivalent category to 'Liverpool-born black' among people born in Liverpool 8 who had Malay fathers.

62 The generation of Malay seafarers who arrived in Liverpool after the Second World War was mostly born in the 1920s and 1930s and so reached formal retirement age in the 1990s. Members of the prewar generation, of course, retired much earlier and so had more time to socialize at the club in earlier decades (e.g. Eusop Awang and Ben Youp) or else returned to

the *alam Melayu* (e.g. Johan Awang who returned to Malacca after the death of his wife). Other aspects of these men's lives are covered in Chapters 2 and 3.

63 In subsequent years there was also mention of the Malaysian Society. Khan-Cheema (1979) notes its existence in relation to encouragement given to Muslim minority groups to apply for Urban Aid funding after Pakistani Muslims secured a capital grant to form the Pakistan Centre in 1976.

5

Diasporic (Re)connections

Liverpool's Malay Club may not have been well known within the city, but it attracted Malay visitors from far and wide. In this chapter I consider histories of non-seafaring travels to 7 Jermyn Street including both individual searches for seafaring ancestors and politically driven interest in diaspora communities among Malay nationalist elites in Malaysia. As I show in the first section of the chapter, efforts to trace the provenance of letters and postcards and to track down a long-lost father or grandfather in Liverpool brought visitors to the club as early as the 1960s. Malaysian government scholarships for Malays to study in Britain, as well as growing affluence in parts of Southeast Asia, increased the possibility for such journeys, often combined with musical or sporting pilgrimages. This continued into the twenty-first century, although increasingly what was found was an ancestral gravestone rather than a living relative. In the second section I move beyond interpersonal or familial motivations for seeking Liverpool's Malay Club to consider growing political and media interest in Malays living beyond the *alam Melayu*. This means examining the Malay nationalist imaginings and aspirations of Mahathir Mohamad (prime minister of Malaysia from 1981 to 2003), and his relation to a cultural movement concerned to study and promote links with 'diaspora' populations across an extended Malay world. By the 1990s economic regionalization and globalization meant that Mahathir's Malay nationalist imperative was no longer merely to compete with Chinese and Indian ethnic communities *within*

From World City to the World in One City: Liverpool through Malay Lives,
First Edition. Tim Bunnell.

Malaysia but also to be able to compete across borders. At one level, as I consider in the third section, Malay men in the city could be deemed exemplary transnational subjects through their having ventured to, and made a living in, distant lands. At another level, however, ex-seamen did not fit the mould of the educated and Islamic *Melayu baru* (new Malay) of late twentieth-century Malaysia.

In Search of Lost Ancestors

Mila ... Where did you say your old man was?
Mafiz Liverpool. But he hasn't been back in ages.
Mila ... and your mum?
Mafiz She's here. She's a seamstress in [the village of] Jemapoh. I'm a mechanic. My dad left when I was a kid. We've been waiting for him. In the beginning we used to get letters, even money.
Mila Never came back?
Mafiz Never heard a thing ...[1]

(Dialogue from *Dari Jemapoh ke Manchester*, directed by Hishamuddin Rais, 1998)

The 1998 film *Dari Jemapoh ke Manchester* (From Jemapoh to Manchester), directed by the Malaysian filmmaker Hishamuddin (Hisham) Rais, tells the story of two boys from a village (*kampung*) in the state of Negeri Sembilan in the 1960s. Yadi and Mafiz both dream of escaping from the village of Jemapoh and travelling to England, though for different reasons. Yadi is bored in the *kampung* where cows outnumber people and there are not even enough *kaki* (friends) left for a decent game of football. He dreams of watching his favourite team – 'Manchestee Uni-ted' – and meeting his handsome idol, George Best.[2] Mafiz, in contrast, is no football fan. He would be happy to *lepak* (hang out) in Jemapoh and listen to the Beatles on his radio, but his nagging mother sees this as evidence of Mafiz's laziness and irresponsibility – just like his absent father (*ayah*). Mafiz's *ayah* had left as a sailor (*kelasi kapal*) and the last contact from him was from the Beatles' home town. The two boys 'borrow' a red Volvo from the garage where Mafiz works and hit the road in search of their respective dreams. On their journey out of Jemapoh, Yadi and Mafiz acquire two worldly companions, Mila and Lini. Together, they head for Singapore, gateway to Liverpool, Manchester and the rest of the world.

References to Liverpool and Manchester in the film draw upon Hisham's personal travels to and experiences in Britain, as well as his childhood in Jemapoh. In the 1970s he was among the student leaders who supported anti-government protests in Kuala Lumpur. When the Abdul Razak Hussein government cracked down, Hisham's fellow student leader (and future deputy prime minister) Anwar Ibrahim was detained under the Internal Security Act (ISA) which allows for detention without trial, and so Hisham fled the country, taking a raft from the northern Malaysian frontier town of Glodok over the border to Thailand (Keshvani, 1999). After several years of mostly stateless wandering, he was eventually offered asylum in Belgium.[3] In the mid-1980s Hisham moved from Brussels to London to study filmmaking at Central London Polytechnic. It was in London that he first met Malay ex-seamen such as Man Tokyo, whose knowledge of the Japanese language, acquired while working in dockyards in Japan, had enabled him to secure parts in British war films.[4] On his eventual return to Malaysia in 1995, Hisham was held in remand as a prisoner under the ISA, and it was while he was in detention that the idea for *Dari Jemapoh ke Manchester* came to him (Keshvani, 1999). By the time I watched the film in Kuala Lumpur in 2001, Hisham was in detention again, this time together with five political opposition leaders who were accused of plotting to overthrow the Malaysian government through militant means.[5] I eventually got to meet Hisham after his release and, over *teh tarik* (frothy, sweet, milky tea) in Bangsar Utama, Kuala Lumpur, he confirmed my suspicions: he had met Malay ex-seafarers outside London, including in Cardiff and Liverpool.[6]

Although *Dari Jemapoh ke Manchester* is a work of fiction, postcards were sent 'home' from Liverpool to villages, towns and cities in Southeast Asia. Figure 5.1 is one such example, sent by Carrim Haji Quigus Rahim on 28 January 1989. Carrim was the man from whom Abdul Rahim Daud had rented a room during his studies at Liverpool University in the early 1970s (Chapter 4). Rahim stayed at Carrim's house on Pickwick Street for two years and recalled in interview that his landlord had been from Malaysia.[7] In fact, Carrim was born on the Indonesian island of Belitung – once a major centre of tin mining from where today's Anglo-Australian mining conglomerate, BHP Billiton, derives its name[8] – and had fled to Singapore with a friend after having angered Belitung's raja (hereditary ruler or 'king') for reasons that remain a mystery. Carrim left behind a wife named Aca and a young daughter named Nuratin.[9] In a pattern that is familiar from life geographies sketched in previous chapters, Carrim obtained oceangoing seafaring work in Singapore, arrived at London (in March 1948) and eventually moved to Liverpool.[10] His friend, Usman, stayed in Singapore and became a Singapore citizen. Official seafaring documentation in Britain records that Carrim himself was born on 10 June 1920 in Singapore, but this was a fiction which allowed him to obtain a British seaman's card.[11] Carrim

Figure 5.1 Postcard sent by Carrim Haji Quigus Rahim, 1989. Image courtesy of Noegroho Andy Handojo.

and his English partner in Liverpool, Vera, never had children of their own but signed off together in postcards and letters sent to Carrim's daughter and grandchildren back in Indonesia. The example below was sent to one of Nuratin's grandchildren in Jakarta in January 1989, and reads on the reverse side: 'Your grandmother, Vera, and grandfather live in this city.'[12]

Postcards and letters fomented a desire to visit Britain. Carrim's second grandson, Noegroho, grew up on Belitung island knowing that he had a grandfather in 'London' (a toponym which in Indonesia to this day is commonly used to refer to the whole of Britain). Noegroho received exotic stamps, coins and birthday money as well as letters and postcards.[13] Carrim maintained regular contact with his best friend Usman, and many of the things sent by post from Liverpool to Belitung travelled via Singapore. After completing his bachelor's degree in geography at Universitas Indonesia in Jakarta, Noegroho applied to a master's programme at the University of Leeds in Britain. His application for a scholarship was unsuccessful, and so he never made the trip that would have enabled him to visit the adopted home of the grandfather that he had known from a distance all his life.[14]

None of Carrim's family from Belitung ever made it to Liverpool before he died in 2004, but other families in the *alam Melayu* did visit from as early as the 1960s. Fadzil Mohamed had a Malaysian cousin, Mustafa, who came to Liverpool in 1967, by which time the Beatles had marked the city on mental maps of popular music fans worldwide, and Liverpool 8 had become fashionably countercultural. Famous poets in the city lived in 'Fashionable Liverpool 8' in the 1960s: Roger McGough on Huskisson Street; Adrian Henri on Canning Street. An evening of Allen Ginsberg's poetry reading in 1965 had ended in a West Indian club off Falkner Square (Bowen, 2008). All of these locations are close to the site of the Malay Club and the Fadzils were living at Hope Place, which is also nearby (although technically outside the Liverpool 8 postal district). Their Malaysian cousin knew that the family was living in Liverpool because Fadzil had visited his sister in Singapore while a ship that he was working on docked there in 1961.[15] Fadzil's oldest child, Farida, went on holiday to the Lake District with her newly discovered Malaysian 'uncle' and his friends. Farida's younger brother, Paul, recalls being driven around Liverpool in a car full of Malays in search of Penny Lane which had been popularized through a song by the Beatles.[16]

The opportunity to study in Britain also enabled Omar Othman to meet up with his father – just once – after 20 years of separation. Omar's father, Othman bin Haji Alias (aka Osman Iaji) was from the village of Serkam, Malacca and, like many other Serkam men, went to Singapore to find work after the Second World War.[17] Omar was four years old when his father went to work at sea: 'He came back late afternoon and he said, "I have found a ship and I'm going off tomorrow." He left the following day. And that's it, he never came back.'[18] Omar was taken back to Malacca by his mother and was raised there. It was only when Omar was attending boarding school in Ipoh (a town in the Malaysian state of Perak) that he began to receive letters from his father, initially from Ceylon but then from 'all over the place'. In 1966 Omar won a scholarship to study in London and so finally got the chance to visit his father, who had by that time settled in Liverpool. They spoke on the telephone when Omar was in London and his father asked, 'when are you coming to see me?' The following week, Omar left London for Liverpool with two student friends. When they arrived at the house where Osman Iaji was staying, the three boys tried to trick him about which of the three was his son, but Osman knew immediately.

Osman Iaji was unwell, suffering from respiratory problems. He had married in Liverpool but the marriage did not last long and so he had no family there. During the time when Omar went to visit in 1966, his father was staying with a fellow Malacca man and his English wife. Omar and his friends spent the night at the Malay Club on Jermyn Street before going back to visit his father again. Omar asked his father if he would like to 'come home' (to Malaysia) after Omar's studies were over and promised that he would visit again during the Christmas break in his studies. However, before he was able to make this return visit from London, on 10 December 1966 Omar received a telegram from Liverpool saying that his father had passed away. By the time Omar arrived in Liverpool for the second time, his father's body was being washed, 'so we met once before he died and once after he died.' Osman Iaji was buried at Anfield cemetery. There was an unusually large number of Malays home from sea at the time so the funeral was very well attended. More than four decades later, Fadzil Mohamed, who was among those present, remembered young Omar shivering in the cold December weather during his father's funeral.[19]

Two wider issues arise from Osman Iaji's family (re)connections. The first concerns the way in which travels in search of lost ancestors extend to the generation after his son Omar. During my fieldwork in Liverpool in 2008, I received an email message from Osman Iaji's grandson, Ahmad Izham Omar (one of Omar's sons), who had travelled to Liverpool from London with his wife and children to look for his grandfather's grave (and also, as he admitted, to 'see the birthplace of the Beatles and go to Anfield').[20] Izham's father, Omar, had long forgotten the location of the cemetery having not been back since the funeral in December 1966. I was aware that Malay seamen who died during the 1960s had mostly been buried in the Anfield cemetery, near to the home of Liverpool Football Club which was already on Izham's travel agenda, and I passed this information on to Izham. The moment when Izham found Osman Iaji's grave (see Figure 5.2) was described in Izham's blog:

> I ran through the graves, looking for a name. One by one the tombstones passed in a blur. My pace quickened and my heart beat harder. My feet were getting wet from the morning dew on the grass in the cemetery. But nothing distracted me as I was looking for a name. THE name. I saw the last three tombstones at the end of the cemetery section. My heart beating even faster, I ran toward them, leaving my family far behind. I got to the last three tombstones. I couldn't believe what I saw. There, on a cold and windy June morning in Liverpool, England, was my grandfather's lost grave.[21]

In 2008 a steady stream of ancestors of Malay seamen continued to trickle to Liverpool, often combining their searches with trips to more mainstream tourist attractions.[22] The current generation is able to draw upon a greatly expanded range of technologies of reconnection. In the 1960s Osman Iaji's whereabouts were known to his son Omar through letters and postcards sent back to Serkam (and on to Ipoh), and they

Figure 5.2 The grave of Osman bin Haji Alias, Anfield cemetery, 2003. Photograph by the author.

were able to speak on the telephone when Omar reached London. Four decades later, Izham's search for the grave of his grandfather involved internet Google searches, mobile phone messages and even a global positioning system (GPS) device.[23]

A second issue that arises from Osman Iaji's family reconnections concerns the way in which they extend spatially beyond a nexus between Liverpool and various sites in Malaysia. As mentioned above, Osman Iaji's family in Serkam received letters from Ceylon and other parts of the world. Osman Iaji had remarried in Ceylon (which became Sri Lanka in 1972) before he left for Liverpool. In the late 1970s Omar received a letter from a woman in Sri Lanka announcing that she was his 'half-sister'. They communicated by letter over the years but never met – until 2008. In that year, Omar's Sri Lankan half-sister visited Malaysia because her son, who was planning to get married, happened to be working at the Hilton Hotel in Kuala Lumpur. On the flight from Colombo to Kuala Lumpur, Omar's half-sister asked a flight attendant if she was familiar with the address on the back of an old photograph of Omar, his wife and his first child. Remarkably, one of the flight attendants knew the place and so Osman's half-sister headed there.

In Izham's words, 'my half-aunt took a car to that place, found the first sundry shop there and showed the owner the photo. The guy took a look at it and said, yes, that's my cousin, and straight away he called my father.'[24] Families formed in sites along British colonial maritime Malay routes were thus connected through non-seafaring labour mobilities associated with postindependence economic development in the *alam Melayu* – a region in which Kuala Lumpur had become established as an employment destination for foreign migrants well before Omar met his Sri Lankan half-sister and her son there.

Diaspora Envy and Worldly Malay-ness

Malaysia's Malay-centred ethnonationalist turn at the end of the 1960s, in combination with the country's rapid economic growth in subsequent decades,[25] fomented popular and state interest in all things Malay, including overseas populations. Even before independence, Malay political elites had recognized the existence of dispersed communities that identified at least partly as 'Malay'. It was noted in the previous chapter that Tunku Abdul Rahman visited Kirkby College outside Liverpool, and that it was from there that he announced plans for Malayan independence. As chief minister of the Federation of Malaya, Tunku Abdul Rahman had also sought to incorporate overseas Malay groups, such as the Cape Malays of South Africa, into *Merdeka* celebrations in Kuala Lumpur.[26] However, it was during the premiership of Mahathir Mohamad, beginning more than three decades later, that efforts to reposition Malays for a world of economic regionalization and globalization added political weight to efforts to find, study and promote links with overseas 'diaspora' communities.[27] By the 1990s a state-sponsored Malay corporate class had become well established within Malaysia, but looked with growing envy at the more-than-national economic activity of transnationally connected Chinese and Indian Malaysians. This fomented a 'novel and suddenly unrequited Malay longing for a diaspora of their own and brought it to the centre of Malaysian national life' (Kessler, 1999: 34), (re)invigorating long-standing Malay cultural and 'pseudo academic' interest in Malays overseas (p. 32).[28]

In the early 1980s, Gabungan Persatuan Penulis Nasional Malaysia (GAPENA, Malaysian National Writers' Association) developed a 'Dunia Melayu' (Malay World) programme under the leadership of Ismail Hussein (Tomizawa, 2010). This rose to public prominence following the organization of the first Malay World Assembly in 1982. The event was officially opened by Mahathir, who had become prime minister the year before, and centred upon issues of Malay language and culture in Malaysia.[29] However, attention was also given at the Malacca symposium to the 'problems' faced by the 50,000-strong Malay community in Sri Lanka who were said to need 'the help of countries in the Malay Archipelago to revive their language and tradition'.[30] According to Hisao Tomizawa (2010: 32), a second symposium that was held in Sri Lanka three years later 'contributed to the general awareness among scholars, researchers, journalists and culturalists about the existence of the Malay stock (*rumpun Melayu*) outside the *Dunia Melayu* Motherland (*Dunia Melayu Induk*) which covers Malaysia, Indonesia and Brunei'. As such, although the term *dunia Melayu* has often been used interchangeably with *alam Melayu* and *nusantara*, it is clear that the Dunia Melayu movement was from the outset concerned with much wider (more-than-regional) Malay worlds. While this initially meant 'retracing footsteps of Malays' only as far as Easter Island and Madagascar,[31] it was also during the period after the first symposium that Malays in Liverpool and elsewhere in Britain began to attract the interest of prominent Malaysian political figures. Having made a donation on behalf of the Malaysian government to the London-based Persatuan Masyarakat Pekerja Malaysia United Kingdom (PMPMUK, Malaysian Workers' Association of the United Kingdom) in 1984, the deputy foreign minister, Abdul Kadir Sheikh Fadzir, requested that a full report about Malays in Britain be presented to Mahathir.[32]

Extension of the Dunia Melayu movement beyond GAPENA's cultural activities into the realm of Malay politics and political economy occurred during a late twentieth-century period of technological and economic shifts in which diasporic networks and global connections caught the attention of Malay political elites in Malaysia (Kessler, 1999; Bunnell, 2004a). In particular, while diasporic Chinese and Indian communities seemed to be well placed to succeed in an increasingly border-crossing (or even 'borderless') global economy, nationally bound Malays did not. Mahathir was, as Clive Kessler puts it, afflicted by 'diaspora envy'.[33] As prime minister (and president of the United Malays National Organization, UMNO), Mahathir proffered the need for a 'new Malay' (*Melayu baru*) subject – one not merely able to compete economically with Chinese and Indian co-nationals within Malaysia, but able to think, act and 'compete with the best' in wider worlds (Shamsul, 1999: 105).[34] The chief minister of the state of Selangor, Muhammad (Mat) Taib (1993), published a book-length elaboration of the *Melayu baru* in 1993. The following year, Mat Taib became one of the three vice presidents of UMNO and the Sekretariat Melayu Antarabangsa (SMA, International Malay Secretariat) was established by the Selangor state government (with Mat Taib as its president) to build and promote relationships with Malay populations distributed throughout the world (Tomizawa, 2010). Among the SMA's declared tasks was 'to build an all-embracing database about the Malay figures (*tokoh-tokoh*), institutions and associations including those related to business' and a database of Malay restaurants across the world (Tomizawa, 2010: 33). Thus, during a decade in which Mahathir famously used urban megaprojects in Kuala Lumpur and surrounding parts of Selangor to project Malaysia on the global stage (Bunnell, 2004a), long-standing Malay cultural and intellectual movements became intertwined with increasingly transnational Malay(sian) economic aspirations (see also Haron, 2005). The Dunia Melayu movement, in turn, became even less delimited to a specifiable geographical region or realm, and about networking – 'commercial as well as cultural' (Milner, 2008: 183) – that was worldwide or global in scope.[35]

Malaysians visiting the club on Jermyn Street in Liverpool in search of Malay ancestors came to include people driven by more than merely personal or familial connections. Increasingly, there was a political imperative to tracing Malay life worlds beyond the conventional boundaries of the *alam Melayu* in Southeast Asia. In 2004 Mohamed Nor Hamid (Mat Nor), who had by then been president of the Merseyside Malaysian and Singapore Community Association (MSA) for around a decade, recalled a visit from the granddaughter of an UMNO politician from Negeri Sembilan.[36] This young woman was studying at a university elsewhere in Britain and had been sent to Liverpool to deliver a RM150 (then around £40) donation to that far western outpost of a globally extended *dunia Melayu.* The woman's grandfather, Mat Nor recalled, had visited Sri Lanka, South Africa and Madagascar in search of diasporic Malays. None of this was particularly novel or exciting to ex-seafarers in Liverpool. Many of them had met 'Malays' in these and other maritime locations decades earlier. Some, such as Osman Iaji, had started families in multiple maritime nodes. Mat Nor had himself met people who identified as Malay in both Sri Lanka and South Africa during his time as a seaman.[37]

The position of the Cape Malays in South Africa in relation to plans for the Federation of Malaya's independence celebrations back in 1957 is worthy of brief further elaboration since it presages difficulties faced by later, postindependence efforts at building diasporic Malay identity around a Malaysian homeland. In the lead-up to independence, Malayan government officials met with a man named Ismail Petersen who said that over the previous two decades he had 'entertained numerous Malayans and Indonesian seamen and visitors passing through Cape Town'.[38] In a letter sent to the UK high commissioner in Cape Town on 21 June 1957, Petersen also said that he had been thanked and congratulated by the Malayan officials, and that they had promised to recommend that Petersen be invited to represent the Cape Malays at Malayan independence celebrations in Kuala Lumpur. This prospect caused concern in the Commonwealth Relations Office in London. In the context of an emerging mosaic of Commonwealth states, it was feared that the South African government would be angered by any implication that 'there was a community in South Africa which owed some kind of loyalty to the Federation of Malaya.'[39] Beyond the perceived undesirability of such transnationally divided loyalties, however, was a sense of the implausibility of mapping Cape Malays back to the political territory of the Federation of Malaya. In a telegram sent to the high commissioner of the Federation of Malaya and the UK high commissioner in Pretoria, the secretary of state for the colonies wrote:

> It is not (repeat not) even possible to argue that South African Malays are in a special ethnographical or even sentimental relation to Malaya. They are in fact a mixed community of several races, some of whom immigrated from Java, most recent major immigration being in 18th century. Am informed that they speak Afrikaans and not Malay, and ... they are all South African citizens.

Such concerns resurfaced in the late twentieth century, and hindered attempts to develop transnational linkages between Malaysia and 'Malays' elsewhere.

The problem was once again at least partly one of political geography or, more precisely, that Malays in Liverpool and various other sites that caught the attention of Malaysian diaspora seekers did not map back to a homeland contained by the territorial boundaries of that nation state. Not only had some Liverpool Malays left Southeast Asia prior to the establishment of new political boundaries in the wake of British colonialism, but many thought of their home in Southeast Asia in terms of sites outside Malaysia, especially in what had become the separate nation state of Singapore. Indeed, of the 13 people listed on the deeds for 7 Jermyn Street, the majority originated from Singapore and not from territories that remained part of Malaysia after Singapore's separation in 1965. Political elites in Malaysia who supported or funded study trips to Malay communities overseas were not interested in finding a *Singapore* diaspora. Geopolitical relations between the two nation states were often fractious, especially during Mahathir's terms as prime minister. The decision to register the Malay Club in Liverpool as the MSA (Merseyside Malaysian and Singapore Community Association) thus created difficulties, not just for a specifically Malaysian Dunia Melayu movement but also for Malaysian student groups seeking funding

Figure 5.3 Ex-seamen at the Malay Club in 1989. Reproduced by permission of Dewani Abbas.

from 'home' for events which incorporated Liverpool's long-standing ex-seafaring Malays. The MSA president, Mat Nor, told me in 2004 that he had 'caught' Malaysian students trying to hide Singapore flags and logos when taking photographs in the Malay Club (in order, he thought, to be able to access funds from Malaysian political organizations such as UMNO who would have been put off by any signs of 'Singapore').[40]

There is evidence of interest in Malay Liverpool from Singapore too but, in contrast to Malaysian political and quasi-academic investment in a Malay diaspora, this has been limited to popular media coverage. As early as 1979 an article in the Singapore Malay-language newspaper *Berita Harian* described the Granby Street area around Jermyn Street as Liverpool's '*kampung Melayu*' (Malay village).[41] And a decade later, a *Berita Minggu* article included a picture of three men at the Malay Club: Encik Buang Ahdar (nicknamed Guy), Encik Arsad Hassan and Encik Jaafar Mohd (Jaafar) (see Figure 5.3).[42] Jaafar, the 'Singapore Malay' of Boyanese ancestry who had settled in Liverpool having served on Blue Funnel Line pilgrim ships (see Chapter 2), was at that time president of what was referred in the Singapore newspaper coverage as the Kelab Melayu Liverpool on Jermyn Street. The *Berita Minggu* article considered that the hearts and souls of ex-seamen in Liverpool (and at another Malay Club in London) were still 'Malay', but there was no mention of their ongoing connections back to Southeast Asia. However, the journalist Dewani Abbas's trip to Liverpool and London had in fact been inspired by the return journey of three British-based Malay ex-seamen to Singapore in 1987.[43] Dewani Abbas's own travels to, and writing about, Malay Liverpool in turn served to forge new family connections. Cik Rohaya in Singapore saw the photograph of her father, Jaafar Mohamad, with his friends at the Malay Club in Liverpool and the two established contact by telephone after almost three decades of separation.[44] It was another decade later before father and daughter were finally reunited face-to-face when Jaafar visited Singapore in March 2000. Dewani Abbas, the same journalist who had met Jaafar in Liverpool in 1989, covered the story of his homecoming for *Berita Minggu*.[45]

Malaysian popular media coverage also facilitated reconnections. In some cases, ex-seamen living in Britain had been presumed dead by their relations in Malaysia until their stories were featured in a documentary made by the Malaysian public broadcaster, Radio Televisyen Malaysia (RTM). The journalist and researcher Zaharah Othman emerged as the authority on Malays in Britain and an important contact for people searching for lost relatives. Although based in London, Zaharah visited and interviewed ex-seamen in Liverpool and Cardiff for a BBC radio documentary and an article that was published in the Malaysian English-language daily, the *New Straits Times*.[46] That article was subsequently posted on a web site for Malays overseas, Rantauan.com, with the title 'The old Malays', and that was where I first found it. I was not the only one. Singapore-based family members of Arsad Hassan – one of the three men who had also been featured in the 1989 Singapore *Berita Minggu* story – contacted Zaharah having read the online version of the article. Zaharah, in turn, put the family in email contact with Paul Fadzil, son of Liverpool-based ex-seaman Fadzil Mohamed (Fadzil). Paul Fadzil recalled that the email included a photograph of Arsad Hassan and read: 'I know that Liverpool is a big city, but I thought you might know him.'[47] Paul's father confirmed that Arsad Hassan was the person in the image, and Paul sent on Arsad Hassan's contact details to his relatives in Singapore by email.[48]

Zaharah Othman's writing on Malay ex-seamen in Liverpool was of historical interest to many visitors to the Rantauan.com portal. Unsurprisingly, however, the city did not feature as prominently in the late twentieth-century electronic networks of students and professionals seeking to forge a virtual 'community away from our own' – or in wider imaginings of a globe-spanning *dunia Melayu* – as it had in the mid-twentieth-century maritime networks that brought the 'old Malays' to Liverpool. Within Britain, in an era of Malay student and professional sojourners (female as well as male), rather than seamen, London was the undisputed centre. Even within the northwest of England, it was Manchester rather than Liverpool that had the largest concentration of Malay students from Malaysia. More widely, although Britain remained a popular destination for Malay(sian) students, the Malay expatriate professional class extended its commercial reach beyond the former colonial centre, including to places that feature diasporic Malay communities. Abdul Rahim Daud, the pioneering student who had rented a room from Mr Carrim in 1970 (see Chapter 4), went on to be posted to both Sri Lanka and South Africa as a senior figure in Telekom Malaysia. Among his management staff in Kuala Lumpur was Suheilah Abu Bakar, whose husband, Mohd Khusairi was the man described in the previous chapter as having arrived in Liverpool as a student following the Toxteth riots. Suheilah Abu Bakar herself had experience of working in Pretoria, South Africa, a country in which Malaysia emerged as a leading foreign investor.[49] It is worth considering the role that the Dunia Melayu movement played in such transnational economic linkages. One scholarly analysis of GAPENA's activities in South Africa considered them as a form of 'non-state' international relations in the 1990s (Haron, 2005). In addition, the growth in mutual cultural interest between Malaysian and Cape Malays in the 1990s had wider political economic implications in terms of labour and tourist flows, especially after Malaysia Airlines signed an agreement with South African authorities to fly to Johannesburg and Cape Town in 1993.

Liverpool was at best marginal to the territories of diasporic opportunity imagined by would-be transnational Malay capitalism in the 1990s. An article published in the Malaysian Malay-language newspaper *Berita Harian* in 1989 painted a bleak social and economic picture of the city, and the implications of its decline for resident Malays.[50] The journalist Ahmad Rodzi Yaakob met two Malay men outside the mosque on Mulgrave Street. Haji Talib Md Sin was a Kampung Serkam man who had first visited Liverpool as a seafarer in 1954. Haji Ngah Musa, from Losong, Kuala Terengganu, had arrived in Britain even earlier, in 1948, but had then led a colourful seafaring life that included jumping ship on the other side of the Malay Atlantic, before eventually settling in Liverpool.[51] Musa contrasted the situation in Liverpool in the 1950s when there had been lots of job opportunities for Malays with the chronic unemployment problems facing Britain in the 1980s.[52] He is reported to have finished work in 1980, after which he volunteered at the local mosque before opening a small stall there selling Islamic literature. In the context of heightened competition for jobs, the article concludes that white people in Liverpool and Britain more generally had come to hold increasingly negative perceptions of 'coloured' people (*orang kulit berwarna*). Although both of the *perantau* (migrants or sojourners) who were interviewed had gone to Liverpool to seek their fortunes (as Haji Talib put it), they now imagined better futures to lie back in Malaysia. Both had reportedly made return visits to their respective home towns and had plans to return to their Malaysian homeland once they were old enough to qualify for pensions in Britain.[53]

Old Malays versus the Islamized New Malay

The geographical location in Liverpool of ex-seamen Talib and Musa meant that they were structurally cut off from the diasporic growth areas of the transnational(izing) Malay capitalist class. Yet to what extent did the lives of these men and other 'old Malays' show evidence of traits that were valorized by proponents of the *Melayu baru* in the 1990s? Liverpool-based Malay men could certainly be said to have been exposed to remedies that were prescribed by Mahathir to overcome Malay economic 'backwardness' in preceding decades (Mahathir, 1970).[54] Mahathir's book, *The Malay Dilemma*, published in 1970, more than a decade before he became prime minister, and coinciding with the onset of two decades of planned economic restructuring under the New Economic Policy (NEP), prescribed two key remedies: capitalist discipline and urbanization. 'Shore jobs' in Liverpool usually meant the discipline of the factory or the docks – in Talib's case it had been a furniture factory – while for those who continued to work at sea, ships have long been (and remain) much more highly regulated as well as spatially confined places of work than is conventionally imagined or romanticized (Linebaugh and Rediker, 2012; Sampson, 2013). Moreover, to the extent that most Liverpool-based Malay men originated from rural *kampung* settlements, their *merantau* may be understood as a form of rural-to-urban migration.[55] In view of the fact that one of NEP's main objectives was the creation of a community of Malay entrepreneurs, it should also be noted that Johan Awang, the founder of Liverpool's first Malay Club, was by no means the last Malay to open a business in the city.[56] To the extent that, during much of the two decades after the publication of *The Malay Dilemma*, the primary concern of Malay nationalists was with Malay entrepreneurs taking their place in the modern, urban-based economy of multiethnic Malaysia, rather than with entrepreneurship overseas, Malays running businesses in the *rantau* (region away from home) of Liverpool were ahead of their time. However, by the time the geography of Malay(sian) economic aspiration underwent global expansion in the 1990s, idealizations of new Malay subjectivity had become inflected with class and religious shifts in Malaysia (Shamsul, 1999; Chong, 2005) which were at odds with forms and practices of Malay-ness prevailing among old Malays in Liverpool.

Melayu baru is, in Terence Chong's words, 'shorthand for the new Malay middle class' (Chong, 2005) which emerged during the period of the NEP. As such, the term connoted not merely the developmental effects of capitalist regimes and urbanization – although these remained important in articulations of the *Melayu baru* in the 1990s[57] – but also certain kinds of occupational status or social position. By such systems of evaluation, (ex-)seamen did not count.[58] Similarly, *Melayu baru* did not mean those Malays working on the shop floor of factories in Malaysia's expanding industrial zones (or those working in what was left of industrial manufacturing on Merseyside), but implied their bosses, the middle-class 'professional and technical' as well as 'administrative and managerial' categories (Abdul Rahman, 1996: 63). In sum, men working in poorly paid jobs (or, worse still, not working and claiming social security benefits)[59] while waiting to qualify for their pensions in a faded British imperial port city were not embodiments of the kind of Malay subject that came to be idealized by political elites in Malaysia.

In contrast, one man from Malaya who was depicted as having 'made it' in Britain was Mohamed Aris, reportedly the first Malay to become a mayor of a town in Britain. Mohamed Aris had left his *kampung* in Johor in 1957 not as a seaman but in order to pursue undergraduate studies in Manchester. Interviewed by *Berita Harian* journalists while visiting family in Malaysia in June 1989, Mohamed Aris is reported to have affirmed the mantra that Malays can prosper and succeed (*boleh maju*) anywhere in the world.[60] The racism and the apparent difficulty of securing employment experienced by the two men interviewed by Ahmad Rodzi Yaakob in Liverpool – whose report on ex-seamen Talib and Musa appeared in the same newspaper the following month[61] – contrasted sharply with Mohamed Aris's political achievement. Talib and Musa in Liverpool had surely followed Mohamed Aris's prescriptive philosophy of 'when in Rome do as the Romans do.'[62] However, new Malays were those able to prosper rather than merely to survive overseas. Unlike Mohamed Aris, ex-seafaring Liverpool Malays' continued socioeconomically marginal positioning located them outside the subject position of *Melayu baru* that rose to prominence in political and popular discourses in Malaysia in the 1990s.

Like middle classes elsewhere, *Melayu baru* came to be defined not only in terms of occupational status and wealth, but also in terms of particular styles, attitudes and modes of comportment. One scholar notes the cultural capital required by the emergent Malay capitalist class in Malaysia to negotiate barriers of culture and language: 'The possession of global commodities like the English language, internationally recognized MBAs, and other global tastes in food and clothing mark the *Melayu Baru* as a global class with strong hints of cosmopolitan flavor' (Chong, 2005: 578). Ex-seamen in Liverpool certainly did not have international educational qualifications and, in many cases, spoke 'broken', grammatically incorrect English, despite having lived in Britain for decades. This was mentioned in both English- and Malay-language media coverage in Malaysia (and indeed in Singapore). During my fieldwork in Liverpool, Malaysian students often joked that the *Pak Cik-Pak Cik* (Malay elders) could not even speak Malay particularly well, having been exposed mostly to *bahasa Melayu pasar* (marketplace Malay) – and a somewhat antiquated (*kuno*) version of it, at that – rather than the modern version of the language which was standardized in Malaysia after independence.[63] So while they had negotiated barriers of culture and language in their urban social lives – performing ordinary or working-class forms of cosmopolitanism (see Chapter 3) – Liverpool Malays were nonetheless linguistically excluded from middle-class cosmopolitanism both in Britain and in Malaysia.[64]

It is also significant that reformulations of Mahathir's understanding of Malay development during his time as prime minister emphasized the importance of culture and identity in the face of going 'global'. This marked a shift that is evident from comparison of *The Malay Dilemma* (1970) with Mahathir's later book, *The Challenge*, a collection of essays which were written in the 1970s and published in English in 1986 (Mahathir, 1986; originally published in Malay in 1976). While *The Malay Dilemma* presumed a singular pathway to modernization following experiences in the West, *The Challenge* allowed for the possibility and desirability of non-Western, 'Asian' forms of development. This had much to do with what came to be referred to as the 'East Asian miracle' (World Bank, 1993), or the rapid state-led economic development of countries such as Japan and South Korea. The 'rise' of such Asian economies contrasted sharply with industrial decline in parts of the West, and especially Britain, during the 1970s and 1980s. As prime minister, Mahathir adopted a Look East policy while caricaturing the West as suffering irreversible decline and a 'perversion of values' (Mahathir, 1986: 91). Modernization, in other words, became imaginatively decoupled from Westernization. In light of shifting uneven geographies of economic rise and demise, Malays who had gone west to Britain – and especially to the far western outpost of deindustrializing Liverpool – may increasingly have been imagined to have moved away from the emerging leading edge of economic progress in Asia. In addition, Malay adaptation to the economic and cultural environment of Liverpool – doing what the Liverpudlians do – could now connote not only loss of identity but also the risk of having assimilated into systems of degenerate values and attitudes. There was, in other words, a danger of

Liverpool-based Malays having become 'too Western' to fit in with newly Asian-centred visions of modernization associated with Mahathir's reconfigured understanding of a 'fully developed' Malaysia. As for the children of Malay seamen in Liverpool, one of the ex-seamen featured in the Malaysian press is reported to have highlighted a cultural divide between Malays in Malaysia and those raised overseas, especially England.[65]

While there was a general trend during the Mahathir era of looking away from the West and towards Asian values and attitudes – or of recasting the West as occidental Other to emergent Asian visions of progress – it was the centrality of Islam to performances of *Melayu baru* subjectivity, above all, that distinguished this from prior modern Malay subject positions. The shift may be understood in the context of Islamic resurgence, or *dakwah*, from the 1970s that has been a noted feature of social and political transformation in Malaysia after the time when the Malay men who are central to this study left the *alam Melayu* (Hussin, 1993). Shamsul A.B. (1999: 103) notes a '*dakwah-isation* of the Malay new middle class' but also suggests that there are at least two major *dakwah* factions – 'the "moderate" (modernist) and "radical" (fundamentalist)' (p. 102). Mahathir's essays in *The Challenge* may thus be understood as modernist attempts to reconcile Islam and modernity. Writing at a time when he had become a prominent member of UMNO and a cabinet member, Mahathir railed against a 'retreatist' tendency among (fundamentalist) Muslims in Malaysia that could only jeopardize the position of the Malays and Islam by exhorting believers to 'turn their backs on the world' (Mahathir, 1986: 81). Malay economic development and progress were cast as religious imperatives since it is 'the mastering and use of modern ways which can safeguard the position and security of Muslims' (p. 81).

As prime minister, Mahathir oversaw a period of Islamization which contrasted markedly with the largely secularist orientations of his predecessors. The extent to which Mahathir's pro-Islam posture was an expression of his commitment to the religion and of him having been personally affected by the 'tide of Islamic resurgence' continues to be subject to debate (see Muhammad Haniff, 2007: 298). Sven Schottmann (2011: 367) argues that Mahathir's Islam should be seen as 'something more substantial and original than the mere appeasement of Islamist opponents'. Equally clearly, however, Islamization was at least partly a response to growing critiques of UMNO couched in religious terms and associated electoral opposition from Parti Islam Se-Malaysia (PAS, Pan-Malaysian Islamic Party). Mahathir sought to strengthen his, and UMNO's, Islamic credentials by co-opting the Islamic youth activist Anwar Ibrahim – the man whose detention under the ISA following student protests in 1974 had spurred Hishamuddin Rais to flee Malaysia.

What is important here for new performances of Malay-ness, and so ultimately for 'old Malays' in Liverpool, is that Islamization extended way beyond Malay politics and public policy. Shamsul (1999: 102) writes of a 'mainstreaming' of Islam into 'the everyday activities of Malaysia's multi-ethnic-oriented economy and society'. Although the practices of Islam in Malaysia remain heterogeneous, overall levels of religiosity certainly rose during the Mahathir era, and Malay ethnicity was increasingly conflated with Muslim identity (Khoo, 1995; Martinez, 2004).

The Malaysian journalist Ahmad Rodzi Yaakob met the two ex-seamen who featured in his 1989 *Berita Harian* report at the mosque on Mulgrave Street in Liverpool 8. Both men whom he interviewed carried the title Haji and were involved in religious activities: Talib sold food items at Liverpool's halal centre on Granby Street, while Musa sold religious reading material at the mosque. Such markers of religiosity meant that these two men fitted well into the Islamized *Melayu baru* subject position. But how representative were they of Malay ex-seafarers in Liverpool at that time? There is no doubt that there had always been deeply and visibly religious individuals among Malay seamen who came to or through Liverpool.[66] Religious beliefs inflected household eating practices and rhythms either side of the war (see Chapter 3) and burial arrangements at least as far back as the 1960s, as evidenced by the funeral of Osman Iaji (see above). Johan Awang's butcher's shop on North Hill Street, the first shop to be opened by a Malay in the city, was halal. In addition, among those who had not been overtly religious as young seafaring men, there were those – including Musa – who (re)discovered their faith and changed their conduct accordingly in later life.[67] Nonetheless, in the late 1980s and even up to the time when I began to conduct fieldwork in Liverpool from 2003, one was at least equally likely to find Malay ex-seamen in certain public houses (pubs) in Liverpool 8 as at the Al-Rahma mosque. To what extent was this to do with a generation of mostly secular Malays who liked to drink and gamble? To what extent was it a reflection of 'degeneration' of Malays who had adapted too well to local 'culture' in the godless *rantau* of Liverpool?[68] Conversely, was frequenting and consuming alcohol in pubs simply part of the everyday lives of some men in Liverpool who continued to include 'Malay' and 'Muslim' as components of their identity? The work of Andrew Yip has pointed to the need for scholars to attend to micro-scale dimensions of how Islam (among other religions) is lived rather than reproducing essentialist views of religious belief systems (Yip, 2009). Clearly, that agenda is beyond the scope of this book. The point here is to ask whether the focus on Musa and Talib in Ahmad Rodzi Yaakob's *Berita Harian* article reflected essentialized expectations of conduct among Malays in late 1980s Malaysia. Did the fact that Ahmad Rodzi Yaakob met Talib and Musa outside the mosque reflect his expectation that this was where Malays would or *should* be found?[69] Or was it just a coincidence that his *Berita Harian* article featured two of the Malay men in Liverpool whose performances of Muslim-Malay-ness conformed much more closely to the normative expectations of the newspaper's readers in Malaysia than did the lives of many of the men at the Malay Club on nearby Jermyn Street?[70]

Irrespective of the unrepresentativeness of Musa and Talib, Malay ex-seamen in Liverpool had certainly not been cut off from Islamization in Malaysia or from revivalism in wider Islamic worlds. Malaysian students brought their (Islamized) senses of what it meant to be a 'good Malay' with them to the city and I heard stories at the Malay Club of disagreement between 'modernist' and 'fundamentalist' interpretations of what this implied (to use Shamsul's terms).[71] Of course, there were also young Malay men and women who relished the prospect of studying in Britain precisely to escape from the tightening grip of religious social restrictions in Malaysia. Nonetheless, as noted in the previous chapter, the trend was increasingly for the Malaysian government to prioritize the funding of mature (graduate) students to study overseas; and this typically meant middle-class Malay families with mainstream Malaysian conceptions of Malay-ness. As such, when Mohamed Nor Hamid (Mat Nor) became president of the club in 1994, he sought to tread a difficult middle ground. On the one hand, he wanted Jermyn Street to continue to be a place of association for Malay ex-seamen who had become accustomed to conducting 'un-Islamic' activities there and to non-Muslim British descendants of such men.[72] On the other hand, he sought to 'clean up' the place to be more attractive to Malaysian student families and to religious ex-seamen such as Musa and Talib. While this dilemma was itself evidence of Malaysianization, vectors of religious influence were not a one-way street from Malaysia to Liverpool. *Dakwah* in Malaysia formed part of a worldwide Islamic resurgence, driven in particular by developments in the Middle East from the 1970s, and many Malaysians in fact gained their first exposure as students in Britain (Hussin, 1993). At the beginning of the twenty-first century, Liverpool's Al-Rahma mosque remained a site of remarkable ethnic and national diversity, where Malaysian students and some old Malay ex-seafarers congregated with men from across the multiethnic Islamic world, and were thus inevitably confronted with different ways of being Muslim.

While there is no doubt that the mosque in Liverpool 8 gave rise to transethnic or cross-national interactions, the cosmopolitanism of Islamized *Melayu baru* also served to close down certain possibilities for encounters with difference. This is evident when social practices of ethnic Malay Malaysian students are contrasted not only with those of ex-seamen but also with earlier generations of Malay students in Liverpool. I noted in the previous chapter that Malayan students attending Kirkby College (1951–1962) happily ate at a restaurant in Chinatown with Mat Nor.[73] It was commonplace at that time for Malay students to eat at Chinese restaurants which were not halal, even if they did not consume pork themselves. One person who confirmed this in interview was Baharuddin Marji, a former resident staff member at Kirkby College, whose donation to the Al-Rahma mosque was noted in the previous chapter.[74] It may be contended that the liberal eating practices that he recalled were historically specific to the immediate post-independence period and, even then, confined to English-speaking, urban elites who were not representative of interethnic relations between ordinary Malayans (see Khoo, 2009). Yet one Chinese Malaysian man who studied in Liverpool in the early 1970s noted that, at that time, 'Malays would have a beer.'[75] Even those who were strict about not drinking alcohol or eating pork would still go along to pubs and restaurants with friends who did – 'eating together-in-difference' as Jean Duruz and Gaik Cheng Khoo (2015) have put it. In contrast, the Chinese *kopitiam* (traditional coffee shop) in Malaysia, which was once a space of transethnic and transreligious interaction, is increasingly seen as a no-go zone for 'good' Malays (i.e. practising Muslims). Cultures of hospitality remain very important in contemporary Malaysia, but are now performed, by default, in halal ways such that non-Muslim groups are reduced to the perpetual status of guests.[76] Baharuddin and his wife kindly took me to a Chinese restaurant in Petaling Jaya (greater Kuala Lumpur) after I interviewed them and they ate with chopsticks rather than spoon and fork, recalling the cosmopolitanism of the Kirkby College era. However, in keeping with the prevailing expectations as to what constitutes 'proper' Malay food consumption in Malaysia today, the restaurant was certified as halal (see also Fischer, 2008, 2011).

Another factor that renders Liverpool Malays 'un-Malay' in contemporary Malaysian systems of evaluation is their non-Muslim families. I have noted that an overwhelming majority of Malays who settled in Liverpool married English or Irish women who, in many cases, were the reason for staying in the first place. In contemporary Malaysian terms, there is nothing problematic about this so long as the wife adopts Islam and their children are raised as Muslims. However, this was simply not the case for almost all of the women who married Malay seamen in Liverpool. What is more, it was mostly the mothers who ran the households, especially in cases where their husbands were working at sea and so tended to be away for long periods. As was noted in Chapter 3, eating habits did change in many families when 'dad' was home, although even men who would not eat *babi* (pork) often enjoyed drinking Guinness or other alcoholic drinks. And even though Ben Youp attended prayers at the house of Ali Hizzam before the opening of the Al-Rahma mosque, his daughter became a Church of England Sunday school teacher.[77] Similarly diverse consumption and religious practices have been noted in accounts of the families of Malay seamen in the docks and Tiger Bay areas of Cardiff. In an article written for Tiger Bay's International Folklore Festival in 1994, Marcia Brahim Barry recalled growing up with a Malay father from Malacca and a Roman Catholic mother of mixed Welsh, French and Nepalese ancestry:

> My father was a Mohammedan but my mother and us kids were Catholics. This is an accepted part of our lives, both sides respecting and tolerating each other's religion and culture. I still recall my dad when he was on shore-leave seeing us off to early daily morning mass. Both my brothers were altar-boys so they had to serve daily mass. When we arrived home from church my father would have lit the fire and our breakfast would be waiting for us – laid out on the kitchen table.[78]

Such family dynamics are almost inconceivable in contemporary Malaysia, or at least in peninsular Malaysia.[79] The transethnic and inter-religious lives and homes of Malay seamen in British port cities in the middle decades of the twentieth century contrast sharply with the late twentieth- and twenty first-century 'cosmopolitanism' of middle-class *Melayu baru, global* or *korporat* (Sloane, 1999).

Liverpool-based Malay ex-seamen and their family members have been welcomed (back) into the homes of family in Malaysia and Singapore. This applies to men who, like the father of Mafiz's character in *Dari Jemapoh ke Manchester*, had done little more than send a postcard back to the *kampung* as well as to others who had sustained regular contact and/or remitted money over the decades. There is no doubt that this is evidence of kindness and hospitality as much as kinship obligation. Nonetheless, reconfigured conceptions of Malay-ness, especially following decades of Islamization in Malaysia, meant that there were Malays returning to the *alam Melayu* who felt a need to (re)learn how to 'be Malay'. There were men who would definitely not have been found at the Al-Rahma mosque by visiting Malaysian journalists in 1989 who began to join Friday prayers there after making return visits to Malaysia.[80] Further tutelage and encouragement were widely available from the latest cohorts of Malay students in the city. However, despite such possibilities for transnational ethnoreligious regeneration, Liverpool Malays were not the kind of diasporic Malays whom elites in Malaysia were looking for. Proletarian ex-seamen in the 'inner city' of economically blighted postimperial Liverpool were irredeemably outside of new Malay-ness in terms of both social class and geography. Material and imagined geographies of Malay modernity had changed and Liverpool-based Malay men had to look back to Southeast Asia – and especially to Islamized visions of development in Malaysia – for lessons in how to be a modern, advanced Malay.

Notes

1 Mila ... *Kau kata tadi ayah kau di mana?*
Mafiz *Di Liverpool. Tapi dah lama dia tak balik.*
Mila ... *Mak kau?*
Mafiz *Ada. Tukang jahit di Jemapoh. Aku kerja jugak, aku ambil kereta. Lama dah ayah aku pergi. Aku lagi kecil lagi. Dah lame kami tunggu. Dulu ada surat, kadang-kadang ada duit.*
Mila *Tak pulang-pulang?*
Mafiz *Sekarang ... Satu habuk pun tak ada.*

2 One film studies scholar pointed to 'a sense of latent homosexuality between the two central characters' (McKay, 2011: 14).

3 Steven Gan, '500 days in Kamunting', *Malaysiakini*, 23 August 2002, available at: http://m.malaysiakini.com/editorials/22761 (accessed 5 October 2015).

4 For more on Aman Majid (Man Toyko), see Zaharah Othman, 'In their element at sea', *New Straits Times*, 27 March 2000, p. 5.

5 Steven Gan, '500 days in Kamunting', *Malaysiakini*, 23 August 2002, available at: http://m.malaysiakini.com/editorials/22761 (accessed 5 October 2015).

6 Personal communication with Hishamuddin Rais, Kuala Lumpur, 21 February 2004.

7 Interview, Kuala Lumpur, 6 November 2008.

8 See Tim Bunnell, 'Laskar Belitung di Liverpool' [A sailor from Belitung in Liverpool], *Kompas*, 12 September 2009.

9 Carrim and Aca's daughter Nuratin was born in 1944 but it is not clear how long after this Carrim left. Interview with Noegroho Andy Handojo (son of Nuratin, grandson of Carrim), Jakarta, Indonesia, 2 December 2009.

10 He first shipped out of Liverpool on the *Miguel de Larrinaga* in October 1950. BT 372/089.

11 BT 372/089.

12 '*Di dalam ini kotalah, neneknya Vera dan kake tinggal.*' Carrim died on 23 August 2004. His gravestone records that he was born on the island of Belitung, not in Singapore.

13 Interview with Noegroho, Jakarta, Indonesia, 2 December 2009.

14 Noegroho did, however, get to meet both Carrim and Vera when they visited Indonesia in 1989.

15 Notes from conversation with Fadzil Mohamed, Liverpool, 14 June 2008.

16 Interview with Paul Fadzil, Liverpool, 29 September 2004.

17 See Chapter 2.

18 Interview with Omar, Kuala Lumpur, 7 November 2008. The remainder of this paragraph and the next paragraph are based on this interview.
19 Notes from conversation with Fadzil Mohamed, Liverpool, 14 June 2008.
20 Email communication, 2 June 2008. Anfield is the home of Liverpool Football Club.
21 'The grave in Liverpool', 27 June 2008, http://www.8tv.com.my/off_the_record/The_Grave_In_Liverpool.html (accessed 1 July 2008, no longer available).
22 Beatles fan, Izham, was on a tour of George Harrison's house when I contacted him.
23 Deborah Loh, 'Mana saya mau letak ini?' [Where do I want to put this?], *The Nutgraph*, 9 July 2009, available at: http://www.thenutgraph.com/mana-saya-mau-letak-ini/ (accessed 27 March 2014).
24 Cited in Deborah Loh, 'Mana saya mau letak ini?' [Where do I want to put this?], *The Nutgraph*, 9 July 2009, available at: http://www.thenutgraph.com/mana-saya-mau-letak-ini/ (accessed 27 March 2014).
25 By the 1970s Malaysia had followed Singapore's lead into export-oriented industrialization and the two countries experienced annual economic growth rates of 8 and 9 per cent respectively during the decade. Despite a severe downturn in the middle years of the subsequent decade Malaysia still registered an average growth in real GDP of 5.4 per cent during the 1980s (Drabble, 2000).
26 CO 1030/842, 'Celebrations on independence of Malaya'. I am grateful to Lai Chee Kien for alerting me to this file.
27 The use of scare quotes around the term 'diaspora' signals recognition that the overseas groups concerned do not satisfy all definitions of diaspora, particularly in that their geographies emerged from individual choice rather than forced collective dispersal. However, influential academic as well as popular uses of the term today are sufficiently broad to encompass the experiences of Liverpool-based Malays, for example as 'labour and imperial' diasporas (Cohen, 1997).
28 It should be noted that there has since emerged a (separate) body of important scholarly research which is concerned to examine the Malay world beyond conventional or predetermined boundaries, and to foreground transregional historical dynamics and cultural interactions (see Mandal, 2013 and the papers that this introduces).
29 Zainah Anwar, 'One language, one culture: Dr M', *New Straits Times*, 19 December 1982, p. 1.
30 'Malays in Sri Lanka need outside help', *New Straits Times*, 20 December 1982, p. 5.
31 'Retracing footsteps of Malays', *New Straits Times*, 7 August 1985, p. 3.
32 'Malaysia ambil perhatian nasib Melayu di UK' [Malaysia pays attention to the fate of Malays in the UK], *Berita Harian*, 13 September 1984. I have been unable to find any trace of this report or, indeed, whether it ever materialized. A subsequent news report notes how the organization received a contribution of RM73,000 from the Terengganu sultanate towards the cost of purchasing a building of its own in London ('Impian

masyarakat Melayu London hampir tercapai' [The dreams of the Malay community in London have almost been realized], *Berita Harian*, 8 November 1986). PMPMUK traces its origins to the Persatuan Melayu United Kingdom, which was established in Liverpool in 1951 ('Mempererat hubungan pekerja Melayu di Britain' [Tightening the connections among Malay workers in the UK], *Berita Harian*, 25 January 1988).

33 In this context of what Kessler has referred to as a broader 'entangling of geopolitical and scholarly ambitions' (p. 33), it is unsurprising that there are clear examples of connections between the broader Dunia Melayu movement and ruling UMNO. The former director of the Malay World and Civilization Institute (ATMA) at Universiti Kebangsaan Malaysia, which had close links and overlaps with GAPENA, for example, became an UMNO member of parliament.

34 Shamsul A.B. considers the 'new Malay' as 'the group that Mahathir feels will carry the "Malay flag", as it were, into the next century, competent, skilled and able to compete with the best in Malaysia and the world' (p. 105).

35 By November 2000, Ismail Hussein was quoted as having said that his obsession was to 'build a global Malay Tribe (*Suku Melayu Dunia*)' (cited in Tomizawa, 2010: 34).

36 Interview, Liverpool, 29 September 2004. Negeri Sembilan is another state in peninsular Malaysia (coincidentally, the one in which Jemapoh is located).

37 Interview, Liverpool, 3 September 2004.

38 CO 1030/842, 'Celebrations on independence of Malaya'.

39 CO 1030/842, 'Celebrations on independence of Malaya' (Telegram from the Secretary of State for the Colonies, 4 July 1956). British colonial officials were also concerned to follow an emerging set of protocols for decolonization within the Commonwealth, and the preparations for Malayan independence referred back to earlier procedures in Ceylon and Ghana (Stockwell, 2008).

40 Interview, Liverpool, 29 September 2004.

41 'Kampung Melayu di Bandar Liverpool' [A Malay village in the city of Liverpool], *Berita Harian*, 21 October 1979.

42 Dewani Abbas, 'Tetap Melayu walau di bumi "Mat Saleh"' [Still Malay although in the land of 'white people'], *Berita Minggu*, 3 October, 1989.

43 Dewani Abbas, 'Gembira kembali ke tanahair: bersua lagi dengan saudara-mara selepas 38 tahun di England' [Happy to return to the homeland: meeting up again with their relatives after 38 years in England], *Berita Minggu*, 25 January 1988. Among the three men was London-based Encik Aman Majid (aka Man Tokyo), whom Malaysian student leader, exile and filmmaker Hishamuddin Rais had met while in exile in London, and also a Liverpool-based ex-seaman, Haji Mohamed Omar Almaskaty.

44 Even prior to this, in 1984, Rohaya had been told that her father was in Liverpool, after he was visited by another relative working for an airline. *Berita Minggu*, 19 March 2000.

45 'Temu lepas 40 tahun berpisah' [Meeting up after 40 years of separation], *Berita Minggu*, 19 March 2000.

46 Zaharah Othman, 'In their element at sea', *New Straits Times*, 27 March 2000, p. 3.

47 Notes from conversation with Paul Fadzil, Liverpool, 31 March 2008.

48 Arsad Hassan is also the 'Mr Hassan' that my former colleague's aunt told me about prior to my pilot visit to the Malay Club (see Prologue).

49 Notes from conversation, Liverpool, 2 July 2008. Rahim's Chinese Malaysian classmate in Liverpool, Tan Chian Khai (CK), also worked for Telekom Malaysia in South Africa. Given his fluency in the Malay language, CK and his wife, Rosalind, suggested that they were in some ways 'more Malay' than the so-called Malays of South Africa, echoing the definitional concerns of British colonial authorities decades earlier. Interview, Kuala Lumpur, 25 February 2008.

50 Ahmad Rodzi Yaakob, 'Melayu Liverpool tidak pernah lupakan tanahair' [Malays in Liverpool never forgot the homeland], *Berita Harian*, 12 July 1989.

51 Notes from conversation with Musa, Liverpool, 29 September 2004.

52 In this respect, he echoed the findings of the Singapore journalist who had visited Jermyn Street a decade earlier. See Chapter 4, and 'Kampung Melayu di Bandar Liverpool' [A Malay village in the city of Liverpool], *Berita Harian*, 21 October 1979.

53 This is taken from a version of the story that was published in the Singapore *Berita Harian* three days after the Malaysian version. 'Dua perantau ingin kembali ke tanahair' [Two migrants/sojourners wish to return to their homeland], *Berita Harian*, 15 July 1989, p. 7.

54 There is also evidence that Malay seamen themselves sought to contest some of the colonial stereotypes that drove – and were arguably perpetuated by – Mahathir's political treatise *The Malay Dilemma* (Mahathir, 1970). Zaharah Othman recounted a story of Pak Yahya Bahari, for example, who claimed to have been spurred to cycle around the world in 1959 after reading a British encyclopaedia description of Malays as 'a complacent and lazy race'. Zaharah Othman, 'In their element at sea', *New Straits Times*, 27 March 2000.

55 It should be reiterated that the mobile life geographies traced in this book reveal that the Malay *kampung* – and especially the coastal villages from which many seafarers originated – were often much less cut off from urban life than is imagined in Malay nationalist discourse, including in Mahathir's *The Malay Dilemma* (see also Chapter 2; Rigg, 1994; Kahn, 2006; Thompson, 2007).

56 By the time that Jaafar Mohamad returned to Singapore in March 2000, for example, he was running Jaafar Cafe at 137 Granby Street, just round the corner from Jermyn Street.

57 Muhammad Taib's (1993) political treatise on *Melayu baru*, for example, echoed Mahathir's call for the urbanization of Malays (*membandarkan Melayu*) made more than two decades earlier (Mahathir, 1970; and see Thompson, 2007).

58 Or, at least, ordinary seamen would not have counted, but those Malays who underwent training to become merchant navy officers or captains may have done.

59 The 1979 Singapore *Berita Harian* article noted above reported that five or six out of every 10 Malay men in Liverpool was unemployed and in receipt of social security ('dole') payments. 'Kampung Melayu di Bandar Liverpool' [A Malay village in the city of Liverpool], *Berita Harian*, 21 October 1979.

60 'Anak Melayu pertama jadi Datuk Bandar di England' [The first Malay to become a mayor in England], *Berita Harian*, 15 June 1989.

61 *Berita Harian*, 12 July 1989; 'Dua perantau ingin kembali ke tanahair' [Two migrants/sojourners wish to return to their homeland], *Berita Harian*, 15 July 1989, p. 7.

62 '*Masuk kandang kambing mengembek, masuk kandang lembu menguak.*' Cited in 'Anak Melayu pertama jadi Datuk Bandar di England' [The first Malay to become a mayor in England], *Berita Harian*, 15 June 1989.

63 Zaharah Othman, for example, referred to the 'old Malays' as 'a curious linguistic fossil, speaking the quaint kind of Malay that you only hear in old Malay movies'.

64 This resonates with the kind of 'double' social exclusion that Helen Sampson (2013) notes in her work on seafarers, in contrast to the idealized notion of transnationals who are included in dual national contexts.

65 This was a cultural gap (*jurang budaya*) that Haji Talib was said to be keen to bridge, by marrying his son to a Malaysian Malay girl. Talib's eldest daughter had already reportedly married an engineer who worked for Malaysia International Shipping Corporation. Ahmad Rodzi Yaakob, 'Melayu Liverpool tidak pernah lupakan tanahair' [Liverpool Malays never forgot the homeland], *Berita Harian*, 12 July 1989.

66 Ben Youp's daughter, Joan Higgins, for example, recalled that a man named Yassin, who stayed in the Youp's house on Upper Huskisson Street, used to 'pray all the time'. Interview, Liverpool, 12 September 2004.

67 Musa, who was a regular mosque-goer by 1989 – and continued to be in 2004 when I met him at the Malay Club – was very open about having been a 'very bad man' in his youth, not only in terms of drinking but also in terms of fighting and stealing cargo from ships to sell in port. Personal communication, Liverpool, 29 September 2004.

68 It certainly seems that activities that took place at the Malay Club in the 1970s and 1980s which would not have been permitted when it was run by Johan Awang on St James Road. One Malay Singaporean man who arrived in Liverpool in 1979 to begin his studies recalled visiting 7 Jermyn Street while his parents were in town. They were 'not very impressed' with what appeared to be a 'gambling den and drinking place'. Interview with Hadi Roslan, Cheshire, 13 September 2004.

69 To the extent that this was the case, it resonates with Clive Kessler's (1999: 32) wider critique of Malaysian interest in a diasporic *dunia Melayu*, where the search for signs of 'Malay culture' outside the *alam Melayu* were filtered through the 'somewhat limiting lens of their own preoccupations'.

70 There is mention of the club as Persatuan Malaysia-Singapura (Malaysia-Singapore Association) in Ahmad Rodzi Yaakob's article as somewhere that Malays in Liverpool met up, but in the past tense ('*pada masa dulu*').

71 Interview with Mohamed Nor Hamid (Mat Nor), Liverpool, 29 September 2004.

72 Mohamed Nor Hamid said in interview that he had resisted efforts by another ex-seaman together with an earlier cohort of Malaysian students to put the MSA under the 'umbrella' of the Liverpool Islamic Society. Interview, Liverpool, 29 September 2004.

73 Or, more precisely, that any anxiety that they felt in doing so concerned the size of the bill rather than the content of the food.

74 Interview, Kuala Lumpur, 24 February 2008.

75 Interview with Tan Chian Khai, Kuala Lumpur, 25 February 2008.

76 This has important political resonances in Malaysia given that the imaginative construction of peninsular Malaysia as home to the Malays (*Tanah Melayu*) positions others as migrant 'guests' (Khoo, 2009).

77 Interview with Joan Higgins, Liverpool, 12 September 2004.

78 Marcia Brahim Barry, 'My family, my cosmopolitan community', *Butetown Carnival Magazine*, 1994. Tiger Bay Community Arts.

79 Tolerance of religious intermarriage is, however, much greater in East Malaysia (see Jehom, 2008 on the case of Sarawak).

80 Among them was Fadzil Mohamed whose transformative travels to Malacca, via Kuala Lumpur, are considered in the next chapter.

6

Relocating Expectations of Modernity

The global spatial shift of industrial production that had blighted Atlantic port cities meant rapid industrialization and urbanization in East and Southeast Asia. Liverpool-based Malay men who made return journeys to the *alam Melayu* thus encountered a region that was not only geopolitically very different from the one they had left as young seamen (Chapter 4) but that also unsettled their previously *Eropah*-centred 'expectations of modernity' (Ferguson, 1999). In the first section of this chapter, I focus on Kuala Lumpur, which emerged as the economic as well as political centre of the nation state of Malaysia and its main international gateway in an era of jet travel. Not prominent in earlier stages in the lives of most of the Malay men who settled in Liverpool, as national capital Kuala Lumpur subsequently grew rapidly and was shaped by processes of Malayization (from the 1970s) and Islamization (from the 1980s). In the 1990s iconic architecture was deployed to make Kuala Lumpur globally visible and images of its high-rise skyline were disseminated through tourist marketing material, cinematic representation and media coverage of international events that were hosted there. The accounts of Malay ex-seamen returning from Liverpool frequently centre on much more mundane markers of transformation, not least domestic bathroom and toilet facilities. As I consider in the second section of the chapter concerning return visits to villages around the historical port town of Malacca, ex-seamen commonly narrate an excremental transition that occurred in Malaysia during the decades when

From World City to the World in One City: Liverpool through Malay Lives, First Edition. Tim Bunnell.

they were away in Liverpool. Trips to Malaysia also often set in motion profound transformations of the men themselves – taking on board contemporary Malaysian conceptions of what it means to be a 'good' or 'proper' Malay. In the third and final section, I examine return journeys to Singapore, a very different social and political context from Malaysia but a city-state which had also undergone profound economic and material transformation – 'from Third World to First'. The allure of the modern that had attracted young Malay men to *Eropah* was increasingly imagined to reside in the very region that they had left behind.

Kuala Lumpur: Journeys to the New Centre of the Malay World

In the autumn of 2004, in Belle Vale, Liverpool, I watched a video recording of the BBC's coverage of the 1998 Commonwealth Games, which took place in Kuala Lumpur. The venue for my viewing was the living room in the home of ex-seaman Ali Kechil. While Ali was in the kitchen making me a cup of tea, the BBC's studio presenter passed over to David Coleman – a voice familiar to sports-watching British television viewers – inside the newly built Bukit Jalil stadium, because the opening ceremony was about to commence:

> The city of Kuala Lumpur was awarded the celebration of these Games six years ago. In that short time it's been transformed. There's been a tremendous acceleration of development, new highways, a new light railway, a superb sports complex – indeed it could be the envy of the world. And also 4,000 new hotel rooms opened this January. The prime minister adopted the slogan 'Malaysia can', and Malaysia has done.

Ali returned from the kitchen as the opening ceremony began. It was already clear to me that he was much more comfortable talking about late twentieth-century Malaysia – and especially the spectacular transformation of its capital city, Kuala Lumpur – than about the mid-twentieth-century maritime routes that had brought him from Bayan Lepas, Penang, via Singapore, to Liverpool. We chatted over tea while watching Ali's video recording of 'Kuala Lumpur 1998'.[1]

The capital city of Malaysia had not always received this kind of international attention. Kuala Lumpur barely features in the life stages of ex-seafarers before they settled in Liverpool. Even Port Swettenham, which was built to serve Kuala Lumpur, is more prominent in ex-seafarers' early life geographies. In large part this is due to the simple fact that Kuala Lumpur is not, and never was, a port town. However, another set of explanations has to do with the city's wider historical commercial position. While Kuala Lumpur became the administrative centre of the Federated Malay States (FMS) in 1896, as considered in Chapter 2, it was Singapore which was *the* commercial centre of British Malaya during the first half of the twentieth century. Port Swettenham was completed in 1901 as a rival to Singapore, but ended up becoming 'primarily a feeder to it' (Huff, 1994: 11). It was only after independence that 'provincial' Kuala Lumpur began to emerge from the shadow of Singapore (Gullick, 1983: 166). Large-scale national infrastructure building was focused in and around the capital of the Federation of Malaya. This included construction of a new international airport at Subang, south of Kuala Lumpur proper (Lai, 2007), through which Ali eventually returned, in 1994 to (what had by then become) Malaysia. Opened in 1965, the airport at Subang formed part of Malaysia's main industrial corridor extending from Kuala Lumpur to Port Klang (as Port Swettenham was renamed) (Hamzah, 1965). Relatives who went to meet Ali at Subang expected him to be a doddery old man: 'They expect me to come down from the plane with a walking stick.'[2] He recalled with glee how surprised they all were when he bounded down the steps from the aircraft onto the runway. Ali was, in turn, surprised by the transformation of Kuala Lumpur. An already blistering pace of development was being 'accelerated' – as television commentator David Coleman put it – in the lead up to the 16th Commonwealth Games.

In the BBC television coverage of the Games, Kuala Lumpur was presented as the centre of an ethnically and culturally diverse, yet harmonious, nation state. At one point Coleman referred approvingly to 'the multicultural experience which is Kuala Lumpur'. Leaving aside the question of whether this was an accurate depiction of Kuala Lumpur or urban Malaysia more broadly in 1998, it certainly contrasted starkly with the conditions which prevailed in George Town, Penang when Ali lived and worked there in the 1950s,[3] and with the way that Malaysia was depicted in the press in Liverpool at the end of the subsequent decade. British Colonial Office records detail racial 'disturbances' that broke out in Penang at the conclusion of a Chinese procession to celebrate the centenary of the George Town Municipal Commission on 2 January 1957. Violence continued over the following two weeks and, in a telegram sent to the secretary of state for the colonies on 19 January from the Federation of Malaya administration, it is noted that: 'For the last six months there has been an undercurrent of inter-racial disharmony in Penang.'[4] Sir Donald MacGillivray, British high commissioner in Malaya, attributed the disharmony to 'Malay impatience for independence and their desire that Penang should be integrated on similar terms with the Malay States in the Federation'. He concluded: 'The sooner there is a settlement of constitutional issues the better.'

Although Tunku Abdul Rahman did secure early independence for the Federation of Malaya later that year, as was noted in Chapter 4, his *laissez-faire* economic policy in what became Malaysia from 1963 left British commercial interests largely intact. The political and economic mode of development which prevailed during the subsequent decade fomented economic frustration among the Malay middle classes (Jomo, 1995). Tunku Abdul Rahman's Alliance government did introduce initiatives for Malay rural development, including land distribution for the cultivation of cash crops (Shamsul and Lee, 1988), but the modern economy of Malaysia remained largely controlled by ethnic Chinese in urban centres such as George Town and Kuala Lumpur. None of these developments impacted directly upon Ali Kechil. Through his work as a quartermaster with Blue Funnel Line in the 1950s, Liverpool had already become his 'second home' and, in 1958, he decided to stay there. Ali obtained employment initially at the Adelphi Hotel – where he got to meet various stars of the entertainment business, including Cilla Black – before moving on to work on the docks and thereafter as a bus driver.[5] In the newly independent nation state that he left behind, Malay economic frustration contributed to low levels of support for the Alliance of ethnically based parties in the election of 10 May 1969 and electoral animosity escalated into renewed racial violence (Comber, 1983).

The riots that took place in Kuala Lumpur on 13 May 1969 were much more destructive than those that took place in Toxteth, Liverpool 13 years later. A report in the *Liverpool Echo* on 14 May 1969 entitled 'Shoot to kill curfew in Kuala Lumpur' described a 'sudden outbreak of violence between Chinese and Malays' which had resulted in 'hours of street clashes' and cases where motorists had been 'dragged from their cars and killed'. Ali said that the news became the talk of the Malay Club on Jermyn Street but he could not recall any of the details.[6] Officially, 196 people lost their lives in the Kuala Lumpur race riots, although international correspondents at the time calculated a much higher number of fatalities, the majority of them ethnic Chinese (Kua, 2007). An editorial in the *Liverpool Daily Post* on 19 May lamented that Malaysia's postindependence harmony had been shattered: 'Until a few days ago, Malaysia was a shining light in the Far East, a positive indication that people of many races can work together and blend into one nation.'[7] The reporter, Charles Quant, went on to suggest that with the earlier shared enemy of communist 'terrorism' under control, the different races of Malaysian society had come into increasingly conflictual competition. Official documents in Britain that were declassified decades later, however, point to the conclusion that the 'May 13 Incident' did not occur spontaneously but was planned as 'a coup d'etat by the then emergent Malay state capitalist class' (Kua, 2007: 3). What is not in doubt is that the violence enabled extension of *ketuanan Melayu* (Malay dominance). The post-1969 political landscape was one in which the United Malays National Organisation (UMNO) played a much more dominant role.[8]

Kuala Lumpur emerged from the riots as the capital of a more Malay-centred nation state. Abdul Razak Hussein, who proffered a much more explicitly pro-Malay national economic and cultural agenda, replaced Tunku Abdul Rahman as prime minister. The New Economic Policy (NEP), which commenced in 1971, introduced a range of affirmative action measures to try to 'raise' the Malays to economic parity with the other ethnic groups and especially the Chinese (Gomez and Jomo, 1997).[9] In terms of cultural politics, too, there was a growing emphasis on Malay-ness in national life, with a new cultural policy stating that national culture should be based on people 'indigenous' to the national territory (so-called Bumiputera) (Tan, 1992). In peninsular Malaysia at least, this meant 'Malay' people and so the skyline of the national capital – historically a Chinese-dominated town in demographic as well as commercial terms – came to be marked with attempts to symbolize Malay culture and commerce in modern, often high-rise, architectural forms (Loo, 2013).[10] Prominent examples include: the Bank Bumiputera building which incorporated a five-storey banking chamber on stilts with 'a vast "traditional" Malay-style roof' (King, 2008: 105); and, later, the Menara Maybank, which became the tallest building in the city with its roof shaped like a Malay *kris* (asymmetrical dagger). Perhaps symbolizing the new era of *ketuanan Melayu*, Menara Maybank overlooked areas of Kuala Lumpur where blood had been spilled in May 1969.[11]

The prime minister who oversaw the city skyline's most dramatic 'Malayization' (King, 2008) was Mahathir Mohamad. Mahathir had initially risen to national political prominence as an opponent of Tunku Abdul Rahman's *laissez-faire* economic policy and was expelled from UMNO for writing an open letter demanding Tunku Abdul Rahman's resignation. Although Mahathir was still out of UMNO when the NEP was introduced in the early 1970s, this formed part of a new policy orientation which 'could easily have been following a Mahathir script' (Wain, 2009: 30). In such a racialized political economy, being 'Malay' came to make a big difference for a Malaysian citizen's life chances. Comments made by Ali as the band of the Malay Regiment appeared in his video recording of the Commonwealth Games opening ceremony serve as a reminder that this kind of discrimination was not entirely new to the NEP period. Not only, as the name suggests, are regiment members exclusively Malay but, according to Ali, 'you have to be a pure Malay' in order to qualify. Ali himself was a Penang Malay or Jawi Peranakan, a locally born Muslim with Arab or Indian blood – in his case with an 'Arab' father.[12] Ali described himself (using the Liverpool idiom)[13] as a 'half-caste' and so ineligible to join the Malay Regiment. By this system of evaluation, Mahathir, the Malay 'ultra', would also have been ineligible on grounds of racial 'impurity'. However, in practice, there has long been a degree of flexibility. Ali's brother was admitted to the regiment at a time when it had been 'short of cooks'.[14] And, in 1981, Mahathir – son of Mohamad Iskandar, whose father was from India – became president of UMNO and prime minister of Malaysia. By the time of the 1998 Commonwealth Games, Mahathir was the longest serving prime minister in the history of Malaysia but, not surprisingly, his Indian Muslim ancestry was publicly downplayed, except by political detractors. Whether in politics, in the armed forces, or even in the skyline of the national capital, being seen to be Malay remained important in Malaysia during the Mahathir era (Khoo, 1995).

It was also during Mahathir's tenure that processes of Islamization, which were noted in the previous chapter, intensified. In the 1970s, the decade before Mahathir became prime minister, a wave of Islamic revivalism swept many parts of the world following events such as the Arab–Israeli war and Israel's occupation of Jerusalem. In addition, the oil crisis of 1973 led to a five-fold rise in oil prices which 'boosted the position of the "Muslim bloc" in international politics and consequently led to a sense of pride and confidence in the growth of the Muslim faith, Islam' (Hussin, 1993: 10). It was against this geopolitical and geoeconomic backdrop that Mahathir wrote his essays about Islam's compatibility with capitalist development and material prosperity that were published in English as *The Challenge* (Mahathir 1986; originally published in Malay in 1976). One biographical account was not exaggerating when suggesting that, for Mahathir, 'Malays had almost a religious obligation to change their character and participate wholeheartedly in Malaysia's development' (Wain, 2009: 222). For middle-class corporate Malays, entrepreneurship became 'the main vector of ethnic, religious, and moral worth and a test of virtue and modernity among the beneficiaries of NEP' (Sloane, 1999: 16). State sponsorship of Malay entrepreneurship together with Islamization gave rise to a commercialization of Islamic forms and consumption practices which were most clearly evident in the national capital (Fischer, 2008). The centrality of Malay-ness in Malaysian public life and Mahathir's conflation of Malay and Islamic identity (Martinez, 2004) meant that Muslim celebrations assumed greater prominence in the national calendar. Malaysians going to Britain as students from the 1990s were from a generation that had never known any other national rhythm. One Malaysian mature student friend of mine in Liverpool was horrified to discover in 2004 that Ali did not celebrate Hari Raya (Eid al-Fitr or Aidilfitri) that marks the end of the

Muslim fasting month (Ramadan).[15] In fact, Ali did not even know when Ramadan was to be held during that year, something that is unthinkable in Malaysia. For three decades, Ali had done as the Liverpudlians do, and this meant adopting practices and rhythms out of sync with Malaysia and especially its Islamized Malay middle class.[16]

Completion of the NEP's 20-year course in 1990 opened possibilities for a shift in political focus, away from domestic ethnoracial divisions and towards Malaysia's place in a wider globalizing world (Khoo, 1995). Mahathir's official vision was to turn Malaysia into a 'fully developed' nation by 2020. Malay nationalism had certainly not gone away, but it was folded into what appeared to be increasingly multicultural national aspirations. As considered in the previous chapter, processes of economic regionalization and globalization gave rise to a growing belief among Malay elites in the need for more worldly, even global, forms of Malay subjectivity (*Melayu global*). However, Mahathir's political discourse in the 1990s emphasized that such new Malays formed part of a wider Malay*sian* nation as opposed to a merely Malay ethnic grouping. Moreover, rather than merely being objects of Malay 'diaspora envy' (Kessler, 1999), Malaysia's non-Malay (Chinese and Indian) communities also came to be valorized for their transnational economic connections to China and India (Bunnell, 2002). Multicultural representation became a key marketing tool for Malaysia in efforts to attract investment and tourists. As was evident from the BBC's Commonwealth Games coverage, Kuala Lumpur took centre stage in mediated imaginings of a vibrant and dynamic multicultural nation state (Silk, 2002; van der Westhuizen 2004). From the late 1980s, Mahathir had taken the development of Kuala Lumpur in particular as his personal project. The 1998 Games marked the culmination of a decade during which the city and its wider urban region had been materially and symbolically reconstructed for global audiences (Bunnell, 2004a).

Mahathir's vision for Kuala Lumpur in the 1990s bore some similarities with Liverpool's rebuilding at the beginning of the twentieth century. Both looked to New York City for lessons in modernity. In Liverpool in the 1910s, this resulted in the construction of the Liver Building, Britain's first skyscraper.[17] In the case of Kuala Lumpur, construction of the tallest twin towers in the world represented an effort to effect 'Manhattan transfer' (King, 1996), or to gain some of the global visibility of that iconic skyline (Pile, 1999). With their 73-metre spires, the Petronas Towers topped out taller than the twin towers of New York's World Trade Center and the Sears Tower in Chicago, which had eclipsed the World Trade Center towers as the tallest building in the world. As part of the wider Kuala Lumpur City Centre mega-development on the site of the former colonial racecourse, the Petronas

Towers were purported to define a new 'gateway' to the economic opportunities of Malaysia and elsewhere in a booming east. In an earlier era, the Liver Building and the other so-called 'graces' on the waterfront had marked a monumental 'western gateway to the world' (Lane, 1997: 1). This was an era when city boosters saw Liverpool not as a provincial city, but as being in the same 'world city' league as London.[18]

As Ali and other Liverpool-based Malay ex-seamen returning to Southeast Asia in the 1990s observed, in the decades that they had been away the geography of uneven development had changed and it was no longer Liverpool or even London where the monumental urban transformation was taking place. The architect César Pelli, who had designed the high-rise One Canada Square building in London's Canary Wharf financial district, contrasted receptiveness to his Petronas Towers in Kuala Lumpur with negative reactions to 'the first true skyscraper in England'. Canary Wharf, he argued, sits uneasily at the edge of a city that is very ambivalent about skyscrapers, whereas 'the Petronas Towers are for a city that is embracing them wholeheartedly.' Malaysia, he added, 'sees itself as moving forward to the future whereas some think that Britain had its best days in the nineteenth century'.[19] Comparison of infrastructural development trajectories in Liverpool and Kuala Lumpur provides some further evidence to substantiate Pelli's generalization. From 1893 Liverpool had boasted the world's first electrically operated overhead railway, but this had closed in 1956, two years before Ali decided to stay in Liverpool and began work at the Adelphi Hotel (Sykes *et al.*, 2013). By the time Ali returned to Kuala Lumpur in 1994, that city boasted a newly opened monorail and a light rail transit system was nearing completion. The latter was opened in time for the 1998 Commonwealth Games.

It was ironic that the big chance to showcase the postindependence national development of Kuala Lumpur came in the form of the Commonwealth – formerly 'Empire' – Games. During the preceding seven decades, the Games had largely been the preserve of the first British dominions: New Zealand, Canada, Australia and Britain between them hosted the Games 15 times between 1930 and 1994. Malaysia sought to make the most of the rare opportunity for a 'developing country' to host the Games, and 'splurged' (van der Westhuizen, 2004: 1277). The cost of the new Bukit Jalil stadium alone ran to RM1.2 billion (in the range of £200 million and £300 in a period of exchange rate volatility) and another RM300 million (£50–75 million) was spent on upgrading existing facilities in and around Kuala Lumpur. As Janis van der Westhuizen (2004: 1284) notes: 'sport is one of the few arenas of society in which the state could forcefully both design and shape the idea of Malaysia as the model modern, sophisticated Islamic society, both multicultural and at the cutting edge of the next "Asian century"'. During the 1998 Commonwealth Games, the host feed to foreign broadcasters, including the BBC, focused on the modern landscape of Kuala Lumpur which was dominated by the twin towers headquarters of the state oil conglomerate. Petronas also sponsored the Games. Images of Malaysia's multicultural modernity were beamed to more than 500 million television viewers across the former British Empire. Ali, re-watching the coverage with me in Belle Vale, Liverpool, six years after the Games, described the Petronas Towers to me as 'cracking' (as in 'great', not disintegrating). The building was still under construction during Ali's first return trip to Malaysia in 1994, but he made a point of visiting during a subsequent stay in 2002.[20] Liverpool-born descendants of other Malay ex-seamen went to Kuala Lumpur in order to watch the Games live, combining sports tourism with efforts to reconnect with their roots.[21] These are small pieces of evidence that 'an essentially second order games' (van der Westhuizen, 2004: 1278) was successfully used to 'extend Malaysia's marketing power'.

There is no doubt that Ali was wowed by the new urban centre of the Malay world, not only through direct experience but also through televisual and even cinematic encounters. It was seeing the Petronas Towers in the Hollywood blockbuster *Entrapment,* as much as watching the Commonwealth Games on television, that inspired him to visit the Petronas Towers. More generally, Ali was so taken with Mahathirist Malaysian development that he bought a Malaysian national brand of car – a Proton Impian – in Liverpool. Yet by the time of the 1998 Commonwealth Games in Kuala Lumpur, the Malaysian dream and, indeed, the wider Asian economic 'miracle', appeared to be fading. The Asian economic crisis which began in 1997 ended 10 years of rapid growth and had particularly destructive consequences for Malay business elites who had benefited from political patronage under Mahathir's premiership. Among the companies that were bailed out by the Malaysian government (with money from Petronas)[22] were privatized enterprises responsible for two of the light rail systems in the capital. Another was the Malaysian International Shipping Corporation which had, in turn, acquired the shipping assets and debts of Konsortium Perkapalan, a company 51 per cent owned by the prime minister's son, Mirzan Mahathir (Wain, 2009: 107). The economic crisis also became a political crisis in Malaysia. Anwar Ibrahim, the former student leader who had risen to become deputy prime minister and finance minister after having been co-opted into UMNO by Mahathir (Chapter 5), was sacked on 2 September 1998. While this was ostensibly because of corruption and moral impropriety in his private life, Mahathir feared his deputy was planning to challenge for leadership at a time when the prime minister faced negative international opinion for his handling of the economic crisis (Wain, 2009). This political farce tarnished Malaysia's international reputation and many Malaysians were ashamed at the lurid and unsavoury nature of the political conspiracy against Anwar Ibrahim. None of this stopped Ali from wanting to go back and to follow Sean Connery and Catherine Zeta-Jones – the stars of *Entrapment* – up the Petronas Towers.

Although *Entrapment* was a box office success and so projected Kuala Lumpur to large cinema audiences around the world,[23] Mahathir took little satisfaction from this international exposure. The Petronas Towers initially appear in the movie spliced together with riverside 'slums' which were filmed in the town of Malacca, not Kuala Lumpur. According to Mahathir, this was a deliberate Western misrepresentation, and a denial of the urban transformation that had taken place in the years leading up to the Games as well as more than four decades of postindependence development (Bunnell, 2004b). In part, it was sensitivity to colonial stereotypes of tropical urban uncleanliness and underdevelopment that had driven efforts to project a clean, modern image of Kuala Lumpur during the Games. Mahathir complained that a Western 'conspiracy' was undoing the material and representational work that he had overseen. Yet for Ali, and other Liverpool-based ex-seamen returning to the *alam Melayu* after many years away, Malaysia was already 'developed' and 'modern' beyond recognition. Moreover, this applied not only to the skyline of the national capital, Kuala Lumpur, but even to the material environment of villages around Malacca which had supplied so many Malay seafarers to the Straits Steamship Company before independence.

Tandas-ization: Excremental Transition in Malacca

Mahathir was not the first person to get anxious over imaginings of the state of development and cleanliness in Malacca. For Mohamed Nor Hamid (Mat Nor), returning to Tanjung Keling after more than two decades in Liverpool, it was memories of the toilet facilities in his home village, rather than riverside slums in town, which were the focus of concern. Mat Nor was able to make a non-seafaring return trip (*balik kampung*) earlier than most other members of the postwar generation of Malay seamen who formed families in Liverpool. Making use of some redundancy money from work on the docks, he returned to his home town with his British family in 1978. He recalled how his biggest fear on going back was the state of the *jamban* (rudimentary squat latrine) at his mother's house – not for himself, he stressed, but for his wife and children. They all arrived safely at Kuala Lumpur's international airport in Subang and took a bus to the city centre. At Pudu bus station in Kuala Lumpur, Mat Nor bumped into some of his old friends from Singapore who were working as taxi drivers. They had moved to the new centre of Malay economic opportunity – Kuala Lumpur – and one of them drove Mat Nor's family to Tanjung Keling. Mat Nor returned to a hero's welcome – reminiscent, he said, of the way in which people returning from the *Hajj* were greeted during his childhood.[24] But there was still the issue of the *jamban* at his mother's house.

Mat Nor's excremental anxieties proved to be completely unfounded. His mother's house had undergone significant upgrading during the years that he had been away to include all modern toilet facilities within a tiled bathroom. In fact, Mat Nor recalled, no one even seemed to use the word *jamban* anymore; it had been replaced by *tandas* (bathroom), at least in polite company.[25] In any case, Mat Nor's family did not end up staying at his mother's place, but in an even more impressive house belonging to a lawyer friend. This man had stayed in Mat Nor's room in Liverpool as a law student during a period when Mat Nor was away working at sea, and was insistent on reciprocating. According to Mat Nor, the *tandas* in the lawyer's bungalow was actually much 'posher' than his own home in Liverpool. There had been progress in Liverpool too – Mat Nor recalled how, during winters in the 1950s, he had been forced to urinate in a bottle in his rented room when he could not face the freezing cold of the outside toilet[26] – but it did not seem to have kept pace with development in Malaysia, even in the coastal villages outside Malacca town from where so many Malay seamen hailed.

The charisma and controversies of Mahathir, and the sheer scale of his developmental ambitions from the early 1980s, attracted a great deal of attention from academics as well as in the media. Yet the Malaysian economy grew more rapidly during the decade *before* Mahathir became prime minister than it did during his time in office (Wain, 2009). Even in the 1960s, prior to the 1969 Kuala Lumpur riots at least, Malaysia was seen as a 'developing-world success' (Wain, 2009: 24). A Blue Funnel Line promotional film from 1966 noted that 'Malaysians like many other peoples are developing a taste for higher living standards' and that 'demand continues to grow for more sophisticated consumer goods.'[27] What changed during the 1970s was that industrializing Malaysia started to make many of the products that had previously been bought from Britain. The rise in affluence in Malaysia during that decade stands in marked contrast to Liverpool's postimperial economic decline that was considered in Chapter 4. However, the capital flows that accounted for the improved toilet conditions in Mat Nor's mother's house were not all to do with structural economic change or the so-called new international division of labour. Mat Nor learned during his return visit in 1978 that the improvements had, in part, been paid for with money he had wired back to his mother in Tanjung Keling over the years. Not all Malay men in Liverpool remitted money to their families in Southeast Asia, and not all Malay family homes in Malaysia had undergone such a thoroughgoing excremental transition as Mat Nor's mother's house by the late 1970s. The old-style squat toilets presented physical problems to some elderly ex-seamen returning to Malaysia in subsequent decades.[28]

Developmental transformations in and around Malacca town were certainly not as visibly spectacular as those that are evident in the skyline of late twentieth-century Kuala Lumpur, but the town had become highly significant to nation building in Malaysia. While Kuala Lumpur became the undisputed new centre of Malay commerce and entrepreneurship, Malacca came to assume a symbolic centrality to Malay-centred national histories. It will be recalled from Chapter 4 that at the beginning of the 1970s Malaysia's second prime minister, Abdul Razak Hussein, heralded the launch of the Malaysian International Shipping Corporation in terms of the re-emergence of a 'golden age of the Malacca Sultanate' when 'our merchant ships roamed the seas far and wide.'[29] In the fifteenth century, Malacca had not only been a powerful sultanate but also the hearth of Islam in Malaysia (Sandu and Wheatley, 1983). In the context of the new cultural policy and Islamization, the town came to feature very prominently in official, Malay-centred narrations of Malaysian history. The construction of a new (replica) fifteenth-century sultan's palace based on a drawing in the *Sejarah Melayu* (Malay Annals) exemplifies how material landscapes were reworked to conform to Malay-centred national history (Cartier, 1998). Relatedly, (mostly Malay) heritage and conservation retained a prominence in Malacca in the face of national modernization even during the developmentalist Mahathir era. In 1989 Malacca was designated Malaysia's historic town (*bandar sejarah*) by the federal government. It was no doubt because of such intertwined cultural and political significance – rather than the fact that so many twentieth-century seafaring diasporic Malays were from villages outside Malacca town – that the first *Dunia Melayu* symposium was held in the town in 1982 (Tomizawa, 2010; and see Chapter 5).[30]

Under the influence of rising numbers of domestic tourists as well as conferences and conventions, newly built hotels, restaurants and malls marked parts of Malacca town beyond the designated heritage area, especially during the 1990s. Nearby coastal villages, including Tanjung Keling, had seen the development of resorts catering to middle-class Kuala Lumpur residents seeking to escape from the hustle and bustle of city life even in earlier decades. During his first return trip to Malacca in

Figure 6.1 Fadzil Mohamed (on the right of the group) on the beach at Tanjung Keling in February 2008. Photograph by the author.

1978, Mat Nor discovered that some land which he should rightfully have inherited had been sold by his brother to ethnic Chinese developers from Kuala Lumpur.[31] It seemed to be no mere coincidence that this brother was 'away' in Indonesia for the duration of Mat Nor's stay. The land, which led onto the beach, was later developed into a resort. I saw this development during a trip to Tanjung Keling with another Liverpool-based Malay ex-seaman, Fadzil Mohamed, in 2008 (see Figure 6.1). I learned from his son, Paul, that Fadzil undertook some 'anti-British' activities on that section of beach as a child. Partly out of fear of spiders around the *jamban,* he said, Fadzil used the beach as a toilet, making and filling shallow holes which were covered with sand after use. Fadzil recalled with glee the thrill of watching British soldiers sunbathing around those thinly covered holes at the weekend and wondering where the terrible smell was coming from.

More than half a century later, Fadzil saw the bathrooms in his nephew's house as the clearest sign of Malay development. This nephew, Alias, is the son of Fadzil's sister, Hamidah. It was Hamidah, and her husband Haji Hassan, who put Fadzil up when he first arrived in Singapore in 1946.[32] Alias was born in Singapore and worked there as a policeman. He moved back to Tanjung Keling after retirement and built a bungalow – with five bedrooms, all with en-suite bathrooms, as Fadzil told me on several occasions – on Malay reservation land inherited from his wife's mother.[33] I was invited to the house in February 2008 when I met up with Fadzil and two of his children, Paul and Farida, in Malacca.[34] Fadzil had stayed at the house during a previous trip and would have been very happy to have stayed there again, but Farida and Paul preferred the independence of staying in a hotel. I met them all at the centrally located Mahkota Hotel the night before we went to Alias's place, having taken a bus from Pudu bus station in Kuala Lumpur. By 2008 the Malacca buses stopped at the recently opened Malacca Sentral bus terminal, described in my guidebook as the 'most modern' in Malaysia. It certainly contrasted with the grimy chaos of Pudu, but Malacca Sentral is also located some distance from the town and so I took a taxi over to meet the Fadzils at the Mahkota Hotel. The young driver of the taxi was from Kampung Serkam but he had no knowledge of his village's seafaring connections to Liverpool. I eventually met Fadzil, Paul and Farida in the lobby of the hotel and we went to eat together at a food court nearby. Although we passed Mahkota Parade, Malacca's 'premier shopping and entertainment complex', which appeared to be more upmarket than the mall in Liverpool where I had met with the Fadzils in the past, the main indicator of Fadzil's developmental evaluations lay elsewhere. Tomorrow, he said, he would take me to Alias's house which (in case I had forgotten) had five bedrooms, all with en-suite bathrooms.[35]

The next morning, Alias came to pick us up from the hotel. We headed to Malacca airport where another relative was working. One of the men at the airport told Fadzil that he had seen news in the Malaysian press about the death of another Liverpool-based ex-seaman, Ngah Musa.[36] Fadzil said that Musa had been his friend, and added that there were very few Malays left in Liverpool. My attention shifted to a huge advertisement for the Mahkota hospital. It turned out that visitors flying into Malacca were mostly Indonesians seeking medical care.[37] During that time in 2008 there was only one flight each day across the Straits of Malacca (from Pekanbaru), but massive expansion was planned and construction work had already begun on lengthening the runway to accommodate bigger aeroplanes. As we headed back to Tanjung Keling in Alias's Proton, Fadzil recalled taking bullock carts (*kereta lembu*) along the *tanah merah* (red earth) which had connected Tanjung Keling to Malacca town after the Second World War. Fadzil also noted how a small island off the coast at Tanjung Keling had seemed much further away during his childhood. While this may highlight, in part, the unreliability of human memory, it is likely that the island really had become closer given widespread reclamation along the coastline. The most visible sign of development, however, was a high-rise hotel which Fadzil thought had been built on the land sold off by Mat Nor's brother.

Election campaign flags along the side of the road spurred Alias into some critical commentary on the Malaysian government and its 'corrupt ways'. Alias's political position became even clearer when we arrived at his house – the one about which I had already heard so much from Fadzil. One thing I had not been told about was that the bungalow was built on a piece of land large enough to include a significant garden. Alias told me how, after the controversial sacking and arrest of Anwar Ibrahim in 1998, he had supported Parti Keadilan Nasional (National Justice Party) and had even allowed the party to hold public talks (*ceramah*) in his garden during the 2004 general election. The Parti Keadilan Nasional had fared badly in that election, however, and Alias had since shifted his allegiance to the Parti Islam Se-Malaysia (PAS, Pan-Malaysian Islamic Party). Alias's oppositional political views did not seem to have much effect on Fadzil, who was clearly both impressed by, and proud of, the signs of development all around him, especially the 'posh' *tandas* attached to each of the bedrooms in Alias's house.

While seemingly unmoved by – or impervious to – political critique of the government that had overseen the social and economic transformation of Malaysia, Fadzil's trips 'home' did have profound effects upon him. His son, Paul, said that Fadzil's view of Malaysia as 'modern' after his first return trip in 2004 had made him noticeably prouder to be associated with Malaysia.[38] In addition, as was noted at the end of the previous chapter, Fadzil took on board some contemporary Malaysian notions of what it meant to be a good Malay Muslim. On returning to Liverpool, he started to attend prayers at the Al-Rahma mosque on Fridays, putting him into closer contact with mosque-going Malaysian students who gave encouragement and respect to Fadzil as he (re)discovered Islam. Somewhat less positive, in Paul's view, was the fact that his father became increasingly judgemental towards other people's supposedly un-Islamic activities. One example was that Fadzil had taken to scolding Muslim shop owners in Liverpool for selling alcohol. He had known some of these people for many years and had perhaps even bought alcohol from some of them in the past. Fadzil also stopped eating Chinese food after his trip back to Malaysia.[39] These new taboos were in evidence during the time when I was with the family in Malacca in 2008. When we crossed the road from the Mahkota Hotel to get some food, for instance, it was clear that Fadzil wanted to avoid the non-halal section of the food court despite the fact that his children were keen to diversify their diet beyond the Malay food offerings. While Fadzil found that Malaysian domesticity had undergone a modern transformation to be 'just like in Europe',[40] this Liverpool-based man was also transformed through adopting modern Malaysian senses of 'proper Islamic consumption' (Fischer, 2008) and, by extension, of being Malay.

Returning to Singapore: From Third World to First

Fadzil had gone to Kuala Lumpur after the Second World War and worked there before eventually moving to Singapore.[41] The area around Kuala Lumpur at that time, he recalled, was still 'jungle' and Fadzil did not enjoy his work as a *peon* (menial labourer) in a British family.[42] He left after less than a year and headed south to stay with his mother's family in Skudai, a town in southern Johor. It was following a fire for which Fadzil was blamed that he packed his bag early one morning and walked across the causeway to Singapore. In addition to the fact that his sister, Hamidah, was living there, Singapore in that immediate postwar period also possessed the bright lights and commercial promise that attracted men from across an extended Malay world, as indeed it had done before the war (Iskandar, 1989; Kahn, 2006). While the People's Action Party (PAP), which governed Singapore from 1959 onwards, takes credit for having transformed Singapore 'from Third World to First' (Lee, 2000), for young Malay men such as Fadzil, Singapore was already a beacon of affluence and modernity long before the PAP came to power. Singapore was where young men got a taste of *Eropah* (literally Europe), learning how to dress fashionably and how to dance. Both of these attributes, I was told by several men in Liverpool, proved to be very attractive to women in ports around the world.

Another young man who travelled across to Singapore from the peninsula at around the same time – but who may not have been so concerned with dancing or womanizing – was Mahathir Mohamad. He left Alor Setar in Kedah in 1947 to study medicine at Singapore's King Edward VII College of Medicine (Khoo, 1995). When he was not involved in his medical studies, Mahathir wrote newspaper articles under the pseudonym Che Dat to supplement his income. The writing of Che Dat in the late 1940s highlighted the significant developmental gap that already existed between each side of the causeway connecting Singapore to the rest of British Malaya. Mahathir was also angered by, and ashamed at, what he saw as the impoverished position of Malays in Singapore (see Khoo, 1995; Wain, 2009: 11). He felt that Singapore Chinese looked down on the Malays (Wain, 2009: 12), a belief that inflected Mahathir's antagonistic relations with Singapore as prime minister decades later. Economic development strategies in Malaysia, including during the Mahathir era, clearly drew upon the policies and experiences of Asian tiger economies, and Mahathir's Look East policy, for example, may have borrowed at least in part from Singapore. Yet the geopolitics of separation in 1965 and Mahathir's long-held personal antagonism meant that the city-state to the south of the peninsula was not publicly cited as a developmental model or inspiration.

Singapore certainly had a head start over most of peninsular Malaya in terms of economic development on account of its long-standing position as the commercial centre of British colonial Southeast Asia. A passenger onboard one of Liverpool's Blue Funnel Line ships remarked on the modern appearance of Singapore before the Second World War.[43] The important assets that Singapore took into the period of decolonization included 'a natural world-class harbour sited in a strategic location astride one of the busiest sea-lanes of the world' (Lee, 2000: 24). Nonetheless, it was far from certain that this attribute alone would translate into postindependence economic success, especially after Singapore was expelled from Malaysia. The memoirs of Singapore's first prime minister, Lee Kuan Yew, suggest that the prospects looked very bleak at this juncture:

> All of a sudden, on 9 August 1965, we were out on our own as an independent nation. We had been asked to leave Malaysia and go our own way with no signposts to our next destination. We faced tremendous odds with an improbable chance of survival. Singapore was not a natural country but man-made, a trading post the British had developed into a nodal point in their world-wide maritime empire. We inherited the island without a hinterland, a heart without a body. (p. 19)

Lee fostered a siege mentality among Singaporeans, compelling them to 'do things better and cheaper than our neighbours' (p. 23), but few observers gave the newly formed city-state much chance of prospering independently from the Malaysian geobody.

The prospects for Malays in Singapore seemed particularly bleak. From having formed a numerical majority in Malaysia, those officially defined as Malay in Singapore became a small minority in the newly formed state which was predominantly ethnic Chinese. As Lee recalls:

> We feared that pro-UMNO Malays would run amok when they realised they had been abandoned by the Malaysian government and were once again a minority. Our policemen were mostly Malays from the kampungs of Malaya and their loyalty would be strained if they had to take action against Malay rioters who wanted to rejoin Malaysia. (p. 23)

Among the Malacca men who stayed on in Singapore to work as policemen was Fadzil's brother-in-law, Haji Hassan. It was his son, Alias, whose house in Tanjung Keling I visited with Fadzil in 2008 in the account above. Alias had followed in his father's footsteps, working as a policeman in Singapore, and only moved to Malacca after retirement. Others, like the taxi drivers whom Mat Nor met in Kuala Lumpur during his first return visit to Malaysia, moved out of Singapore much sooner in search of better employment opportunities. Many Singapore Malays continued to work at sea – a job which allowed passage to lands whose economic future appeared to be more assured than Singapore's – although the jobs were not always easy to obtain by the 1960s. A Malay man named Yussof Ismail who grew up in the Paya Lebar area of Singapore, for example, was reported in a *Berita Harian* newspaper article in 1995 as recalling that he had to wait two years before he got the opportunity to work at sea in 1971. At that time, he said, 'many young men in my kampung were unemployed. Without work, they either stole or begged.' Compared to this, the grass seemed much greener elsewhere and Yussof noted that New York City in particular was (still) widely perceived to be a modern 'heaven on earth' (*syurga dunia*): 'When I arrived in New York, I took the opportunity to jump ship. Many others did the same because back in the kampung we always heard that New York was the best place.'[44] Seafaring was one of a limited range of employment opportunities that Malays in Singapore considered to be open to them, and Yussof Ismail was among those – along with dozens of men on the opposite side of the Atlantic, in Liverpool in preceding decades – who decided not to go back.

Some of the men who settled in Liverpool had more specific, non-economic reasons for *not* wishing to return to the *alam Melayu*. The fire for which Fadzil was blamed, and the role of this incident in spurring him to head for Singapore, has already been noted.[45] Another man, who requested anonymity, was motivated, in part, to use Liverpool as his seafaring base, rather than return to Singapore, in order to evade an arranged marriage. Given the ethnic tensions which simmered in Singapore when the PAP came to power in 1959, it comes as no surprise that yet other Malay men went to sea in order to flee political entanglements and associated physical danger. Singapore-born Malay ex-seaman Rahman told me in Liverpool in 2006 that when a telegram inviting him to join a ship was delivered to his family's house on Jalan Buntu in 1961, he was reluctant to leave, having already worked at sea in the 1950s.[46] It was his mother who persuaded him to return to the sea, saying that under the new PAP government 'there was always clash between Malays and Chinese.'

Later in the same interview, Rahman swore that it was Allah rather than just his mother who had convinced him to leave Singapore. From the late 1950s Rahman had become involved in an organization known as Angkatan Revolusi Tentera Islam Singapura (ARTIS, Singapore

Islamic Revolutionary League) and, after returning from one of the group's meetings at the university on Bukit Timah, he found Special Branch officers waiting outside the house on Jalan Buntu. Rahman recalled that he was one of 18 Malays who were arrested and sent to the nearby prison at Changi. Rahman had attended school with the man who interrogated him, Inspector Sidek: 'He was surprised to see me, he said "why you mix with them?". I said "mix with what?" "They want to kill Chinese" [Sidek replied]. I said, "who want to kill Chinese?" I said, "I don't intend to kill Chinese".' Rahman recalled making a lengthy statement in prison:

> I said I've been at sea, I have been all over the world. I say we want Malay, Chinese in the market together, and we want all the three years old children, make one special school for them, put them to school. So when they know each other from those years, from the beginning, until they grow together, they won't fight, so they know each other. So put Malay teacher there, put India teacher there, put Chinese teacher there so they can learn three language there. A lot of things my statement there you know, all finished about 40 pages, but some of them I can't remember.

There was clearly a connection here with the perception of Malay economic marginality:

> I say, you can see [for] yourself, all Chinese got the chicken farm, this and that. What Malay got? Nothing. So I want them [the government] to join them [together] even if Malay have to work with Chinese to learn.

According to Rahman, the authorities in Singapore were eventually satisfied that he did not intend to pursue violent means to achieve his goal of 'mixing' the racial groups, and he said that he was the first of the 18 men to be released. Purportedly unbeknown to Rahman, some of the other ARTIS detainees had been spreading very different messages in their visits to Malay villages across Singapore: 'But I don't know some of them want to kill Chinese inside there. It is very, very dangerous to mix with people like that.'[47] It was in this context, during his time in detention at Changi, that Rahman said that he had a religious experience: 'Before I go out from the prison at night I was dreaming that Allah can see me.... I say "so what's going on now?" He said, "Rahman, you keep away from all these, your time has not come yet, just keep away ... don't mix with them".' The next morning, a Special Branch officer came to the prison with papers for Rahman's release. He returned to the house on Jalan Buntu where he received the telegram inviting him to join a ship.

In the short term at least, it was perhaps fortuitous that Rahman left on that ship in 1961 because ethnic relations were at times even worse during the subsequent decade. According to Michael Leifer, 'communal strife between Malays and Chinese' resulted in 33 deaths and more than 600 injuries between July and September 1964 alone (Leifer, 1964). Lee Kuan Yew's memoirs note 'two bloody Malay-Chinese riots' in that year (Lee, 1998: 18). One followed a procession to celebrate Prophet Muhammad's birthday on 21 July 1964 when, instead of the usual religious sermons, 'there were political speeches designed to stir up Malay feelings of hatred' (p. 556). Malay–Chinese clashes broke out as the procession headed towards the Geylang Serai area, and the news began to spread: 'All over the island, Malays began killing Chinese, and Chinese retaliated. The casualties came to 23 dead and 454 injured, and when the body count was made at the mortuary there were as many Malay as there were Chinese victims' (p. 558). Although the curfew was lifted on 2 August, tensions continued to be inflamed by the politics of Singapore's inclusion in, and eventual separation from, Malaysia. Even at the end of the 1960s, Singapore's ethnic relations were influenced by events in Kuala Lumpur. In the week following the violence of 13 May 1969 in the Malaysian capital, some Chinese men in Singapore 'took revenge for what had happened in Kuala Lumpur' (Lee, 2000: 38).

In marked contrast, by the time Rahman made a return visit to Singapore in the 1980s, the situation had improved in line, he thought, with the vision that had been detailed in his prison statement:

> The first time when I go back [after] about over 20 years, that's when I see change. First I want to go to fish market. So when I go to fish market I see this Malay woman sell the fish, you know. I say, 'Oh my God, that's what I want, you know.' Before you don't see Malay in market like that. I say, 'Oh my God this is dream come true now.' And I see children you know go to nursery, Malay, Chinese and India, I say, 'Ah, they used my [Changi prison] statement.'[48]

When back in Liverpool, Rahman went to the docks with his British wife and saw the Singapore flag flying on a Neptune Orient Lines ship. He recalls shouting up greetings to the crew and being thrilled to see the ship's ethnically mixed composition. Certainly, after the experience with ARTIS and the riots of 1964, the PAP had taken a much more interventionist role in managing interethnic relations as part of its wider authoritarian nation-building efforts. There was an important social geography to this as ethnic enclaves, including Malay *kampung* areas, were considered to be 'hotbeds of radicalism' (Aljunied, 2009: 128).[49] People who were moved into new public Housing Development Board flats across the island were subject to an ethnic quota system stipulating the proportion of residents who were Chinese, Malay, Indian or 'other' (Sin,

2003). The apparently happily mixed crew of the Neptune Orient Lines ship that Rahman met in Liverpool approximated Singapore's Chinese-Malay-Indian-Others (CMIO) multiracial 'grid' (see Goh, 2010: 571). The spectre of ethnic violence has continued to haunt Singapore multiculturalism,[50] but the city-state has not witnessed any repeat of the interracial conflict of the 1960s and the subsequent decades of peace and stability formed the basis for rapid economic development.

So spectacular was Singapore's economic growth in the decades after Rahman left that by the 1990s GDP per capita exceeded that of the former colonial centre. Lee Kuan Yew, who served as prime minister until 1990, concluded that, in material terms at least, Singapore had 'left behind our Third World problems of poverty' (Lee, 2000: 13). Economic growth was initially achieved through a successful policy of export-oriented manufacturing production from the late 1960s (Huff, 1995). The fact that Kuala Lumpur had emerged as a commercial and symbolic centre of the *alam Melayu* did not imply any diminution in Singapore's trade position. On the contrary, Singapore expanded its horizons beyond the region, identifying itself as a 'global city' many years before that term became common currency in anglophone academic social science (Oswin and Yeoh, 2010) and, in turn, becoming increasingly disconnected from immediate neighbouring countries (Rahim, 2009). In line with the definition of global city famously proffered by Saskia Sassen (1991), Singapore became a centre for advanced producer services, enabling global reach in financial and managerial as well as industrial terms. Financial and business services replaced manufacturing as the main engine of growth after 1979, this sector of the economy growing at an annual average rate of 9.9 per cent up to 1992 (Huff, 1995). Postindependence Singapore also cemented the position that it had inherited as a regional aviation hub and, in contrast to Liverpool, expansion of air transportation was accompanied by continued growth in shipping.[51] During the 1990s Singapore became the world's busiest port, a mantle that had been held by Liverpool decades earlier.[52]

Singapore's continued expansion as a port gave Liverpool-based Malays who continued to work at sea the chance to call in and visit relatives. Among them was Fadzil Mohamed. He visited his brother-in-law Haji Hassan's house on Jalan Jagung on two occasions as a seaman, the first in 1961 and the second in 1973 (see Figure 6.2). It would then be another three decades before Fadzil visited Singapore again, as part of a return trip to Southeast Asia that was centred primarily on Malaysia. However, by the end of the 1970s, as unemployment rates in Britain (and especially in and around Liverpool) soared, there were other Liverpool-based men who were deliberating a permanent move back to Singapore for economic reasons. As was considered in Chapter 4, they included Ali Musa who planned to fly back to Singapore to make

Figure 6.2 Fadzil Mohamed's visit to Singapore in 1973. Photograph courtesy of Fadzil Mohamed.

job enquiries after he had signed off the ill-fated MV *Derbyshire* in Japan. Ali Musa's son, Charles, recalls his father saying of Britain: 'This country's finished, I'm going home.'[53] Ali Musa never made it to Singapore or even to Japan, and Charles said that he often wondered how different his life would have been if his father had survived long enough to have arranged a move back to increasingly prosperous Singapore. Although Charles lost contact with his Singapore relatives in the two decades after his father's death, he was able to reconnect through various internet searches in 2003. By the time that I interviewed Charles in Liverpool in 2010 he had made a visit to Singapore himself and was keen for his daughter – Ali Musa's granddaughter – to explore employment opportunities through relatives of the grandfather she never got to meet.

The Singapore that Ali Musa had hoped to return to in the early 1980s had already undergone significant transformation during the quarter of a century that he was based in Liverpool, and not merely because of the apparent absence of ethnic violence. When Rahman visited Singapore, he was impressed as much with the rise in living standards as with the interethnic 'mixing'. In line with the focus of attention in the return visits of Fadzil to Malacca, Rahman recalled: 'I was surprised. They all have nice house and nice toilet.'[54] Such developments only compounded Rahman's sense of regret at having had to leave Singapore in the first place. He recalled how during a subsequent trip back there, he met another former member of ARTIS. In the 1960s, Rahman said, there had been a handsome reward for this man's capture and Rahman recalled that he felt like handing the man in and claiming the money as 'compensation'. According to Rahman, he said to the man: 'If you put me as your leader [i.e. of ARTIS] before, we shouldn't be like this and I wouldn't be in England, I would stay here.' Rahman's British passport as well as commitment to his family in Liverpool precluded any possibility of him moving back to Singapore on a permanent basis, and he clearly harboured a sense of having been marooned: 'Even though I am here [in Liverpool], you know, my heart is still there [in Singapore].' Gesturing to the other adult family members in the room when I interviewed him in Liverpool in 2006, Rahman added that 'when they all go to work I am always playing Malayan records', as a way of imaginatively transporting himself back to Singapore.[55]

Another man from Singapore who was keen to spend more time back 'home', if not to move back permanently to Singapore, was Jaafar Mohamad. As was noted in the previous chapter, this Singapore-born man of Boyanese ancestry was reunited with his daughter in Singapore in March 2000 after 40 years away in Liverpool. In Singapore media coverage of his homecoming, Jaafar was reportedly hoping to travel back and forth between Liverpool and Singapore every two or three months, in order to see his grandchildren in both locations.[56] Perhaps unsurprisingly, this level of post-retirement transnational mobility did not transpire. Apart from the expense of long-distance flight tickets, insurance costs increase markedly for elderly travellers, an issue that was raised at the Malay Club by several men planning trips back to Malaysia as well as to Singapore. In addition, especially in the case of Singapore, the rise in costs of living associated with rapid economic growth meant that British pound sterling-denominated pensions did not go as far as many returning ex-seamen hoped or expected.[57] This raises a wider issue, in Jaafar's case, that his desire to make regular trips to Singapore arose partly *despite* – rather than because of – some of the changes that had taken place during the decades that he had been based in Liverpool. In addition to the costliness of Singapore and feelings of unfamiliarity that arose from changes to the material environment of the city, Jaafar said that his old Malay friends there no longer socialized like they did in the past.[58] But at least he still had friends there, whereas in Liverpool when I interviewed him there in March 2008, he complained that there was no one left ('*kawan-kawan tak ada lagi*').[59] The winter weather in Liverpool was also a factor in Jaafar's comparative judgements as the cold aggravated his angina. Between the time when he first went back in 2000 and when I interviewed him in Liverpool in 2008, Jaafar had gone back to Singapore for extended periods of time almost every year, mostly scheduled to avoid the coldest periods in Britain.

A common denominator in recollections and evaluations of ex-seamen and their family members whom I met or interviewed was that Liverpool had lost the attractions that had compelled them to drop anchor in the city during the two decades after the Second World War. The reasons for this change of perception ranged from the intensely personal to the macrostructural. In Jaafar's case, it was at least in part the loss of friends in Liverpool – through their having died or moved away – that drew him back to Singapore in later life. Yet the case of Ali Musa that was described in detail in Chapter 4 (and referred to above) is evidence that there had also long been those for whom the allure of material development, which had first attracted them from Southeast Asia to *Eropah*, now worked in reverse. While political leaders in Singapore boasted of a transition from 'Third World to First', Liverpool had arguably shifted the other way. From 1993 Merseyside was accorded Objective 1 status as a region of the European Union (EU) whose development is 'lagging behind' and in need of 'structural adjustment'.[60] This meant that Liverpool was awash with social and community funding which organizations such as the Merseyside Malaysian and Singapore Community Association (MSA) could tap (see Chapter 4). But Objective 1 status also meant that the city (and the wider Merseyside region) was in receipt of a form of regional developmental assistance that may be likened to flows of aid to former colonial territories in what was once termed the Third World. An Objective 1 region was one in which per capita GDP was less than 75 per cent of the EU average. Liverpool came to qualify for this increased level of 'aid intensity' (Meegan, 2003: 63) in the early 1990s, around the same time that Singapore's per capita GDP exceeded that of Britain. At the end of that decade, a caller to a radio show responding to a recently screened film about sacked dock workers in Liverpool specifically articulated the wider point: 'We're becoming a third world country' (Sekula, 2000: 421).[61] In this context, and also bearing in mind Singapore's long-standing commercial importance, the phrase 'Third World to First' might be deployed more accurately to characterize return trips to Singapore made by Liverpool-based ex-seamen than as a description of Singapore's own economic transformation after independence.

If in the late nineteenth century Singapore had been likened to antecedent maritime 'world city' Liverpool – 'the Liverpool of the East' – by the last decades of the twentieth century the leading edge of development appeared to be moving in the opposite direction. Redevelopment of the second Ocean Building in Singapore involved what was perhaps the last enactment of world city command from Liverpool – plans for a new

28-storey tower requiring final approval from headquarters in Liverpool in 1970 (Seet, 2011). Those plans formed part of a comprehensive refashioning of Singapore's Golden Shoe central business district from 1968. In contrast, most of Liverpool's equally ambitious 1960s schemes for city centre renewal were never realized (see Murden, 2006). In Singapore in the late 1970s work began on cleaning up and converting warehouses along the Singapore River to become dining and entertainment venues, while port activities were expanded along the west coast of the island (Dobbs, 2003). Liverpool, too, saw riverside redevelopment in the 1980s, but in that urban context it was to rejuvenate derelict and abandoned port facilities along the River Mersey, while dock operations concentrated at Seaforth and Bootle came to have 'little direct effect upon the economic fortunes of Liverpool' (Murden, 2006: 477). It was a telling sign of changing times and tides that the organization leading the redevelopment of the Albert Dock, the Merseyside Development Corporation, sought investors from the 'Far East' (Meegan, 1999). In a different register, in Singapore, Housing Development Board public flats, such as the one in Yishun where Jafaar stayed during his return visits to Singapore after 2000, emerged as models for replication internationally (Chua, 2011). Again, in marked contrast, high-rise overspill estates on Merseyside – such as the one in Kirkby to which Jaafar's family in Liverpool had moved – were cast as examples of the failure of modernist design and planning, where (as one local newspaper headline put it), 'dreams rapidly became nightmares' (cited in Murden, 2006: 413).

Such examples are clearly highly selective and I have already acknowledged that men such as Jaafar were capable of making much more nuanced comparisons of shifting geographies of urban development between Liverpool and Southeast Asia. Equally clearly, however, over the decades that Jaafar had lived in Liverpool, the city and wider Merseyside region had undergone what James Ferguson (writing in the context of post-mining boom Zambia) termed 'a demotion in the worldwide standing of things' (Ferguson, 1999: 12). For Liverpool-based Malay ex-seamen, as for the men connected to the Zambian mining industry boom in Ferguson's work, this wider loss of standing translated into diminished individual and collective senses of self-worth. In fact, it is possible that Liverpool-based men experienced such shifts with particular intensity given that their 'expectations of modernity' were not merely unrealized (in Liverpool) but imaginatively relocated to the very territories that they had left behind as young men and to which they returned in later life. For elderly ex-seafaring Malays who continued to meet at Liverpool's Malay Club, as for most academic and media commentators, the leading edge of global economic change was certainly not in Liverpool, nor indeed in the (north) Atlantic or Europe more broadly, but in Asia, including some of those parts of Southeast Asia that I have referred to as the *alam Melayu.*

Notes

1 The interview took place on 30 September 2004.
2 Interview with Ali Kechil, Liverpool, 27 September 2004.
3 Ali Kechil was born in 1932 in Perak, one of what were then the Federated Malay States (now a state in Malaysia), but his family moved to the island of Penang, initially to Bayan Lepas and then to George Town. He worked as a *peon* for an Indian shipping company in George Town and then as a chandler before beginning seafaring work (as a quartermaster) with the Straits Steamship Company. He began work as a quartermaster with the Blue Funnel Line in the mid-1950s and decided to sign off from that company in Liverpool in 1958.
4 CO 1030/759, 'Racial disturbances between Malays and Chinese in Penang, Federation of Malaya'.
5 Interview, Liverpool, 27 September 2004.
6 Notes from conversation, Liverpool, 30 September 2004.
7 'Editorial: The malaise of Malaya', *Liverpool Daily Post,* 19 May 1969.
8 In Kua Kia Soong's (2007: 4) words: 'The eclipse of the Alliance's predominance in the Malaysian political landscape at the 1969 general elections and the perceived threat to UMNO's supremacy provided the signal for the state capitalists to implement their plan to seize state power in the name of "Malay dominance".'
9 It was as part of this that growing numbers of Malay students were eligible for a range of scholarships to universities in Britain, including in Liverpool (see Chapter 4).
10 This was accompanied by a corresponding 'roll back' of the historically prominent presence of non-Malay cultural symbols in urban public space (Loo, 2013: 3).
11 I owe this connection to the work of the Malaysian artist Nadiah Bamadhaj and, in particular 'KL in 1969' from her 'Taking It Personally' series. References to the *kris* are among the 'racist and fascist taunts' which are 'standard fare' at UMNO assemblies (see Kua, 2007: 9). Work on Chinese spaces in Kuala Lumpur has noted that the Maybank Tower was also perceived to have disrupted the 'good fortune' of Chinatown in terms of *feng shui* principles (Loo, 2013).
12 Hadhrami traders visited Penang from the tenth century though significant settlement only began after the establishment of Penang as a British trading post in 1786. These men married 'native' women and the descendants of these unions became known as Jawi Peranakan. The relationship between this group and 'Malay' is historically complex. From the early nineteenth century, 'Penang Malay' denoted people of diverse origins,

including Hadhramis. However, particularly in the twentieth-century period when Ali Kechil grew up on Penang island, people of '*darah keturunan Arab*' (Arabic ancestral blood) were often seen as impure or not 'proper' Malays. The distinction worked both ways with 'Malays' of Arabic descent seeing themselves as superior to 'real Penang Malays' who lived in 'backward' rural villages on the mainland. Ali Kechil's own identification with Malay-ness was similarly complex and contextually variable.

13 See Chapter 3.

14 Interview with Ali Kechil, 30 September 2004.

15 Personal communication with Sharidah Sharif, Liverpool, 15 November 2004.

16 See also Chapter 5.

17 Stuart Wilks-Heeg (2003: 42) notes more widely: 'As is typical of cities with global articulations, the desire to mark Liverpool's standing in the world economy came to be reflected in the built environment, most evidently in the redevelopment of the pier head.' While skyscrapers in Manhattan would have dwarfed the buildings along the waterfront, one postcard celebrating the building of the *Titanic* in 1912 showed it standing vertically, dwarfing New York City's recently constructed Woolworth Building (see Milne, 2006: 274).

18 Kuala Lumpur, too, rivalled and was referenced in relation to a city to the south – Singapore – which was indisputably superior in economic terms. With Singapore having become a separate city-state, however, Kuala Lumpur's rivalry with Singapore is not intranational in the way that Liverpool has been relegated to the status of a provincial city in a London-dominated UK.

19 Cited in Rowan Moore, 'The tallest – and guess where it is?' *Daily Telegraph*, 6 May 1994 (see also Bunnell, 2004a).

20 He also had a series of family photographs as proof of this visit, as well as a metal memento skyline of Kuala Lumpur on his mantelpiece, which included the Petronas Towers.

21 Among them was Farida Chapman, daughter of Fadzil Mohamed, who had first visited Malaysia on a package tour with her sister two years earlier, and used the Games as an 'excuse' to go back. Notes from conversation, Liverpool, 29 July 2006.

22 Barry Wain (2009: 155) notes that Petronas reported by law to the prime minister, rather than the finance minister: 'It was Dr. Mahathir's favourite piggy bank, to be raided in emergencies and on other special occasions.'

23 The film grossed more than $212 million in box office takings worldwide, almost $88 million of which were taken in the USA. See 'Entrapment', Box Office Mojo, available at: http://www.boxofficemojo.com/movies/?id=entrapment.htm (accessed 8 August 2012).

24 Interview, Liverpool, 10 September 2004.

25 This is a linguistic and developmental shift that was noted by other ex-seamen in Liverpool, including Ali Kechil and Fadzil Mohamed. As Mat Nor put it: 'I didn't know about this *tandas* business. I saw all the shower, bathroom, everything … good old days not like that, you see.' Interview, Liverpool, 10 September 2004.

26 Interview, Liverpool, 29 September 2004. He also noted having had to pay a half-crown (a coin worth two shillings and sixpence or 12½ pence) to use a public baths at that time in the 1950s.

27 *The Blue Highway* (Gerard Holdsworth Productions and Blue Funnel Line, 1966) dir. John Haggarty (shown as part of exhibition at Merseyside Maritime Museum, 18 November 2004).

28 In a trip to Malaysia with Mat Nor in 1995, for example, Majid was forced to use a specially adapted chair – with a hole cut through the seat – that could be perched on top of squat latrines.

29 Cited in 'Important break-through for the country', *Straits Times*, 9 December 1970.

30 Fifteenth-century Malacca certainly is important to Malay diaspora discourse, as a maritime trade centre with worldwide reach during the 'Golden Age' of the Malacca sultanate (Kessler, 1999).

31 Land issues, especially in relation to inheritance, featured in several ex-seafarers' stories of return journeys to Malaysia and in some of the diasporic connections that preceded them. Family members of the late Youp bin Baba (Ben Youp) in Tanjung Keling, for example, made contact with his descendants in Liverpool through Mat Nor. They apparently needed a copy of Ben Youp's British death certificate (from 1978) for land inheritance purposes. This reconnection had spurred a granddaughter of Ben Youp in Liverpool to visit her distant family in Malacca as part of a holiday in Southeast Asia in 2004. Interview with Joan Higgins (daughter of Ben Youp), Liverpool 12 September 2004.

32 See Chapter 2.

33 The category of Malay reservation land raises further inheritance issues, particularly in terms of whether Liverpool-based descendants of Malay ex-seamen could inherit land. Malay reservation land can only be transferred to Malays but, as has been considered in previous chapters, most children and grandchildren of Malay ex-seamen in Liverpool do not satisfy constitutional definitions of Malay-ness in Malaysia, in that they are not Muslims and/or that they do not habitually speak Malay.

34 The material in the remainder of this paragraph and in the two subsequent paragraphs is taken from field notes made in Malacca on 20–21 February 2008, unless otherwise noted.

35 The first time that I was told about the five bedrooms and en-suite bathrooms was during an interview in Liverpool (29 September 2004). I emphasize this here not as a form of mockery but because the domestic developments that they represented clearly had a profound effect on Fadzil and other ex-seamen returning to Malaysia (and Singapore) – as much, if not more so, than the more internationally well-known transformation of the skyline of the national capital, Kuala Lumpur.

36 This is Haji Ngah Musa who had been interviewed by the Malaysian journalist Ahmad Rodzi Yaakob in 1989 (see Chapter 5). Musa's death was reported in the press in Malaysia which, presumably, was how the man working at the airport had come to hear of the news. See, for example, 'Jenazah Ngah Musa selamat dikebumikan' [Ngah Musa's body safely

buried], *Utusan Malaysia Online*, 27 January 2008, available at: http://www.utusan.com.my/utusan/info.asp?y=2008&dt=0128&pub=Utusan_Malaysia&sec=Dalam_Negeri&pg=dn_09.htm (accessed 11 February 2008).

37 Recent scholarship has examined such medical travel between Indonesia and Malaysia (e.g. Ormond, 2015).

38 Notes from conversations, Liverpool, 18 December 2005 and 5 July 2008.

39 Notes from conversation with Paul Fadzil, Liverpool, 21 February 2008.

40 Notes from conversation with Fadzil, Liverpool, 11 October 2004.

41 See also Chapter 2.

42 Notes from conversation, Liverpool, 24 May 2008.

43 S.A. Townley who arrived on board the *Ulysses* on Tuesday 27 September 1932 remarked in his dairy (which was published by the Blue Funnel Line): 'We drove through the town, which is well built and covers a very large area with imposing buildings and very good roads everywhere. The town is planned on very generous lines – no congestion anywhere.' OA 828.666, 'The Diary of a Ulysses Passenger', circa 1933, p. 22.

44 Cited in '"Hilang" di New York' ['Lost' in New York], *Berita Harian*, 1 July 1995.

45 Fadzil's children also believed that the fire incident was the reason why Fadzil was initially so reluctant to make a return visit to Malaysia. As has been noted, two of Fadzil's children visited Malaysia – including to watch the Commonwealth Games – in the 1990s, paving the way for him to make a return visit. Although he needed some encouragement, even coaxing, to make the first return visit in 2004, he subsequently made annual visits and regretted not having gone back earlier. Notes from conversation with Paul Fadzil and Farida Chapman, Liverpool, 5 July 2008.

46 He first arrived in Britain by aeroplane in 1952, having been recruited in Singapore. Interview, Liverpool, 17 October 2006.

47 ARTIS was one of two Malay/Muslim underground organizations which historical accounts suggest were plotting to overthrow the PAP government (Aljunied, 2009).

48 Interview with Rahman, Liverpool, 17 October 2006.

49 Destruction of *kampung* areas itself generated tension and protests, especially in the 1960s (see Kahn, 2006).

50 Syed Muhd Khairudin Aljunied (2011: 158) notes that when four Malays were detained without trial in April 1987 for 'manufacturing rumours about an imminent clash between Chinese and Malays in Singapore', the main message in local media coverage was that 'such intended acts of violence could revive tensions and disharmony that characterized the island-state during the colonial period.'

51 As late as 1970 Liverpool remained 'the largest exporting port in the British Commonwealth, putting it ahead of Hong Kong, Sydney and Singapore' (Sykes *et al.*, 2013: 299), but its position diminished sharply thereafter, and 'Manchester's airport was favoured over Liverpool as the northern English hub' (p. 307).

52 This is certainly what young Malayans arriving in the city to attend Kirkby College in the 1950s believed (see Shaari, 2009).

53 Interview with Charles Musa, Liverpool, 22 March 2010.

54 Interview, Liverpool, 17 October 2006. This contrasts with the 'indescribably primitive and disgusting' sanitary arrangements that one British reporter recalls of Singapore in the 1920s, especially during public holidays when the 'nightsoil coolies' did not come around to empty the *jamban* (Peet, 1985: 59).

55 Or, more precisely, to a Singapore that exists in the songs of P. Ramlee whom Rahman cited as being among his favourite singers.

56 'Temu lepas 40 tahun berpisah' [Meeting up after 40 years of separation], *Berita Minggu*, 19 March 2000.

57 Certainly not as far as they did when Mohamed Nor Hamid (Mat Nor) first returned to Malacca in 1978. After 1997, however, the Asian financial crisis helped as both the Singapore dollar and the Malaysian ringgit lost value against the British pound.

58 Notes from conversation with Jaafar, Liverpool, 10 October 2004. Most of Jaafar's Malay friends had become teetotalers. Although Singapore has not experienced the kind of state-sponsored Islamization that has occurred in Malaysia, wider processes of Islamic revivalism and a 'Malay ethnic resurgence' in Singapore from the 1980s associated with Malays' position as a minority in an ethnic Chinese-majority population (Aljunied, 2011: 146) meant that Jaafar returned to a Singapore in which (as in Malaysia) Islam and Malay identity have increasingly been conflated.

59 Interview, Liverpool, 9 May 2008.

60 'Provisions and instruments of regional policy: Objective 1', Summaries of EU Legislation, available at: http://europa.eu/legislation_summaries/regional_policy/provisions_and_instruments/g24203_en.htm (accessed 12 February 2014). Merseyside had earlier (from 1989) had Objective 2 status as a 'declining industrial region' (Boland *et al.*, 1995; and see Chapter 7).

61 This is taken from Allan Sekula's documentation of the struggle of the sacked dockworkers in Liverpool. Sekula's documentation also included an image of a group of these men listening to the radio show in which callers responded to a recent broadcast of a film that the dockers co-wrote.

7

Community in the Capital of Culture

Spectacular urban and economic transformation in Southeast Asia certainly compelled revision of returning Malay ex-seafarers' imagined geographies of uneven development. Yet Kuala Lumpur and Singapore were not the only cities that feature in the life geographies of Liverpool-based Malay ex-seamen to undergo a thorough makeover. From the last decades of the twentieth century Glasgow and Liverpool adopted entrepreneurial reimaging strategies as part of efforts to turn around their economic fortunes. In the case of Liverpool in the 1990s, processes of culture-led regeneration were bound up with a wider so-called British 'urban renaissance', as well as with the availability of European Union (EU) structural and social funds. I begin this chapter by elaborating the rise of spatially targeted funding for community-based modes of 'neighbourhood renewal'. In the second section, I turn attention to the lead-up to European capital of culture 2008, including how Liverpool's bid differed from that of cities that had previously held the title through its emphasis on ethnocultural diversity – Liverpool as 'the World in One City'. The third and final section examines a coalition of Malaysian students, a social enterprise and selected Malay seafarers which sought to obtain capacity building and cultural funding through the Merseyside Malaysian and Singapore Community Association (MSA) as the Malay Club is registered and known to local authorities. Malaysian students' prior experiences of performing Malay 'culture' in Malaysia were uncannily well suited to the multicultural European capital of culture of 2008.

From World City to the World in One City: Liverpool through Malay Lives,
First Edition. Tim Bunnell.

The Place of Community

My first encounter with a Malay ex-seaman in Liverpool, during my first ever visit to 7 Jermyn Street, was recounted at the very beginning of this book. Dol was at the Malay Club on that day in December 2003 to attend a funding meeting and I greedily tried to squeeze in an interview with him before the formal agenda began. The field notes I scribbled piece together a life geography that subsequently became very familiar to me (and the broad contours of which have been sketched in several of the preceding chapters for other Malay ex-seamen in Liverpool). Beginning seafaring work on Straits Steamship Company boats after the Second World War, Dol gained oceangoing experience on the Blue Funnel Line's Singapore-based ship, MV *Charon.*[1] He was then recruited in Singapore by agents looking to hire seamen who were British subjects, and flown out to London where he joined a ship called the MV *Gladys Moller.* This was the ship on which he first arrived in Liverpool in December 1950. It is important to note, however, that not all of Dol's subsequent time in Britain had been spent living or even based in Liverpool. After he stopped working at sea in the mid-1960s, Dol moved with his English wife to Glasgow, where he worked as a bus conductor. Dol eventually returned to the northwest of England because his wife (who was from Preston) wanted to be closer to her elderly parents.[2]

It was at this point in Dol's narration of his life geography that my interview was cut short by the arrival at the Malay Club of a representative of the John Moores Foundation. The meeting had been arranged so that this charitable organization could find out more about the MSA in connection with its application for funding. I sat in on the meeting and although I was a passive observer for the most part, my presence as an academic researcher who had come all the way from Singapore to study the lives of men such as Dol may have added legitimacy to the application (although it remains unclear to me whether this was the motivation of MSA members for having invited me). The meeting provided me with initial insights into how ex-seafarers from Southeast Asia and Malaysian students who met at the Malay Club presented themselves as a 'community'. What was then the recent award to Liverpool of the status of European capital of culture for 2008 appeared to have expanded recognition of, and the value attached to, diverse ethnocultural communities in the city.

Submitted in October 2003 by Novas-Ouvertures, a social enterprise that was working with the MSA, the application sought a grant of £5,000 towards the purchase of equipment and furniture for the 'clubhouse' of the 'community' on Jermyn Street.[3] A community development manager from Novas-Ouvertures attended the meeting where I met Dol.

Also in attendance was a Malaysian doctoral student who had recently become part of the MSA committee and who had prepared a document on the history and background of the organization that was submitted to the John Moores Foundation along with the funding application form.[4] The document depicted a community established in the 1930s when a generation of seamen before Dol had settled in Liverpool. The men were described as having 'married local women and raised families in the City', and the MSA clubhouse (as the Malay Club was referred to) was identified as the place where the 'elders', 'youngsters' and students interact as a community. However, the term community was also deployed in the same document to refer to an even wider group or spatial unit: 'The Clubhouse and the Malaysian and Singapore peoples have an excellent reputation *within the community*' (emphasis added). In addition, it was noted that other 'diverse groups' from this wider community or neighbourhood – 'the Somalian, African, Yemeni, Pakistani, Bangladeshi community' were those named – attend a 'luncheon club' on Wednesdays at 7 Jermyn Street. The Malay Club, then, was represented as both the defining place of an ethnocultural community, and as a site of interaction with other groups – a community within a community.

'Community' has long been recognized as a term that lends itself to vague and even vacuous usage, especially in political discourse (Paddison, 2001). In the case of the John Moores Foundation application document – prepared and submitted by a community development manager – the frequent use of the term may be understood in the context of a wider 'turn to community' in British urban policy (Duffy and Hutchison, 1997). In particular, community was central to the ideology of the New Labour government that took office in 1997 (Levitas, 2000). Although it continued to be used with 'promiscuous flexibility' (p. 191), community came to denote a particular mode of governance, working through the actions and capacities of local people. So-called 'marginalized' communities, including some black and minority ethnic groups, were those deemed in need of 'increased capacity to help themselves' (Tooke, 2003: 241) in order to be able to participate more effectively in the 'mainstream' of society. In part, the vaunting of communities as actors or agents in social and economic transformation represented 'a response to the top-down, libertarian and market content of the Thatcher agenda' (Murtagh and McKay, 2003: 194). However, the new emphasis on community was also used as a means of distinguishing New Labour from the state interventionist associations of Old Labour (Levitas, 2000). Under Tony Blair's New Labour, 'community involvement' rose to prominence 'across a whole range of British social policy' (Tooke, 2003: 238), including in efforts to foster an 'urban renaissance' (Lees, 2003).

While this changing national political context was undoubtedly significant for the rise of community-based social policy, so too were shifts at the European supranational level. French concepts of partnership, integration and social inclusion were well established in EU spatial planning prior to the formation of the New Labour government. The EU's URBAN Community Initiative, for example, was launched in 1994 (Murtagh and McKay, 2003) with the aim of targeting structural funds at deprived inner-city areas through locally led partnerships. An era of 'partnership' governance from the late 1980s meant that Liverpool and the wider Merseyside city-region were well placed to tap such funding streams (Meegan, 2003). European structural funds were awarded to Merseyside from 1989, when it received Objective 2 status as a 'declining industrial region' (Boland *et al.*, 1995). As was noted in the previous chapter, Objective 1 status followed in 1993, a designation which was worth £630 million over five years (1994–1999) and was considered by some scholars to present 'an important opportunity to escape from the long term spiral of social and economic decline which has plagued Merseyside for so many years' (Boland *et al.*, 1995: 698). Money from the European Social Fund, in particular, promised increased opportunities for funding applications from voluntary sector organizations, including arts and cultural activities and minority group organizations, as part of what have been referred to elsewhere as 'grant coalitions' (Cochrane *et al.*, 1996: 119). In practice, however, the governance process during this period is said to have been dominated by the EU, the national government and its regional arms, with the result that 'social partners were totally excluded from the policy design process' (Boland, 1999: 789). This scenario may have changed even without the incoming New Labour government's community-focused agenda. However, there is little doubt that the new national government from 1997 provided a spur for increasing the involvement of local community representatives as partners in urban governance, bringing Britain into closer alignment with EU policy.

Related to the expansion of community-centred initiatives, another aspect of alignment in the late 1990s that forms an important backdrop to understanding MSA activities was growing emphasis on area- or locality-based policies. Spatial targeting was not part of the original Merseyside bid for Objective 1 assistance in 1993. Its omission was noted in one of the evaluations of the bid and the European Commission was said to have taken up the cause enthusiastically (Meegan and Mitchell, 2001). Together with voluntary sector and other local organizations, the Commission put pressure on the then Conservative government to include a spatially targeted component to the ways in which the funds would be spent. Political as well as technical considerations resulted in enumeration districts being selected as the spatial unit for what were termed 'pathways to integration' in the EU Objective 1 Structural Funds Programme for Merseyside, and 'Granby Toxteth' was among the 38 enumeration districts to be designated a 'pathways' area as it fell into the bottom 35 per cent in terms of deprivation (Meegan and Mitchell, 2001). The New Labour government was itself enthusiastic about spatially targeted policies, although, more widely, there was also a good deal of (neoliberal) policy continuity from the outgoing Conservative government (Jones and Evans, 2008).[5] New Labour's Social Exclusion Unit emphasized the importance of neighbourhoods in urban regeneration policy, but it did not give 'a clear framework for identifying and defining them' (Meegan and Mitchell, 2001: 2168). Subsequently the national Neighbourhood Renewal Fund allocated funds to the 88 local authority areas judged to be the most deprived based on the indices of multiple deprivation for 2000.

The application submitted by the MSA to the John Moores Foundation may be seen in the context of enthusiasm on the part of both New Labour and the EU for community participation and the channelling of associated funds to deprived neighbourhoods in Merseyside as an Objective 1 region (a designation that was retained through the period 1999–2004). MSA documentation that was discussed at the meeting where I met Dol included categorization of the 'community' as a 'Black Racial Minority group' centred in the 'Granby/Toxteth ward ... historical home to the greatest proportion of Black and Ethnic Minority residents in Liverpool'. Reference to the ward locality in the application invoked a recognizable geography of need, while ethnocultural minority characterization chimed in with the John Moores Foundation's aim of assisting 'people who are marginalised, as a result of social, educational, physical, economic, cultural, geographical or other disadvantage' (John Moores Foundation, 2009).[6] In line with the John Moores Foundation's intended role as an 'enabling funder' for groups that find it difficult to raise money, the application noted: 'With regards to capacity building the organisation does not at this stage have the infrastructure to develop their Clubhouse without the support of other agencies.' Not surprisingly, given that the application concerned equipment and furniture for the 'clubhouse', much was made in the application of the importance of the Malay Club building as the social and spatial heart of the community:

> [T]he Clubhouse on Jermyn Street is the only resource available to the community members and is a popular and well-used establishment.
>
> They spend many hours interacting and socializing, offering real community spirit to each other and to the wider community in an environment that does little outwardly to reflect this hospitality and warmth of character.

A key problem, then, was the run-down condition of the clubhouse itself:

> The facilities within the building are dilapidated and of a poor quality. The furniture is sub-standard and has in some cases been reclaimed from skips and abandoned premises. None of the furniture (arm chairs and sofas) meets current fire safety levels and is inappropriate [*sic*] for elderly people with mobility and infirmity issues.
>
> The furniture within the Clubhouse has a demoralizing and negative effect upon the members who use the facilities on a daily basis.

Regeneration of the 7 Jermyn Street home of the Malay Club was thus linked to the social health of the community members (and, by extension, the wider neighbourhood):

> They would have the opportunity to spend time together with their peers and fellow countrymen in comfort as opposed to sitting alone in their own homes. It is the shared experience of spending time with others in a welcoming and cheerful environment that would benefit the members more than anything else.

The residential geography of the people comprising the community who met at 7 Jermyn Street was (perhaps strategically) unspecified in the John Moores Foundation application. As I have shown in previous chapters, Liverpool 8 became an important residential location for Malay (ex-)seafarers and their families – often moving outwards and topographically upwards from the city centre – after the Second World War. The last address in Dol's records as a seaman (in September 1965) was on Harrowby Street, off Princes Avenue, in Liverpool 8. However, I have also noted that there were families who subsequently moved out of the city altogether. In Dol's case, this meant a move initially to Preston and then to Glasgow. Other Malay (ex-)seaman and their families (were) moved to overspill estates in surrounding parts of Merseyside such as Kirkby and Halewood.[7] In the 1980s this outward movement accelerated both voluntarily and because of redevelopment following the riots at the beginning of the decade. In addition, while Malaysian undergraduate students such as Abdul Rahim Daud had rented rooms in the vicinity from the early 1970s – in some cases from Malay seafarers who were away at sea – by the 1990s the Malay student body in the city reflected the Malaysian government's preference for sponsoring graduate students. As we have seen, these mature students were typically accompanied by spouses and children and so preferred to live in parts of the city that were perceived to be safer and more conducive to family life than Liverpool 8. Number 7 Jermyn Street, in other words, had become less the meeting point for an area-based community, and more of a node for a network of people dispersed across (and, in some cases, beyond) the city.

The Malay Club served a very important role, precisely because spatial dispersal precluded other day-to-day forms of association, but one founded upon a rather different spatiality of 'community' than that presumed in national or European policy discourses. The degree of importance that the John Moores Foundation trustees attached to a particular geography of community is unclear. However, in the wider context of policies targeting spatially delimited deprivation and need, it surely mattered that (1) the clubhouse (i.e. the 7 Jermyn Street home of the Malay Club and official registered address of the MSA) was located in one of the Objective 1 pathways areas of Merseyside; and (2) the MSA's members were implied to be an ethnocultural subset of that deprived neighbourhood. The application was successful and, on 11 February 2004, the John Moores Foundation sent a letter to the Novas-Ouvertures community development manager with news that the MSA had been awarded a grant of £5,000.

The John Moores Foundation application was by no means the first attempt to secure funding for activities at the Malay Club. After the registration of the MSA as a charity, and the adoption of its constitution on 23 February 1995, funds had been secured from Liverpool Social Services for the lunch club – which continued to bring Malaysian students as well as Malay ex-seamen to Jermyn Street at lunchtime on Wednesdays when I began my first extended period of fieldwork in Liverpool in 2004. The MSA's annual report for 1998/89 noted:

> The lunch club is an important event for our community as it ensures our more elderly members have access to hot food and affordable traditional Malaysian/Singaporean food at least once a week. Furthermore, it has also become something of a social gathering where our members can socialize in a culturally safe and non-oppressive environment, thus providing an outlet for those who live alone or are isolated from their family and friends.

Also included in the 1998/89 report was a picture of a group of 'Malaysians and Singaporeans' outside the Malay Club during the celebration of Hari Raya (Eid al-Fitr) at the end of Ramadan. As part of a weekend of celebrations it was reported that: 'Between 200 and 250 Malaysian and Singaporean Muslims visited the Centre, where traditional foods and refreshments were provided to mark the occasion.' The Urban Community Chest, an initiative for area regeneration through community capacity building, had supported the event, though the size of the grant and other details were not stated in the MSA records. It was apparent from the report, however, that the smiling faces in the accompanying group picture that had been taken on the steps of the Malay Club masked some wider problems in what was described as having been an 'extremely difficult' year. In the absence of additional funding for essential renovation work in the future, it was reported that 'the building will have to close on Health and Safety Grounds depriving our community of an invaluable resource.' In addition, the chairperson of the MSA, Mohamed Nor Hamid (Mat Nor), began his annual report with reference to 'problems we had with one of our volunteers'. A community development worker who had helped to secure funding for the Eid al-Fitr event had also allegedly been enriching himself.[8]

By the time I visited Jermyn Street in December 2003, the MSA was enjoying a much happier relationship with the Novas-Ouvertures community development manager who attended the John Moores Foundation meeting. Her role centred upon knowledge of what the MSA needed to demonstrate – which boxes needed to be ticked in the systems of evaluation of potential funders – in order to secure financial assistance. At the meeting with the John Moores Foundation, the community development manager answered most of the questions, while Dol said very little. The overall impression that was given to the John Moores Foundation representative at that meeting was that a fully functioning community could be fostered or regenerated by means of small amounts of financial investment. The following month, the MSA submitted another application for funding, this time to the Merseyside and Halton Neighbourhood Renewal Community Chests which administered financial resources from the national Neighbourhood Renewal Fund.[9] This application concerned a series of cultural events and activities, and made mention not only of the 'community' (and its involvement in neighbourhood social activity) but also two other words that had risen to prominence in Liverpool: culture and capital. Described as fitting in with the 'cultural aims' of the city's European capital of culture bid success, which had been announced in June 2003, the proposed events also promised to 'share and de-mystify the cultural and traditional heritage of the MSA community and encourage the wider community to engage and help to embed the MSA community into the mainstream'.

Glasgowing and Beyond: Towards Multicultural Regeneration

> One of Liverpool's key problems is that it faces undoubted negative perceptions – not internationally, but in the UK. We would use 2008 for exactly the same purpose as Glasgow – to change perceptions of the city

> by demonstrating the exciting, creative and rich culture of Liverpool. (Liverpool Culture Company, 2002: 703)

In formulating culture-led regeneration strategies, Liverpool city authorities looked up to Glasgow. From the late 1980s the city in which Dol had worked as a bus conductor after leaving Liverpool was reimaged and came to be vaunted as a model in urban regeneration policy circles. Of more specific relevance to Liverpool's European capital of culture aspirations was the widely held view that Glasgow's status as European city of culture in 1990 had formed an important component of its urban regeneration. Proponents of the Liverpool European capital of culture bid looked to Glasgow as the 'gold standard' to which they aspired (Liverpool Culture Company, 2002: 703).[10] Certainly, of all the cities that had been accorded the title of European city or capital of culture[11] since the mid-1980s, Glasgow's cultural and economic history was the one that mapped most closely onto Liverpool's own experiences. Like many other cities in Britain and elsewhere in northern Europe, both Glasgow and Liverpool suffered from processes of deindustrialization. However, these wider structural trends were experienced particularly acutely in Glasgow and Liverpool given the extent to which their prior prosperity had been bound up with British imperial trade.[12] Both cities claimed historically to have been the 'second city of the empire' (Lane, 1997; MacKenzie, 1999) but the maritime commercial activities that underpinned such competing claims were greatly diminished by the time Glasgow became European city of culture in 1990. Prior to Glasgow, European city of culture status had been conferred upon Athens, Florence, Amsterdam, (West) Berlin and Paris – all cities with established credentials for Cultural (capital C) tourism. It is not difficult to see how Glasgow appeared as a more appropriate and replicable model for Liverpool's attempts at culture-led urban regeneration from the late 1990s.

Of particular appeal to Liverpool city boosters was the way in which the European capital of culture had been used to turn around negative images or perceptions of Glasgow. According to Liverpool's European capital of culture bid document, 'The key impact on Glasgow was to change perceptions – to transform the city's reputation in the UK and abroad and to restore self-confidence and pride in the city to Glaswegians devastated by years of post-industrial gloom' (Liverpool Culture Company, 2002: 703). Liverpool Culture Company, set up by the city council to deliver the European capital of culture bid, thus referred generically to 'negative perceptions'.[13] The socioeconomic problems of Glasgow and Liverpool had never been reducible to image or perception, but that is not to say that such matters were inconsequential. The sociologist Tony Lane (1997: xiii) notes that both cities had at different times been among those imagined as 'containing a distilled essence of the "British problem"'. Manchester, London and Glasgow had represented the particular urban 'anxieties' of earlier periods. Liverpool's turn came in the late twentieth century, a period of economic globalization in which the material effects of negative imaginings were heightened by the increased mobility of investment capital. If European city of culture status had helped Glasgow to pass on its unwanted mantle to Liverpool, perhaps Liverpool could, in turn, use the same means to escape its own centrality to imaginings of what was wrong with British cities.

Unlike some other major provincial cities in Britain, Liverpool experienced little in the way of positive reimaging during the 1980s and 1990s. Leaving aside the question of whether 'successful' culture-led development elsewhere amounted to much more than an improvement to *image*,[14] Liverpool was described as 'a tale of missed opportunities' in one influential volume on cultural policy and urban regeneration, despite having been a site for experimentation with culture-led urban regeneration as early as 1982 (Parkinson and Bianchini, 1993). Among the initiatives assigned by the Conservative central government's Merseyside Task Force to the Merseyside Development Corporation in the aftermath of the street disturbances of 1981[15] were two major regeneration projects. One was the redevelopment, from 1982, of Albert Dock – the section of the south docks closest to Liverpool city centre – a site that had been redundant for a decade. The architecturally valuable dock buildings could not be demolished and so were redeveloped for a mixture of retail and cultural uses (Jones and Evans, 2008). The Merseyside Development Corporation's second major cultural project was the International Garden Festival which was held on another section of abandoned south docks, near the Dingle, during the summer of 1984 (see Figure 1.1). By the time the final phase of the redevelopment of Albert Dock was completed in 2002, it housed cultural attractions including the Tate Liverpool art gallery, the Merseyside Maritime Museum and The Beatles Story, attracting visitors from around the world.[16] However, much of the International Garden Festival site lay empty and derelict,[17] and it was the image of Liverpool's decay and dereliction which continued to predominate, particularly within Britain. One academic urban planning text notes that the dominant image of Liverpool was that of 'a place struggling to come to terms with its reduced importance and its poverty' (Couch, 2003: 14). Persistent negative images and imaginings – in political discourse, popular culture and the media – served to rub salt into deep socioeconomic wounds. There was a growing conviction among local council leaders that European capital of culture status was necessary for Liverpool to capture some of the good feeling that had been experienced in (some) other parts of urban Britain from the 1990s.

The award of European capital of culture for 2008 to Liverpool was in part testament to the success of the proponents of the bid in highlighting what the title could do for the city. Since Liverpool's 'need' was imagined to be greater than that of its British rivals – Birmingham, Bristol, Cardiff, Newcastle/Gateshead (which submitted a joint bid) and Oxford – the bid inferred that the transformative potential of the European capital of culture in Liverpool was correspondingly greater than in other cities. The Liverpool bid was likened to a 'scholarship' that could be used by the city 'to transform itself and deliver a step change in regeneration, confidence, inward investment and tourism that would last for the foreseeable future' (Liverpool Culture Company, 2002: 703). Securing the award of European capital of culture status in June 2003, of course, was only the first in a series of Glasgow's steps that Liverpool seemed compelled to follow. Louise Ellman (Labour member of parliament for the Liverpool Riverside constituency) therefore greeted news of the award by suggesting: 'This is a magnificent boost for Liverpool but it is also a challenge.'[18] Councillor Mike Storey, leader of Liverpool City Council, was rather more jubilant: 'This decision means so much to the city. It gives us the opportunity to bring real change for the better. This is a day for the people of Liverpool to celebrate.' More widely, as far as European capital of culture proponents were concerned, turning around the economic fortunes of Liverpool became a matter of following the Glasgow course of culture-led regeneration to graduation in 2008.

Not everyone was convinced of the desirability of 'doing a Glasgow'. According to one scholar of that city, for example, Glasgow 1990 had been 'little other than a form of "spin"' and was 'not about tackling Glasgow's structural problems, the social divisions, the inequalities and the poverty' (Mooney, 2004: 337). The implication for Liverpool, of course, was that European capital of culture 2008 might provide an opportunity for a facelift and associated changes in image, particularly in the city centre, but was unlikely to achieve much else. Following this line of argument, what is primarily an exercise in urban reimaging or rebranding would, like Glasgow's cultural regeneration strategies, provide few benefits for the city's poorest residents and areas, and might even gloss over their ongoing problems (Mooney, 2004; Jones and Wilks-Heeg, 2004). Culture-led regeneration and even 'renaissance' in cities such as Glasgow are, accordingly, forms of 'state-led gentrification' (Lees, 2003: 62). There are, in other words, powerful and important critiques that unsettle the fundamental assumption in Liverpool's European capital of culture bid of the desirability of following Glasgow down a road of culture-led urban regeneration policy. However, what critics such as Mooney do share with proponents of the 2008 bid is a sense of Glasgow as a meaningful comparative reference point for Liverpool.

One distinction between the reimaging of Glasgow as European city of culture in 1990 and Liverpool in 2008 that had implications for minority ethnic groups such as the Malays concerns the emphasis given to the 'multicultural' or 'cosmopolitan' demographic composition of the city. In part, the catchphrase the World in One City evoked the self-conscious cosmopolitanism of Edwardian times, revalorizing the wealth of cultural influences and styles that Liverpool had soaked up as a great seaport and 'world city' (Belchem, 2000). However, in contrast to the city's 700th birthday celebrations in 1907, the glossing of Liverpool as a 'cocktail of cultures' in the European capital of culture bid was also a matter of capitalizing upon the demographic legacy of the maritime era. The marketing of Liverpool's multiculturalism and the absence of this trope from Glasgow 1990 marketing is not a matter of significant differences in the demographic composition of the two cities. Dockside areas of Glasgow, like Liverpool (and other British seaports such as Cardiff and London), had highly geographically and ethnoracially diverse populations before the postwar Commonwealth migration.[19] In addition, while Liverpool may have gained particular notoriety for its 'riots' in the 1980s, the histories of racial discrimination and prejudice which partly fuelled them are hardly unique to Liverpool, even if they exist mostly in more diluted forms elsewhere. The attention given to 'difference' in the Liverpool bid, in other words, was not a manifestation of Liverpool being different or exceptional. Rather, it reflected at least in part the increased attention afforded to strategies of marketing cultural diversity in Britain after Glasgow 1990.

During the 1990s visible signs of urban otherness were reimagined as evidence of vitality. Phil Cohen (1999: 11) argues that the conventional tendency to 'represent the city as Other, and then to isolate the Other in the city' was being overturned by a 'dramatic new trope of a multicultural city'. 'Visible subcultures', he suggests, 'are being vigorously promoted as signs of urban vitality and cosmopolitanism, as part of the attraction of a "multicultural city" to lifestyle tourists at home and abroad' (p. 10). While Cohen was writing primarily about the experiences of world city London – which also came to be glossed in the media as the 'world in one city' (Binnie *et al.*, 2006) – a similar re-evaluation of urban 'resources' was underway in less fashionable, provincial cities which had once served as 'immigrant gateways' (Price and Benton-Short, 2008). One clear example is Birmingham, a 'downscaled' (Glick Schiller and Çağlar, 2011: 8) former 'gateway city' (McEwan *et al.*, 2008) which had previously 'spent a lot of energy denying its migrant heritage' (Bhattacharyya, 2000: 170). Gargi Bhattacharyya describes how Birmingham's 'mixed-bag population' had begun to be 'repackaged as a positive asset'. In an essay published in 2000, but based on developments over the preceding decade, she notes that 'Birmingham has started to sell itself as a distinctively multiethnic experience, somewhere cosmopolitan in an urbane rather than a threatening way' (Bhattacharyya, 2000: 170). Such processes served to revalorize previously marginal(ized) urban places as 'multicultural' or 'cosmopolitan' (Binnie *et al.*, 2006). Within the older industrial cities of Britain, and elsewhere in Europe, areas that had housed the immigrant and labouring poor from around the world for over a century became prime sites for redevelopment as the favoured location of the new cultural industries (Cohen, 1997; Glick Schiller and Çağlar, 2009). Of course, this is not the same as saying that the immigrant and labouring poor are the ones who benefit from associated forms of what Cohen refers to as 'multicultural capitalism'. On the one hand, Bhattacharyya (2000: 171) argues that '[n]ow cities have to shift away from an anti-urban bias that hates workers and foreigners as figures of contamination and decay, and start to present these archetypically urban people as the best products of city space.'[20] On the other hand, there was a danger that multicultural regeneration would turn out to be little more than a form of gentrification in which difference is packaged as lifestyle choices for middle-class consumers or the creative classes (Mitchell, 1993; Žižek, 1997; Fish, 1997) in specific urban enclaves and 'quarters' (Bell and Jayne, 2004).[21]

What is clear is that not only did 'mixed-bag' populations of inner-city neighbourhoods begin to find a place in civic representations of provincial cities in Britain in the 1990s but there was also a wider re-evaluation of the place of cities (and their ethnocultural diversity) in national life. Talk of 'urban renaissance' became increasingly audible in New Labour Britain (Lees, 2003), and 'diversity' was, at least for a time, embraced in suggestions as to how British national identity might be repackaged. *Britain™: Renewing Our Identity*, a book published in 1997 by the think tank Demos (which had close links with New Labour), examined the importance of 're-imagining Britain' (Leonard, 1997: 12) in the face of bad press and a national image around the world which was said to be 'stuck in the past' (p. 8). Mark Leonard suggested a need to 'not only highlight Britain's place in the world, but the world's place in Britain' (p. 67), to involve 'all of Britain's ethnic groups in public festivals to celebrate Britain's hybridity' (p. 69). Importantly, this national-level prescription was informed by city-level stories of success in reimaging and rebranding in which ethnocultural resources had been foregrounded. In Liverpool, the city council produced a document that emphasized the importance of 'celebrating diversity' (p. 3) and vaunted its value for tourist, cultural and creative industries (Liverpool City Council, 2002). Published in 2002, *The Cultural Strategy for Liverpool* was a response to a proposal by the New Labour national government's Department for Culture, Media and Sport that all local authorities across Britain prepare local cultural strategies, and preceded Liverpool's European capital of culture bid.

Enthusiasm for celebrating multicultural diversity subsequently faded very rapidly at the national level, but persisted in many British cities, including Liverpool. An important turning point in national political terms for New Labour was the widespread criticism levelled at a report on *The Future of Multi-ethnic Britain* which was funded by the Runnymede Trust and published in 2000. What became known as the Parekh Report,[22] proposed to allow multiple identities and cultural affiliations to develop a sense of belonging to a common (national) political community. The right-wing national press in particular took exception to the suggestion that British citizens might need to re-evaluate their history and identity, or that the historical racial coding of Britishness needed to be abandoned to allow citizens of different cultures and colours to coexist with the same right of claim to the nation. Sadly, the New Labour national government's response was to distance itself from the Parekh Report. In subsequent official documents, such as the 2002 White Paper on migration, 'support for immigration and multiculturalism is muted beyond all recognition: death by a thousand qualifications' (Kymlicka, 2003: 205). The city of Liverpool, in contrast, continued to heed Mark Leonard's (1997: 67) call for 'a concerted effort to rethink our links with the rest of the world', although for the most part this meant pursuit of diasporic links with economically booming cities and countries, rather than world-embracing openness to difference. Perhaps the most prominent were public–private partnerships seeking to capitalize on historical associations and Chinese community links with China, especially Shanghai (Cook *et al.*, 2008).[23] Nonetheless, even such instrumental urban 'diaspora strategies' (Larner, 2007) and the 'weak' form of multiculturalism associated with the marketing of Liverpool as 'the World in One City' in the 2002 European capital of culture bid document (Liverpool Culture Company, 2002) suggested space for minority ethnic groups and 'communities' that had not existed during Glasgow's time as European capital of culture two decades earlier.

Marking Malays(ia) on the Map of the World in One City

The people who socialized at the Malay Club on Jermyn Street during this period were well placed to capitalize on the increasingly positive attention that was being afforded to multicultural diversity in Liverpool.

In addition to the productive relationship that had been forged between the MSA and Novas-Ouvertures, Malaysian students had come to assume a greater organizational role in the MSA. As noted in Chapter 4, students from Malaysia, including many ethnic Malays, had come to Liverpool on government scholarships from the 1960s, and their number increased after 1970. At that time, some students had joined in with activities of Liverpool's resident Malay population, mostly through the club on Jermyn Street. However, by the time that Liverpool was officially rebranded as the World in One City in 2002 the nature of interrelations between student sojourners and settled Malay ex-seamen (and their families) had almost completely inverted. Malaysian graduate students in the city and members of their families, through groups such as the Malay-speaking circle, took the lead in organizing social events in which (at least some of) the ex-seafaring 'elders' were able to participate. It was these student-led events, rather than the more mundane Wednesday lunchtime meetings at the Malay Club, which generated the kinds of colourful and exotic 'community' imagery that chimed with official imaginings of ethnocultural diversity and cosmopolitanism. The 'history and background' document – noted above – that formed part of the MSA's application to the John Moores Foundation sketched a community comprising both British citizens (naturalized ex-seamen as well as their British-born descendants) and citizens of nation states in Southeast Asia (mostly students and young professionals from Malaysia, and their family members). Aizi Razman Ismail, the student who was present at the John Moores Foundation meeting where I first met Dol, had put this document together. Aizi was also head (*penghulu*) of the Malay-speaking circle during that time in 2003. Studying for his doctorate at the University of Liverpool, Aizi had community-organizing skills that were not found among the dwindling numbers of ex-seamen in the city. Apart from his ability to put together official documentation in English, the information and communications technologies that Aizi and his peers used as part of their everyday lives were noted as important for interacting with Novas-Ouvertures, the social enterprise working with the MSA.[24] There were also Malay students and former students who had more specific professional skills that proved very useful, one example being a surveyor who assessed 7 Jermyn Street as part of an earlier application for funds to renovate the building.[25]

Less tangibly, the multicultural recasting of Liverpool entailed ways of seeing and representing ethnocultural difference which were uncannily familiar to Malaysian students.[26] The peninsular territories that eventually became Malaysia had been constructed through European racial categorization as a 'plural society' during British colonial times (Hirschman, 1986). Malaysia (or, at least, peninsular Malaysia) is conventionally understood to comprise, and be governed through, three main ethnic groups: Malays, Chinese and Indians. As was considered in the previous chapter, although Malays (and other so-called Bumiputera groups) occupy a special political position on account of their putative indigeneity, and *ketuanan Melayu* was strengthened after the racial riots of 1969 making Malay-ness more central to Malaysian national identity, 'multicultural' state representations of Malaysian society were (re)emphasized from the 1990s (Bunnell, 2002). One that was prominent during the period when I was conducting research in Liverpool was the Malaysian Tourism Board's Malaysia Truly Asia campaign. If Liverpool was being marketed as the World in One City, Malaysia Truly Asia promised visitors to Malaysia the experience of Asia-in-one-nation. The country was presented as somewhere visitors could experience and consume diverse Asian 'cultures' – usually meaning types of food, styles of clothing and various forms of 'traditional' performance. This may be dismissed as a form of 'boutique multiculturalism' in which difference is depoliticized and aestheticized, such that relations with cultural others remain largely untransformed in any meaningful or progressive way (Fish, 1997). Conversely, multicultural tourist promotion can be seen as having more profound effects in terms of lived identities and prevailing ideologies (Henderson, 2003). Either way, the official scripting of Malaysian multiculturalism was well suited to the context of Liverpool (and other British cities) where ostensibly 'multicultural' or 'cosmopolitan' marketing carries a distinct whiff of colonial exoticism (Keith, 2005). In the case of Liverpool-based Malaysian students, therefore, postcolonial socialization to know, and to be capable of performing, 'their' culture (whether Malay, Chinese or Indian), became a resource in the World in One City.

It was through Mohamed Nor Hamid (Mat Nor), president of the Malay Club (and thereby of the MSA), that Aizi Razman and other students were given the opportunity to put their Malaysian (multi)cultural capital to work. Aizi noted in interview:

> We were invited by Pak Cik Mat Nor [*Pak Cik* being the honorific term for a Malay elder] to come and listen to the briefing from Novas at the MSA and they were saying that there is a lot of money out there that we can bid for. But because the Pak Ciks perhaps did not have the ability to bid properly according to the procedures and requirements, so they were losing out. According to Novas, MSA was really losing out compared to other community organizations in Liverpool. It was just that they didn't have anyone to do the paperwork and that kind of thing.[27]

The proper 'procedures and requirements' that Aizi was referring to included such things as holding annual general meetings (with minutes), report writing, keeping accounts and having an official constitution. These were necessary components of a functioning and viable 'community' in the eyes of organizations such as the John Moores Foundation and wider governance structures. Aizi went on to explain how previously some British family members of Malay ex-seamen had taken on such work.[28] However, that arrangement had apparently ended in conflict as some of the ex-seafaring elders considered it tantamount to a 'take over' of the club. While Aizi was attentive to the danger of Malaysian students being seen as posing a similar threat, members of the Malay-speaking circle, which he headed, had come to play expanded roles in the life of the 'community' assembled at/through the 7 Jermyn Street home of the Malay Club (and official address of the MSA). Another Malaysian graduate student member of the Malay-speaking circle, Sharidah Sharif, was elected as a member of the MSA management committee in August 2003, thus forming a bridge between the Malay-speaking circle and the MSA/Malay Club.

A graduate student at Liverpool Hope University, Sharidah had relocated to Liverpool with her husband and four children in 2002. She made contact with Aizi and the Malay-speaking circle by email even before leaving Kuala Lumpur.[29] After arriving in Liverpool, Sharidah soon became heavily involved in organizing Malay-speaking circle mutual help and social activities. It was through Malay-speaking circle social events that she met some of Liverpool's ex-seafaring elders (*Pak Cik-Pak Cik*), including Mat Nor. As part of the new MSA committee that was formed in August 2003, Sharidah shouldered much of the day-to-day administrative and organizational work. By the time I first interviewed her in September of the following year, Sharidah had become concerned with wider promotion of Malays' historical presence in Liverpool. People in the city, she said, 'know so much about the Somali community and the Yemeni community'. In contrast, 'they don't know anything about Malays.' She spoke enthusiastically of 'trying to position the community' in order to increase its public visibility. Sharidah had lived through the Mahathir era during which Kuala Lumpur's skyline had been transformed in order to mark Malaysia on world maps, and when Malay nationalist concerns had shifted beyond national borders in search of recognition in a globalizing and transnationalizing world.[30] In Liverpool in 2004 Sharidah had come to see it as her mission to put the Malay diaspora on the map of the World in One City.

Despite their awareness of the importance of avoiding being seen as 'taking over' the Malay Club, the growing involvement of students such as Aizi and Sharidah inevitably served to accelerate the processes of Malaysianization. Evidence of this was very clear from the MSA's annual report for 2003, which was compiled by Sharidah as part of the newly elected management committee. This very competently assembled document detailed a range of social activities in which community members had participated over the course of the year. However, the overwhelming majority of the faces in the accompanying photographs were those of Malaysian students, their spouses and children. Descendants of ex-seamen featured in just one of the photographs, and that was of the annual general meeting which was held at the Malay Club on Jermyn Street in August. Mat Nor, who, as the president of the MSA, did appear in a majority of the 12 photographs in the report, noted in his 'Chairman's Statement 2003' that 'the highlight of the year' had been a visit by the high commissioner for Malaysia in the UK, Salim Hashim. The three accompanying photographs of this visit showed women in colourful traditional Malay clothing and headscarves – all suitably exotic for the World in One City. However, with the exception of the wife of the high commissioner, all of these women were from Malaysian student families and none were British descendants of Malay ex-seamen. The photograph depicting a subsequent event in Dover showed a younger, less formally attired group who went to greet a fellow ethnic Malay Malaysian who was aiming to swim across the English Channel from Calais. The swimmer, Malik Mydin, was noted in the annual report as 'the first South-East Asian' to have accomplished this feat. Finally, the report included a picture taken at the Malay Club in Liverpool in which Malaysian flag-waving children were shown singing patriotic songs to mark Malaysian independence day (*Merdeka*), while a handful of seemingly bemused elders (ex-seamen) looked on.

There were undoubtedly many positive aspects of the growing influence of Malaysian students in community organization in general and at the Malay Club in particular. Aizi, Sharidah and many of their fellow Malay-speaking circle members were genuine in their concern for the welfare of the elderly ex-seamen. In interview, Aizi highlighted 'respect for elders' as a key part of 'Malay culture'.[31] Moreover, at a meeting organized by the Malay-speaking circle at the University of Liverpool in October 2004 to welcome new Malay(sian) students to the city, Aizi's successor noted the presence of the elderly ex-seamen and the importance of helping them wherever possible.[32] A range of forms of assistance is mentioned in the MSA annual report of 2003, including the delivery of meals to housebound community members, hospital visits to sick members and assistance with Islamic bereavement arrangements. Students had also carried out much of the work of redecorating and refurbishing the 7 Jermyn Street home of the Malay Club/MSA, shortly before my first visit to the club in December 2003.

The problem with the increased influence of Malaysian students, at least as far as some of the ex-seamen and their family members were concerned, was that they had strong, normative conceptions of

Malay-ness based on their socialization in Mahathir era Malaysia.[33] The most significant change made to the Malay Club was the introduction of a new prayer room for women. Aizi, Sharidah and others were well aware that Islam had not featured prominently in the adult lives of many of the ex-seamen, and were at pains to stress that they had no intention of trying to tell the remaining ex-seamen to change their ways. However, those ex-seamen who continued to live in un-Islamic ways were considered, at best, to have lost touch with their Malay identity. As for non-Malay-speaking, non-halal food eating descendants of the ex-seamen, these people were simply 'not familiar with the Malay culture' – with the exception of those who were married off to Malaysians 'to save them'.[34] There is no doubt that at least some aspects of the Malaysianization of Liverpool's Malay community were appreciated by those ex-seamen who wished to realize themselves in ways that conformed to norms of Malay-ness in twenty-first-century Malaysia, especially those who had returned to the mosque in order to 'cleanse' themselves of un-Islamic pasts. However, other ex-seamen and members of their families felt increasingly out of place in the Malaysianized and Islamized Malay Club. Men who continued to drink or gamble – both commonplace activities at 7 Jermyn Street in earlier periods[35] – were no longer welcomed. No doubt there had always been squabbles and enmities among men who identified at least partly as 'Malay' in Liverpool – an important point to note given the tendency in ethnic and migration studies to presume that co-ethnics are inherent sources of social capital and support (Glick Schiller and Çağlar, 2009) – and there were thus many reasons why some had long stayed away from the club.[36] Nonetheless, there were certainly men for whom 7 Jermyn Street had once been a site of friendship and socialization, but who had come to be increasingly socially isolated through not feeling welcome at the regenerated club.

Despite these exclusions – perhaps even because of them – the Malay-speaking circle and the newly formed MSA committee looked set for effective collaboration. While I have so far noted the importance of the injection of Malaysian students' energies and (multi)cultural skills for the MSA and the Malay Club, the importance of Mat Nor's role as president of the MSA should also be highlighted. In addition to being a very active and spritely septuagenarian in 2004, he had become precisely the kind of Liverpool Malay who fitted in with Malaysian students' conceptions of what elderly Malays *should* be like. He attended the mosque, refrained from cooking Wednesday lunches during Ramadan, and could be relied upon to wear traditional Malay clothes – usually a brightly coloured *baju Melayu* (Malay shirt) and *songkok* (rimless cap) – during cultural events. Above all, Mat Nor was an acceptable British face of an imagined Liverpool 'Malaysian and Singapore community' whose active members were mostly Malaysian citizens. 'The World in One City' in Liverpool's European capital of culture bid document, it should be emphasized, referred primarily to the geographically diverse ancestry of British Liverpudlians rather than to foreign sojourners (see also Bunnell, 2008). Mat Nor anchored the activities of Malay(sian) student sojourners in a local population of ethnically Malay British citizens. Meanwhile, as was noted above, the location of the Malay Club in what was at that time termed the Granby Toxteth ward placed the community within an official geography of deprivation. Malaysian students in Liverpool thus appeared to be well placed to lead efforts to access social and, increasingly, cultural funding.

The Community Chest application that the then recently elected MSA committee submitted in late 2003 was for funding of celebrations designed to 'promote and raise the profile of the MSA and to celebrate their diversity and cultural heritage'. This was noted as being aligned with the objectives of the Community Chest: 'To help black and minority ethnic or other communities find out more about their origins and culture and maintain their traditions.' In line with the wider multicultural reimag(in)ing of the city, the proposed 'planned day of cultural dance, music and song', would serve to 'support the equality and diversity of Liverpool's citizens in light of the cultural aims of the City's success in the Capital of Culture'. As the Novas-Ouvertures community development manager who was working with MSA put it rather more candidly in interview, the key to the application was 'playing the ethnic dance ... to open the purse strings'.[37] The application requested a total of £5,000, of which £1,500 was for entertainment (dancers, singers and musicians). In May 2004 Novas-Ouvertures was informed that the MSA had been awarded a grant of £3,509 from the neighbourhood renewal Community Chest. This figure fell short of the amount requested because the budget for food had been cut substantially, but it appeared to be another step towards putting Malays(ians) on the map of the World in One City. Significantly for the constitutive transnational urban connections that run through this book, not only were the multicultural rescripting and marketing of Liverpool in general reminiscent of urban and national boosterism in Malaysia (and Singapore), but Malaysian citizens played a key role in MSA's efforts to capitalize on (multi)cultural community funding opportunities in the lead-up to 2008.

Notes

1 Interview, Liverpool, 5 December 2003. In between, he worked for a Chinese-owned shipping company which operated in Indonesia. He recalled one ship that he worked on being stopped by a Dutch destroyer because

Dutch authorities were suspicious about the cargo. As a result, he was taken prisoner in Surabaya for three months.

2 It is not clear to me why Dol moved to Glasgow to find a shore job. However, the shared imperial and maritime histories of Liverpool and Glasgow that are elaborated in this chapter meant that this was one of the port cities that many Malay (ex-)seafarers were familiar with in the middle decades of the twentieth century. As noted in Chapter 4, one of the men who was registered as living at 5 Jermyn Street in the early 1970s had previously lived in Glasgow – Amat Rashid, originally from Penang.

3 'Clubhouse' was the term used in the original application to the John Moores Foundation.

4 The document was dated 12 January 2003.

5 As Jones and Evans (2008: 12) put it: 'Committed to the Conservative's spending plans during that early period in order to reassure middle-class voters, there was no sudden abandonment of neoliberal policy principles.'

6 Taken from the John Moores Foundation website, http://www.jmf.org.uk/index.htm (accessed 20 January 2011, no longer available).

7 See Chapter 4.

8 Interview with Mohamed Nor Hamid, Liverpool, 13 October 2004.

9 The local authority of Halton, which borders Merseyside, was (like Liverpool) among the 88 most deprived in Britain.

10 This may be attributed, at least in part, to the way in which a 'Glasgow success narrative' had been celebrated in the Department of Culture, Media and Sport document that initiated the bidding process for the 2008 award (Connolly, 2013: 169).

11 Launched at intergovernmental level in June 1985, the European city of culture concept was the brainchild of the Greek culture minister, Melina Mercouri. It was based on the understanding that: (1) Europe has been and remains the focus of exceptionally rich and extremely varied artistic and cultural activities; and (2) cities have played a key part in the creation and spread of Europe's cultures. In 1999 the intergovernmental nature of the initiative became a Community action, such that the selection now involves the Council, the European Parliament, the European Commission and the Committee of the Regions. The following year 'city of culture' was changed to 'capital of culture' (European Commission, 2010).

12 In Liverpool's case, see Chapter 4.

13 On Liverpool Culture Company and its relationship with Liverpool City Council see O'Brien (2010). O'Brien argues that Liverpool's urban governance model was different from previous European capital of culture winners. The council retained more control than is often the case for the 'professionalized quasi-public agencies' that are conventionally associated with neoliberal urbanism (Leitner *et al.*, 2007: 4).

14 For a critical perspective on the case of Glasgow see Mooney (2004).

15 The 'riots' were discussed in Chapter 4.

16 The development was also said to have been popular with 'locals', with 50 per cent of the visitors in a 1996 visitor survey said to be from Merseyside (Meegan, 1999: 100).

17 See 'Garden festival – 20 years on', *BBC*, 22 April 2004, available at: http://www.bbc.co.uk/liverpool/capital_culture/2004/04/garden_festival/index.shtml# (accessed 29 June 2008).
18 Cited in 'Liverpool named European capital of culture', *The Guardian*, 4 June 2003. The subsequent citation in this paragraph is taken from the same source.
19 As was noted in Chapter 2, Malay seamen were discharged in Glasgow in the mid-nineteenth century (Salter, 1873: 88), while 'Singapore Malays' of Minangkabau ancestry were known to have settled there during the twentieth century (Mokhtar, 1973).
20 Or, as Glick Schiller and Çağlar (2009: 189) put it: 'As the leaders of each city seek to attract capital and to market their city as a globally recognized brand, they may re-evaluate the presence of migrants.' Diversity becomes a marketable asset – 'saleable urban resource for cultural industries'.
21 In a conference presentation in Liverpool in 2008, Steve Higginson described Liverpool Culture Company members' obsession with notions of the 'creative class' and associated possibilities for developing cultural industries in the city. 'Enclosed Liverpool and Culture of Capital', paper presented at Capital, Culture, Power: Criminalisation and Resistance, University of Liverpool/Liverpool John Moores University, 2–4 July 2008. In this respect, Liverpool could perhaps have been described as doing a (Richard) 'Florida', as much as a Glasgow (see Florida, 2002).
22 After the philosopher Bhiku Parekh, who chaired the commission which compiled the report.
23 September 1999 saw a *feng shui* ceremony for commencement of work on an archway at the entrance to Liverpool's Chinatown on Nelson Street to be constructed by Shanghainese workers. The following month, Liverpool was twinned with Shanghai. Subsequently, organizations such as China Link (associated with the Liverpool Chamber of Commerce) and the Liverpool-Shanghai Partnership (involving Liverpool City Council) were established (see Cook *et al.*, 2008).
24 Interview with Novas-Ouvertures Community Development Manager, Liverpool, 7 October 2004.
25 Interview with Aizi Razman, Liverpool, 30 September 2004.
26 And also to me as someone who examined the multicultural 'rescripting' of Malaysia in the 1990s (Bunnell, 2002) and has lived in officially multicultural Singapore since 1999.
27 Interview with Aizi Razman, Liverpool, 30 September 2004.
28 This had been the case, for example, during the time when the 1998 Eid celebrations noted in the first part of this chapter took place. MSA Annual Report 1998/99.
29 Interview with Sharidah Sharif, Liverpool, 21 September 2004.
30 See Chapters 6 and 5 respectively.
31 Interview with Aizi Razman, Liverpool, 30 September 2004.
32 Meeting for incoming Malaysian students, University of Liverpool, 8 October 2004.

33 These conceptions are very much in line with the changes described in Chapter 5 (and in Shamsul, 1999) concerning the 'mainstreaming' of Islam in Malaysian, and especially Malay, social life.

34 Interview with Aizi Razman, Liverpool, 30 September 2004.

35 One of ex-seaman Majid's few recollections of the Malay Club in earlier years was of the gambling that took place there 24 hours a day. Notes from conversation, Liverpool, 10 October 2004.

36 As was noted in Chapter 5, at the end of the 1980s Hajis Musa and Talib stayed away precisely because of the decidedly un-Islamic practices that took place at the club at that time. As Tim Cresswell (2004: 26) notes, places are socially constructed and these constructions are inevitably 'founded upon acts of exclusion'.

37 Interview, Liverpool, 7 October 2004.

8

The Last Hurrah

From Independence Celebrations and Interculturalism to Club Closure

My first extended period of fieldwork in Liverpool in 2004 was timed to begin with the two cultural events that were funded by the Community Chest grant secured by the Merseyside Malaysian and Singapore Community Association (MSA). Both events centred upon celebration of the independence (*Merdeka*) of the Federation of Malaya (what is today peninsular Malaysia), providing further evidence that the community life of Malay Liverpool was running to a Malaysian rhythm. The first event, which I examine in the opening section of this chapter, was held on the date of *Merdeka* day itself (31 August) and consisted of a commemoration service by the River Mersey where there is a monument listing the names of merchant seamen – including many Malays – who lost their lives during the Second World War. A second event, a Malaysian food festival and children's street party, took place the following Saturday outside the Malay Club on Jermyn Street, and I examine this in the second section of the chapter. At the time, both events seemed to be great successes to me.[1] They gave rise to colourful scenes that could be used to present an active community to potential funding bodies, and so serve as resources for bigger, more ambitious community events as the European capital of culture year approached. It transpired that the *Merdeka* events marked the high point of the life of the community that had been forged out of collaboration between Malaysian students and their families on the one hand, and Liverpool-based ex-seamen and their British descendants on the other. Organizational and budgetary

From World City to the World in One City: Liverpool through Malay Lives,
First Edition. Tim Bunnell.

squabbles that I consider in the third section exacerbated a divide between Malaysian students and Liverpool-born descendants of ex-seamen. The largest gatherings held at 7 Jermyn Street after the *Merdeka* events, detailed in the final section of the chapter, each marked the death of one of the few remaining Malay ex-seamen in Liverpool.

Merdeka on the Mersey

In 2004 Malaysian independence day (31 August) fell on a Tuesday. That morning, I drove over to the Malay Club where a small group of Malaysian student members of Liverpool's Malay-speaking circle were talking with the MSA president Mohamed Nor Hamid (Mat Nor) and some Malaysian journalists who had travelled from London to cover the *Merdeka* celebrations. The Pier Head section of the Liverpool waterfront where the celebrations were scheduled to be held from 2.30 p.m. was only around five or ten minutes away by car. However, I left well before 2.00 p.m. as Sharidah Sharif – the Malaysian student who, as secretary of the MSA, had come to form a bridge between that club-based organization and the Malay-speaking circle – requested a ride to a nearby supermarket in order to buy flowers. By the time we reached Pier Head, now carrying several bunches of flowers, there were already small groups of people assembled beside the Liverpool Memorial which overlooked the Mersey ferry terminal. Seemingly oblivious to the presence of a Mister Softy ice cream van on the adjacent Riverside Walk, brightly dressed children of Malaysian students posed patiently for pictures while waving small flags of their home country. At this point in my video recording of the day's events, an unidentifiable voice asks (in English): 'Are they going to do dancing?' Although there was to be no dancing, the event was well suited to the kind of wider 'ethnic dance' that was considered attractive to (multi)cultural funding, and singing was on the agenda.[2] At around 3.40 p.m., considerably behind schedule, the Malay-speaking circle's Aizi Razman Ismail formally initiated the afternoon's proceedings by introducing the flag-waving children as a choir. With a faintly audible stereo accompaniment, the children's choir gave a creditable performance of the Malaysian national anthem, *Negaraku* (My Country), followed by another patriotic song (also in Malay).

In addition to the Malaysian children and their parents, the group of around 50 people who assembled at the waterfront included a handful of Malay ex-seamen and a similar number of their British descendants. The last of these three subgroups of people who together comprised Liverpool's so-called 'Malaysian and Singapore community' was small, in part because the event was held during the afternoon of a working day. Various Malaysian students, however, assured me that the ratio of British to Malaysian citizens would be more balanced at the street party that was scheduled for the coming weekend. I mingled and tried to make conversation with as many people as possible, while my brother – recruited as a volunteer cameraman for the day – filmed the proceedings. Next in the formal part of the event came the introduction of a representative from the students' department of the Malaysian High Commission in London. This man gave a speech in Malay (followed by a much shorter version in English) in which he praised the organizers of the event for demonstrating the spirit of *Merdeka*. I wondered how many of the people present realized that although Singapore gained independence by joining Malaysia for a brief period (around two years) from 1963, 31 August is the date of independence only for the national territory that is today Malaysia. More precisely, 31 August 1957 only applies to West (or peninsular) Malaysia. What are today the East Malaysian states of Sabah and Sarawak, like Singapore, only gained independence from Britain in 1963 (Tan, 2008).

Such historical geopolitical details may be dismissed as merely academic, and I certainly did not raise them in conversation at the riverfront celebrations. However, they assume significance when considering the people in whose name the event was ostensibly being held: Malay men listed on a riverside memorial to merchant seamen who died on board British naval vessels during the Second World War.[3] The wife of a Malaysian student standing beside one of the plaques on the memorial bearing the names of those who died on board HMS *Banka* can be heard in my video recording saying (in Malay) that these Malay men were 'from Malacca, Johor and other places in Malaysia'. Apart from the historical fact that the nation state of Malaysia did not come into being until more than two decades after the *Banka* was sunk in December 1941, the names on the memorial that I have been able to trace were of men recorded as being from Singapore, not (parts of what became) Malaysia. Adnan Bin Hahran, seaman number 8923 and one of HMS *Banka*'s naval auxiliary personnel, for example, who is reported to have died aged 18 on 10 December 1941, is listed as 'husband of bte Chachine of Singapore, Malaya' (Imperial War Graves Commission, 1952). Seaman number 9541, Muhammad Hashim bin Ahmad, who died at the age of 23 while serving on board HMS *Anking* the following year, is described as 'Son of Ahmad bin Aman of Singapore, Malaya'. Men from places in colonial British Malaya (including Malacca and Johor) that did eventually become part of Malaysia, rather than Singapore, were certainly among the Malay merchant seafarers who died on British naval vessels during the war.[4] Nonetheless, contradictions arising from the entanglement of histories and geographies associated with *Merdeka* by the Mersey included the following: an event marking Malaysian independence being held next to a monument to men who died at sea (in 1941/42) two decades before a nation state bearing the name Malaysia came into being (in 1963), and a decade and a half before even its western, peninsular component gained independence from Britain (in 1957); and, the fact that the Malay men whose names appear on the monument originated from Singapore, not from among those parts of colonial British Malaya (such as Malacca and Johor) that today constitute Malaysia.

Mohamed Nor Hamid (Mat Nor) who, in his capacity as head of the MSA, spoke after the representative from the Malaysian students' department, was the one person who mentioned Singapore during the official proceedings. Although he was born in Tanjung Keling, Malacca, Mat Nor had himself been moved to Singapore by his family to attend school there. In his speech beside the Liverpool Memorial, Mat Nor noted that the generation of Malay seafarers in the city before him – the generation which included casualties of the Second World War – included men from Singapore. Otherwise, Mat Nor narrated his geographical biography at the *Merdeka* celebration in ways appropriate for a specifically Malaysian event and audience. Noting that he had arrived in Liverpool in 1952, before *Merdeka*, Mat Nor recalled Tunku Abdul Rahman (chief minister of the Federation of Malaya) coming to London to negotiate the arrangements for independence, and the Malayan students who were at Kirkby College at that time.[5] Later, he went on to say, seamen from what became Malaysia had come to Liverpool in order to carry out cadet training. In a burst of Malaysian patriotism, Mat Nor (who had been a British citizen for several decades and who, having been born in the Straits Settlements, was a British subject even on arrival in Liverpool in 1952) said of *Merdeka*: 'I am very proud, I never forget my homeland.' As such, Mat Nor publicly positioned himself in relation to specifically Malaysian national history and political geography. After he had finished his speech, the Malaysian students' department representative, who was this time introduced as an *ustaz* (Muslim scholar), resumed centre stage. He recited prayers for the dead while church bells – unrelated to the riverside commemoration service, but uncannily well timed – rang in the background.

The *ustaz* was then the first of a succession of men to lay flowers – mostly bunches that I recognized from the earlier supermarket detour – at the foot of the Liverpool Memorial. All of these men have appeared at some point in preceding chapters of this book, some more prominently than others. Mat Nor was first, followed by Majid from Serkam, Malacca, the oldest of the remaining Malay ex-seamen in Liverpool in 2004, and the only one to have visited the city before the Second World War. Majid was followed, in turn, by another Malacca-born man, Fadzil, who was recovering from a recent medical operation and so moved slowly over to the memorial with the aid of a stick. Then came Teddy Lates and Ronnie Bujang, both born in Liverpool of Malay seafaring fathers before the war[6] and who were considered senior enough to be introduced at the event with the honorific *Pak Cik* (elder). Teddy's father, who was from the town of Batu Pahat, Johor, in British Malaya, died on board the *Fort Concord* during the Second World War. His name appears on a memorial at Tower Bridge in London rather than on the Liverpool Memorial.[7] Ronnie's father, Amat bin Bujang, survived the war, but died in Liverpool in 1951. The two men who followed Teddy and Ronnie in placing flowers by the Liverpool Memorial were Hashim and JJ. The latter was introduced at the event as 'Pak Cik Johan', the formal, Malaysianized version of the name of this Eurasian man who had converted to Islam in Liverpool. As was considered in Chapter 2, JJ had moved from his birthplace of Negeri Sembilan, Malaya, to Singapore with his mother during the war. Hashim, meanwhile, was the one Singapore-born Malay ex-seaman who attended the event. A Malaysian graduate student who had taken over from Aizi as *penghulu* (head) of the Malay-speaking circle completed the line-up of people who laid flowers by the memorial. It only remained for Aizi to announce that the *ustaz* would lead prayers for the deceased (*tahlil dan doa arwah*) at the Malay Club later in the evening, and to thank those people who had played a role in the afternoon's proceedings.

Among those who received specific thanks were the reporters from London who were described as 'friends of Puan Zaharah'. This was a reference to Zaharah Othman who, as has been considered in previous chapters, was the Malaysian journalist who had written more than anyone about Malay people in Britain, including ex-seamen. She was also the person who had first informed me of the riverside commemoration service, in an email message that I received while in Singapore. Another message concerning the 47th anniversary of independence celebrations that had been sent around to Malay-speaking circle members, and which was forwarded to me by Sharidah, noted that the event would be covered in the Malaysian as well as the local media. Zaharah Othman was unable to attend the event herself but her husband was among the group of Malaysian reporters who had made the trip north from London for the day. He made a video recording while a young Malay woman took photographs. Their very presence at the event serves as evidence of Malaysian interest in Malay diaspora that was considered in more detail in Chapter 5. Different combinations of subgroups of the community lined up patiently in front of the memorial for the cameras, and the chance to feature in *Berita Harian* (a Malay-language daily newspaper)[8] or on the Malaysian television channel TV3. Mat Nor, looking down from the memorial as if from the deck of a ship, led enthusiastic

Figure 8.1 Independence day at Pier Head. Photograph by the author.

cries of '*Mer-de-ka, Mer-de-ka, Mer-de-ka*'. Then it was time to eat packed lunches prepared by Malay-speaking circle members, and paid for with the MSA's Community Chest funds.

Many of the photographs taken on that day, by professional Malaysian reporters and photographers, by diverse participants in the event and also by me, were well suited to picturing a fundable cultural community. Most of the female Malaysian students who attended, as well as their children, were dressed in traditional Malay clothing. Some of my own photographs captured these colourfully dressed women and children against the backdrop of the Three Graces – the Royal Liver Building, the Cunard Building and the Port of Liverpool Building – the most prominent landscape legacies of Liverpool's maritime world city past and still the city's 'establishing shot' (Hall, 2003: 194) (see Figure 8.1). Not only could such photographs be said to represent Malays as part of the World in One City but they also provided imagery that would (as the community development manager working with the MSA put it in interview) 'look nice' on annual reports, enhance community visibility and so increase possibilities for securing further funds in the future.[9] The photograph that made it into the local press the following day focused instead on the faces of the brightly coloured, flag-waving Malaysian children beside the memorial.[10] Nonetheless, the very inclusion of such an image in the *Liverpool Daily Post* was a sign that the first *Merdeka* celebration had been a success in realizing one of the objectives stated in the MSA's Community Chest application: 'to act as a platform and showcase for the Malaysian and Singapore community' within the city.[11]

Performing Malay-ness on Jermyn Street

Staying on in Liverpool after the *Merdeka* day celebrations, I used the days in the lead-up to the Malaysian food festival and children's street party to research the origins of the men listed on the memorial in the archives at the Liverpool Central Library, and to get acquainted with Jermyn Street and Liverpool 8 more widely. On one occasion, I parked my car at the end of Jermyn Street, near to the Malay Club, and then walked back towards the junction with Granby Street. Only two of the houses on that southwestern section of Jermyn Street appeared to be in use – the Malay Club at number 7 and also, next to it, 5 Jermyn Street where the widow and son of the first president of the club, Bahazin Bin-Kassim, were still living.[12] The first building on the opposite side of Granby Street had a large, gaping hole in the roof. What I at first thought was graffiti across the side of that building was a sign indicating the recent evacuation of another business: the words 'Ken's Barber Shop moved' were accompanied by big arrows pointing to the other end of Granby Street. The light on this clear day seemed to accentuate the faded grandeur of the urban landscape and I took photographs along the length of Granby Street. There were very few people out and about and I went into one of the few remaining shops in order to try to talk to someone. I asked about the Malay presence in the area, but the South Asian shop owner did not seem to be in the mood for conversation. As I walked back towards Jermyn Street, I was stopped by two men who asked me what I was doing. I mumbled something about researching the Malay community, to which one of them replied, 'This is Somali territory.' I apologized and hurried back to my car.

I later learned that there is a sizeable Somali community in Liverpool 8 and that the Somali Community Centre is also on Granby Street, only a stone's throw from the Malay Club. There are also some important similarities between the histories of migration and mobility associated with Somali and Malay(sian) communities. First, like various other minority ethnic groups in Liverpool 8 – the Yemeni (Halliday, 2010), the Kru (Frost, 1999), the Nigerian and the West Indian communities (Uduku, 2003) – both the Malays and Somalis have their origins in trade links between Britain and former colonial territories and protectorates. Many Somali men enlisted as merchant seamen in the British protectorate of Aden (Lawless, 1994) and, as will be considered later in this chapter, in some cases found work on ships that also included Malay crew. A second similarity between the two communities concerns a significant generational divide between distinct waves of migrants/ sojourners. As has been noted, Malay(sian)s who have moved to Liverpool include both ex-seamen who arrived during late colonial times and a subsequent, postindependence generation of Malaysians and their families who came to the city to study or for professional work. The Somali community is divided between a generation of ex-merchant seamen, on the one hand, and refugees who escaped famine in the 1980s and civil war in the 1990s, on the other. A key contrast between the two communities, however, is that while the later generation of Somalis concentrated residentially in Liverpool 8, the same is not true of the families of Malaysian students and professionals (and, as has been noted in previous chapters, many of the original seafaring generation of Malays and their family members also dispersed to other parts of the city from the 1960s). It is no surprise, then, that the Somali community in and around Granby Street in 2004 was much more visible – sustaining several clubs, groups and associations – than the Malays (Uduku, 2003).[13]

Despite the Somali community's significant numerical advantage and apparent territorial claims, during the afternoon of Saturday 4 September the small section of Jermyn Street on the southwestern side of Granby Street which was home to Liverpool's Malay Club became Malay(sian) space. More than 100 people with a range of connections to the *alam Melayu* (the Malay world region in Southeast Asia) gathered on the street outside the club. Although the majority were Malaysian students and members of their families, there was certainly a larger proportion of locally born descendants of Malay seamen at the Malaysian food festival and children's street party than had attended the riverside *Merdeka* commemoration service earlier in the week. Large Malaysian flags were suspended at the entrance to this section of Jermyn Street and above the front door of the Malay Club. The additional inclusion of many St George's crosses and several Union Jack flags among the street decorations made for an Anglo-Malaysian effect, but the only evidence of Singapore in the landscape was in the small MSA sign above the front door entrance to 7 Jermyn Street. Many people in the crowd, especially Malaysian women and children, were dressed in brightly coloured clothing. Malay Club (and, thereby the MSA) president Mat Nor had also entered into the traditional festive spirit, wearing a bright red Malay *baju* (shirt) and a black *songkok* (rimless cap). Retro Malay music was blasted from a sound system so that even in aural terms, the space seemed to have been (re)claimed as Malay(sian) territory.

The formal proceedings began with an introduction by the new *penghulu* (head) of the Malaysian student group, the Malay-speaking circle, who happily announced that all of the food was being provided for 'free' (having been paid for out of the Community Chest grant). He then handed over to Mat Nor, who gave a brief speech of welcome from in front of the entrance to the Malay Club. The newly painted bright red steps contrasted starkly with neighbouring buildings where accumulated historical layers of thick paint could be seen as it peeled from walls and railings. Yet with so many people present and with rays of sunshine breaking through the canopy of the tree-lined street, it was possible to overlook the visible dereliction of the neighbourhood. Chairs had been placed along the pavement on the side of the street where the Malay Club was located and this is where the small group of ex-seamen was seated. Further towards the end of the street on the same side of the road, a group of male students and young professionals from Malaysia were grilling satay sticks on a barbeque. On the other side of the road, Malaysian women stood along the length of two long trestle tables on which sat an impressive variety of Malay food (see Figure 8.2). There

Figure 8.2 Street party on Jermyn Street. Photograph by the author.

was thus something of a gendered spatial divide, although many participants, myself included, wandered between the culinary offerings on either side of the street.

As had been the case at the riverside commemoration service, Malaysian children provided the main entertainment at the street party. Around 20 of them gathered as a choir and, without accompaniment this time, gave a rather lacklustre rendition of the Malaysian national anthem. A key difference of this second cultural event was the presence of a significant number of children who were not Malaysian, but Liverpool-born descendants – mostly third generation – of Malay ex-seamen and British women. The choice of Malay-language Malaysian songs meant that Liverpool-born children were not able to participate actively in the choir. In my video recording of the event, a small boy wandered up to the Malaysian children in the choir, looking like he wanted to be part of the action. But the boy turned away again when he realized that he did not know the words or even understand what was being sung. Of course, Malaysian students who led the organization of the street party had not deliberately excluded this child, but his inability to join in serves as an example of how Malaysianized proceedings could be experienced as exclusionary by Liverpool-born descendants of Malay ex-seafarers.[14]

Some of the subsequent activities on the agenda were more inclusive. One was a drawing competition divided into three age categories, each with a specific theme. I agreed to be the judge for the competition with some reluctance, not wishing to offend all of those children who did not ultimately win a prize at the beginning of my first period of fieldwork in Liverpool. The category of over-10-year-olds was the most keenly contested, with children asked to create pictures that depicted Malaysian national day. Among the entrants who made it to my top three was the British granddaughter of an ex-seaman, whose picture featured a smiling *kerbau* (buffalo). The other two prize-winning entries were by Malaysian children. Perhaps not surprisingly, their pictures reproduced mainstream Malaysian nationalist imaginings: the struggle between Hang Jebat and Hang Tuah;[15] and Malaysia as a population of diverse people and cultures. Introduced as 'Dr Tim Bunnell from Singapore', I also judged and awarded prizes for a children's fancy dress competition. Some of the more memorable competitors included a pom-pom dancer, a sabre-wielding ghost and Spiderman. A Terengganu fisherman was the competitor whose performance seemed to me to relate most closely to the Malaysian theme of the day, although the one Liverpool-based ex-seaman who hailed from that east coast state – Ngah Musa – was not present at the event.

It was not only children who made extraordinary efforts with their attire on that Saturday afternoon on Jermyn Street in September 2004.

One young Malay woman from Malaysia whom I got to know well during a subsequent period of fieldwork attended the street party wearing a *tudung* (headscarf). While there is nothing out of the ordinary about this way of dressing for Malaysian Malay women in general – indeed, adoption of the *tudung* veil is so widespread as to have become part of the default mode of female attire among Malays in Islamized Malaysia (Stivens, 2006) – it was very unusual for this particular woman. Indeed, although most of the other Malaysian women at the street party ordinarily wore a headscarf in public in Liverpool, on no other occasion did I see my friend wear one. In the wake of the riverside commemoration service held on the preceding Tuesday, all of the Malaysians who had been invited to the street party were aware that the *Merdeka* events were being filmed and photographed for audiences back in Malaysia. And so a woman who did not ordinarily wear a *tudung* in Liverpool decided to do so during the street party – a performance of Malay femininity that she considered would be acceptable to her mother-in-law who may have come to see the television footage or photographs back in Malaysia. Performances of Malay-ness on Jermyn Street, Liverpool 8, were thus transnationally inflected – in line with the disciplinary moral gaze of the Malaysian homeland.

Community Conflict and Urban Interculturalism

The only audiences, or potential audiences, which I was aware of while participating in the *Merdeka* events were city authorities and charitable organizations that held the funds that may have made possible similar – perhaps even more ambitious – community events in the future. There is no doubt that the street party, no less than the riverside commemoration service, provided ample resources for picturing a suitably colourful, exotic and smiling segment of multicultural Liverpool. However, behind the smiles – and largely unknown to me until interviews and conversations carried out in the weeks after the street party – were some complex conflicts and community politics. Organizational squabbles, ostensibly over disbursement of funds, reflected broader tensions, particularly between British descendants of ex-seamen on one side and Malaysian students on the other. As was detailed in the previous chapter, in formulating the *Merdeka* events, Malaysian students assumed the role of defining what counted as Malay(sian) and were able to construct and perform this in ways that easily mapped onto the World in One City. A problem arising from this was that official Malaysian definitions of Malay-ness excluded most descendants of former Malay seafarers in Liverpool from even being considered 'Malay'. Malays are officially understood to form the largest of the three main 'communities' in Malaysia and are constitutionally defined as Muslim, Malay-speaking and people who habitually practise Malay custom or *adat* (Nagata, 1974). Communal categories are largely taken for granted, such that most Malaysians (ethnic Chinese and Indians as well as Malays) instinctively know and perform their respective (communal) customs, especially during culturally significant dates that punctuate the national calendar. As was considered in Chapters 5 and 6, Islam has come to feature increasingly prominently in everyday as well as official constructions of Malay-ness in Malaysia. Yet most descendants of Malay ex-seamen in Liverpool are not Muslims.[16] This, along with their inability in most cases to speak more than a handful of Malay words, makes them straightforwardly non-Malay in the evaluations of most Malaysians.[17]

Some of the ex-seamen themselves expressed concern with the Malaysianization of the *Merdeka* events. It is worth recalling that the ex-seafaring generation includes men who are not from territories which today form part of Malaysia, originating instead from what is now the separate nation state of Singapore or even, in a smaller number of cases, from Indonesia. Even those who do originate from places within the boundaries of present-day Malaysia left prior to its formation in 1963 and subsequent separation from Singapore (in 1965). In addition, those who were born in the Straits Settlements (Penang and Malacca in today's Malaysia, as well as Singapore) were legally British subjects before they ever arrived in the British Isles (Bunnell, 2007). Ex-seamen's geographical imaginations of the *alam Melayu* are therefore very different from those of Malaysian students, many of whom have only ever known a map of Southeast Asia in which Malaysia and Singapore are discrete political entities (and nation states with often antagonistic geopolitical relations – Chapter 6). Mat Nor expressed concern that Malaysian students were actively downplaying the significance of Singapore to Liverpool's Malay community and to the history of the Malay Club which had even been officially registered as home to the MSA.[18] Shortly after the Community Chest-funded *Merdeka* events, he even requested that I bring a Singapore flag the next time I came to Liverpool. This was an addition that he thought would make the decor and symbolism of 7 Jermyn Street reflect more accurately the origins of people who had established the Malay Club there. Ironically, given the political moment that was being celebrated in the *Merdeka* celebrations, Mat Nor described a longer history of Malaysian student involvement in the club – including efforts together with ex-seaman Ngah Musa to place the MSA under the umbrella of the Liverpool Muslim Society – as a threat to the 'independence' of the MSA.[19]

Looking back at the two *Merdeka* events in the light of subsequent interviews and research, it is clear that the anxiety felt by Mat Nor and some of the other ex-seamen associated with the MSA resulted from their position as community intermediaries – between their own British-born descendants on one side and Malaysian students on the other. It may be suggested, therefore, that the events were simply flawed or failed exercises in community building. Although they generated images of a community-in-action, the politics of the organization of the riverside commemoration service and the street party did little to suggest that collaboration between Malaysian students and Liverpudlians with Malay ancestors would extend beyond the lives of the first-generation ex-seamen. Rather than merely contrasting such conflictual realities with glossy representations of a Malaysian community in Liverpool, however, it is worth noting that wider critiques of multiculturalism have highlighted a tendency to trade in essentialist and even romanticized notions of 'community'. The *Merdeka* events may be cast in a much more positive light in relation to what Steven Vertovec (2001) refers to as the 'new multiculturalism'. This acknowledges the problematically essentialist and bounded understandings of community that have conventionally been associated with multiculturalism, while also recognizing that critiques of multiculturalism can serve to feed a resurgence of conservative, assimilationist political agendas in Britain and elsewhere (Mitchell, 2004; Bunnell, 2008). Multiculturalism is thus recuperated through combining recognition of cultural difference in the public sphere with an insistence on the fluidity of culture and the multiple and overlapping nature of cultural boundaries (Runnymede Trust, 2000) – or, what Bhiku Parekh (2006: 350) refers to as 'an interactionist rather than static or ghettoized view of multiculturalism'. This may be applied to the *Merdeka* events in Liverpool in that they brought together a diverse range of people, even while being strategically represented as a distinct segment of multicultural Liverpool for the benefit of funders, and in accordance with the categorical logics of wider structures of governance.

The composition of people who attended the commemoration service and especially the weekend street party made the events more than merely performances of a culturally homogeneous ethnic community. Participants included people united only by residence in Liverpool (ranging from overseas student sojourners to born and bred Liverpudlians) and some kind of connection to Southeast Asia (ranging from citizens of Malaysia to local people with seafaring Southeast Asian fathers and grandfathers whom they had never had the opportunity to meet). The wide visible variability of the crowd at the street party in particular emerged as a key theme in follow-up interviews and conversations with people whom I met at the *Merdeka* events – both Malaysian students and British descendants. The latter included 'white' suburban-dwelling descendants of seafarers who, in attending the street party, had ventured (back) to an inner-city site in which some said they would not ordinarily set foot. Not only was the event thus a performance of multicultural or cosmopolitan Liverpool that extended beyond non-white Others (cf. Alibhai-Brown, 2001), but it also provided moments when conventional cultural boundaries and identifications of various kinds were unsettled.

One sign of how what it meant to be Malay (and British) was radically opened in this momentary community-building space was my being asked (by both Malaysian students and British descendants) whether I was Malay or 'part Malay'. In my case, this was partly to do with my ability to converse in *bahasa Melayu* (the Malay language) and my knowledge of the Malay world as someone who has lived in that region for much of my adult life. But the wider point here is that in the time-space of the street party, even a 'white' person who did not have the cultural knowledge associated with my peculiar geographical biography – my brother, for example – could have 'passed' as Malay. The intertwining of Malay/Malaysian/English/British symbols and cultural elements meant that participants (myself included) shared a space of only partial familiarity, one conducive for cultural dialogue which may more properly be labelled 'intercultural' than multicultural (see Amin, 2002: 967). By bringing together people who would ordinarily consider themselves to be ethnoculturally different as part of a momentary quasi-community, the *Merdeka* events may be likened to the 'moments of cultural destabilization', described by Ash Amin (2002: 970) as 'offering individuals the chance to break out of fixed relations and fixed notions, and through this, to learn to become different through new patterns of social interaction'.

Connections across the most clearly evident dividing line in the tensions associated with the *Merdeka* event interactions – that between Malaysian students and British descendants of seafarers – may even be cast as socially and politically progressive. On the one hand, I have already noted how some of the remaining first-generation seafarers unwittingly became intermediaries between conflictual national groups. On the other hand, the events provided opportunities for intercultural connections to be established across national dividing lines. Examples included Malaysian students assisting Liverpool-born descendants to trace relatives in Malaysia and Singapore[20] as well as (ultimately unrealized) plans for a musical event involving both Malaysian students and young members of British families. Clearly, it was very difficult to track such relations – and *possible* relations – not least because of the variety of ways in which they developed (or broke down) following the exchange of phone numbers and email addresses at the street party on Jermyn Street. What is not in doubt, however, is that the *Merdeka* celebrations extended possibilities for forms of 'urban interculturalism' (Amin, 2002: 967) which are not nationally bounded. The two Community Chest-funded events enabled white British citizens and noncitizen student sojourners to find a place – albeit momentarily – in multicultural Liverpool.

For all the positive interpersonal, intercultural social relations and the fact that the events provided visual resources to satisfy the more conventional multicultural imaginings of funding agencies, the organizational momentum that had made possible the Community Chest funding application was lost in the squabbles between Malaysian students and British descendants of ex-seafarers. Wednesday lunch meetings at the Malay Club continued over the subsequent three months that I stayed in Liverpool in 2004, and were still attended by a small number of British descendants and Malaysian students, as well as some of the dwindling number of healthy ex-seamen. Despite this, it is revealing that the only subsequent gathering during that period which matched the *Merdeka* events in terms of the number and diversity of people in attendance was a funeral. The death of Buang Ahdar, an ex-seaman whom I never had the chance to meet, made me realize that the only time when the 'community' ordinarily came together was to mark the death of one of the remaining first-generation ex-seafarers who formed the main intermediaries between their British-born descendants and fellow *alam Melayu*-born Malaysian students. In retrospect, it became clear to me that the beginning of my fieldwork in Liverpool marked the high point of the quasi-community that had been assembled through the *Merdeka* celebrations.

Death in the Place of Community

Buang Ahdar's funeral on 22 September 2004 began and ended on Jermyn Street. From other ex-seamen at the Malay Club during that morning, I learned that Guy (as Buang Ahdar had been known) was from Singapore and had never married. He had been living in a nursing home and died from lung and stomach cancer. I walked with Hashim, himself an ex-seaman from Singapore, over to the Al-Rahma mosque on nearby Hatherley Street (see Figure 1.1). As the men inside the mosque paid their last respects to Guy, I waited outside and talked with the widow of another deceased Malay seafarer who had known Guy well. This and subsequent conversations suggested that Guy had led a very colourful life even by the standards of fellow ex-seamen. In the 1980s, for example, he had been involved in running a notorious nightclub in Liverpool 8.[21] It was only much more recently that Guy had (re)discovered Islam, began attending Friday prayers at the Al-Rahma mosque and even went on a pilgrimage to the Holy Land. Expenses for his *hajj* had been borne by a Libyan friend – one-time owner of the nightclub where Guy had worked – who was also reported to have covered part of the cost of the funeral.[22] Perhaps because of Guy's religiosity in later life, scores of men, most of them not Malay, had gathered at the mosque and boarded a double-decker bus that had been hired for the trip to the cemetery. I sat downstairs next to a henna-bearded Somali man who had worked on board ship with Malays and who proceeded to demonstrate to me his knowledge of the Malay language (*bahasa Melayu*). The bus headed to Everton cemetery. At the Muslim section, the coffin was lowered into a hole that someone whispered to me had cost £1,000 to excavate, while prayers were recited. Members of the ethnically diverse crowd from Al-Rahma mosque, which included several other Malay ex-seamen, then took turns in using spades to place earth onto the top of Guy's coffin before the job of filling the grave was completed by a mechanical digger.

While Malays formed part of the Al-Rahma mosque's congregation, it would be wrong to cast the group of men whose lives are central to my study as merely a subset of a larger Muslim community in the city. Malay ex-seafarers in Liverpool ranged from men who had been practising Muslims throughout their lives to those who had not stepped foot in a mosque for decades and who claimed to have no intention of ever doing so again. This points to a recurring theme of this book, namely, how diverse individual life experiences and associated geographies defy group generalization. Nonetheless, among Malay ex-seamen in Liverpool it is possible to identify a prevailing trend towards increased religiosity in later life. With few exceptions, Islam did not feature prominently in youthful seafaring life stages or in later onshore family life.[23] However, as in the case of Guy, stories of secular pasts – at sea or onshore or both – were often narrated in the context of wider life histories which also included a shift to – or back to – faith in later years.[24] For any given individual, it is impossible to ascertain the extent to which such a transition may be attributed to a general tendency towards increased religiosity associated with heightened awareness of mortality in old age; the growth of Islam in Britain in general or Liverpool in particular; and/or a more specifically Malay/Malaysian Islamic revivalism transmitted to Liverpool via ex-seamen's return trips to Southeast Asia (Chapter 6) as well as through the travels of Islamized ethnic Malay Malaysian students in the opposite direction. All these factors are pertinent but the point here is that their relative significance inevitably varies from one individual to the next.

Variation in the degree of religiosity among living and deceased ex-seamen made for complex and often conflictual deliberations over appropriate burial arrangements and the relative place of the mosque and the Malay Club in funeral proceedings. It may be recalled from Chapter 4 that support for the construction of the Al-Rahma mosque was galvanized in the 1960s after a Malay ex-seaman, Osman Eusof, died and was 'buried as a non-Muslim' (Khan-Cheema, 1979: 48). Another Malay man was said to have been cremated in Liverpool during the same period, something which is categorically disapproved of in Islam.[25] The growth of the Al-Rahma mosque congregation and the fact it came to include increasing numbers of Malays (both ex-seamen and students) meant that cremation of Malay ex-seamen was much less likely to have occurred in subsequent decades. At the same time, rising religiosity among Malays in the city (again, among students as well as some of the remaining ex-seamen), and the fact that a growing proportion of them were Malaysian citizens who found it difficult to conceive of being Malay without also being Muslim, also fomented new forms of conflict over perceptions of appropriate burial practice. Once again, such conflict largely mapped onto a division between British descendants of Malay seamen on one side and Malaysian students on the other. In general, the former considered it important that the burial wishes of individual Malay men be respected, even if that meant being buried as a Christian; the latter considered that Malays are, by (Malaysian constitutional) definition, Muslims and that they should be buried accordingly.[26]

Ex-seamen were not so much caught in the middle of this contest as themselves divided. At the lunch gathering that followed Guy's burial, a handful of ex-seamen discussed how Malays that they knew of had been buried as Catholics, in one case with a cross on his chest.[27] In another case, a Malay man had been buried in the Catholic section of a graveyard because he had requested to be laid to rest in the same grave as his wife. This man was also said to have given clear instructions that after he died he wanted his friends to buy a large bottle of whisky to share at the Malay Club.[28] That wish went unfulfilled because, in contrast to the late 1980s, whisky drinking had come to be seen as inappropriate for 7 Jermyn Street. As was noted in Chapter 5, religious Malay ex-seamen interviewed by a visiting Malaysian journalist outside the Al-Rahma mosque in 1989 – Haji Talib and Haji Musa – referred to the Malay Club in the past tense as a place of social interaction. By the time I began fieldwork in Liverpool 14 years later, it was 'un-Islamic' Malays who had come to feel out of place at 7 Jermyn Street, although some of them still came back when there was a death in the community. The lunch at the Malay Club that followed Guy's burial attracted even more of the remaining ex-seamen than had attended the *Merdeka* events – including those at opposite ends of the spectrum of religiosity – as well as several British descendants, and a much larger number of Malaysian students.

Whether they were buried as Muslims or not, the death of each ex-seafaring Malay meant one less person to act as an intermediary between Malaysian and Liverpool-born 'Malays'.[29] In addition, even those ex-seamen who were still alive – numbering around 20 men at the beginning of my fieldwork in 2004 – were becoming increasingly frail and so less and less capable of performing intermediary or organizational roles at the Malay Club. Mat Nor had by then served as president for a decade, devoting considerable energy to the maintenance of 7 Jermyn Street and, most importantly, preparing lunch on Wednesdays. The squabbles that surrounded organization of the *Merdeka* events, layered on top of existing enmities between different groups of ex-seamen, seemed to sap his enthusiasm for the leadership position. Although the lunch meetings continued during my fieldwork in 2004, there was no further serious talk of community collaboration. When the day-to-day running of the Malay Club became too much for Mat Nor in late 2005, there was no obvious successor from among the remaining ex-seafaring men. Leadership of the club (and thereby also, officially, of the MSA) thus passed for the first time to someone with no direct connection to seafaring. Wan Mohamed Rosidi Wan Hussain was a Liverpool-based Malay man from Malaysia who significantly, was *not* part of the group of Malaysian students who had worked with or as part of the MSA in organizing the *Merdeka* events. As a young professional, family man, Wan Rosidi understandably did not have the time that Mat Nor had invested in the day-to-day running of the Malay Club. Although the fact that Wan Rosidi worked as a surveyor initially raised hopes that he would be well placed to oversee improvements to the physical condition of the 7 Jermyn Street building, it soon became evident that he saw the most important aspect of his position as overseeing Islamic funeral arrangements when community members passed away. The funerals of ex-seamen that gathered a 'community' at the Malay Club also marked its gradual demise as a place of social interaction.

Wednesday lunchtime meetings continued but, by mid-2006, were being held only on a monthly basis. It was symptomatic of the post-seafaring transition – and imminent death of the established place of the Malay community in Liverpool – that the biggest event of 2007 that bore the name of the Merseyside Malaysian and Singapore Community Association was not held at 7 Jermyn Street. Rather, an evening gathering that was arranged to coincide with the opening of an exhibition chronicling the life and works of Sir Thomas Stamford Raffles was held at the Liverpool Central Library.[30] The attraction of this major national exhibition was trumpeted in the local press as a 'coup for the city' and the opening night gave a handful of Malay ex-seamen a chance to meet up. However, such a one-off gathering was no substitute for regular social interaction at the club. My own fieldwork trips to Liverpool after 2005 increasingly centred on sites other than the Malay Club. In the case of Hari Raya (Eid al-Fitr) celebrations in 2006, the locus was the two residential tower blocks, Crete and Candia, where several Malaysian student families were renting apartments.[31] A handful of ex-seamen joined the flow of Malaysians visiting successive 'open houses' across the two towers. More generally, 182 Boaler Street, then home to Sharidah Sharif and family, became a hub for Malaysian visitors to (as well as for students based in) the city.[32] A final, very important set of research sites, were cafés in Liverpool city centre where Fadzil Mohamed met with members of his family for breakfast on Saturday mornings. During my longest continuous period of fieldwork in Liverpool in 2008, it was through NoshNCoffee café at the Clayton Square shopping centre that I was kept abreast of any 'new memories' that Farida Chapman and Paul Fadzil had gleaned from their father, and of any news regarding other Malay ex-seafarers in his friendship network.

By the time I began six months of sabbatical leave in Liverpool in March 2008, 7 Jermyn Street had ceased to function as a club and had been boarded up following a series of break-ins. The last time that it had opened had been during the previous December, for a gathering that followed the death of Ngah Musa.[33] The building had deteriorated to a condition that fitted in with the more general state of dereliction on Jermyn Street and surrounding streets. A report for the London-based Empty Homes Project described arriving on neighbouring Cairns Street (see Figure 1.1) on a dark winter evening in 2007 as 'like wandering onto the set of an apocalyptic movie'.[34] As on Jermyn Street, derelict properties on Cairns Street far outnumbered those still occupied and residents spoke of 'the slow death of a once thriving community'. While according to the Liberal Democrat councillor Frank Doron, this process had 'happened naturally over a number of years', people who continued to live on Cairns Street alleged a more intentional running down of the area to allow for demolition and gentrified redevelopment.[35] Doron is reported to have claimed that, 'I am not one for letting the bulldozers *run amok* [emphasis added] but this is about listening to what communities themselves feel is the way forward.' Of course, for all the important battles being fought by residents' associations across the city – including in the Granby Street area – in a context where houses, clubs and whole neighbourhoods were being boarded up, there would be little in the way of a community to be listened to before the bulldozers were summoned to unleash their peculiarly Malay mode of destruction.[36]

The overwhelming majority of former residents had (been) moved out of the neighbourhood and even the building that housed the Granby Residents' Association had been deemed structurally unsafe and so was forced to close. Nonetheless, a determined group of remaining residents continued to meet at a local school to resist demolition and promote refurbishment of the local housing stock.[37] Hazel Tilley was among this group and, in interview in August 2008, this resident of Cairns Street who had been living in the area for more than 30 years also recalled having gone to buy curry from the 'sticky and smoky' Malay Club in previous decades. There was no longer any such option 'around the corner' on Jermyn Street. Nor was there any specifically Malay community equivalent to the Granby Residents' Association. In the case of the Malays, the absence of a local community voice was attributable, in part, to the dispersal of families from Liverpool 8 over several decades of 'urban regeneration' that I have examined in previous chapters, and partly to the dwindling number of first-generation ex-seamen. In addition, however, closure of the Malay Club less than four years after the Community Chest-funded party that had been held on Jermyn Street meant that dispersed members of a would-be Liverpool Malay 'community' now had no meeting place to return to in Liverpool 8. As Fadzil's daughter Farida put it during one of our Saturday breakfast cafe meetings in the city centre in 2008, 'I feel now that we're losing touch with the Malay community because there's nowhere to go.'[38] Number 7 Jermyn Street, a place of lively community activity in 2004, was closed and boarded up during Liverpool's year as European capital of culture.

Notes

1 The events also proved to be an excellent way of establishing contact with a diverse range of potential informants whom they brought together.

2 As noted in the previous chapter, the community development manager who worked with the MSA to secure the Community Chest funding spoke of the importance of 'playing the ethnic dance'. Interview, Liverpool, 4 October 2004.

3 See Chapter 3 for consideration of the lives (and deaths) of some such men.

4 The tradition of seamen from Malacca working on British steamships was considered in Chapter 2. One Malay seaman from Johor who died during the Second World War was the father of Liverpool-born Teddy Lates, who attended the *Merdeka* event (see below).

5 See Chapter 4.

6 In Ronnie Bujang's case, see Chapter 3.

7 This discovery was made with help from the research team of a British television personality, Robert Kilroy-Silk, who apparently also lost his father

during the Second World War. Personal communication with Teddy Lates, Liverpool, 15 September 2004. Teddy participated in the unveiling of another, much smaller monument to 'Black Merchant Seamen' in Falkner Square Gardens, in Liverpool 8 in 1993. See 'Black Seamen', *Nerve,* 12 (Summer 2008), p. 22.

8 Zaharah Othman, 'Melayu England' [England Malays], *Berita Harian,* 3 September 2004.

9 Interview with Novas-Ouvertures community development manager, Liverpool, 7 October 2004.

10 'Children pay tribute to lost sailors', *Liverpool Daily Post,* 1 September 2004.

11 This is taken from the original Community Chest application material.

12 For coverage of the opening of the Malay Club under Bahazin's leadership, see Chapter 3.

13 I noted in Chapter 4 that, according to Mat Nor, Somali as well as 'black' community groups were the chief beneficiaries of new social funds that came to Liverpool 8 in the aftermath of the riots of 1981. In historical research carried out on Granby Street during the previous decade (1970s), Fred Halliday (2010: 50) refers to it as the 'Street of the Yemenis' on account of the number of Yemeni shopkeepers located there.

14 Similarly, Joan Higgins (daughter of Ben Youp) said that her granddaughter wanted to join in with the singing and came to feel linguistically left out. Interview, Liverpool, 12 September 2004.

15 These are two warriors from Malacca who are central to a folk story, known to all Malaysian children, which affirms loyalty to traditional leadership as the pre-eminent virtue.

16 There are some important exceptions, including Haji Talib whose three daughters all married Muslim men – two from Yemen and one a Malay engineer working with the Malaysia International Shipping Corporation. See Ahmad Rodzi Yaakob, 'Melayu Liverpool tidak pernah lupakan tanahair' [Malays in Liverpool never forgot the homeland], *Berita Harian,* 12 July 1989; and see Chapter 5.

17 This applies not only to Malaysians who are themselves (classified as) 'Malays'. It is worth recalling from Chapter 5 the comments of Tan Chian Khai (CK), who studied in Liverpool in the early 1970s and subsequently worked for Telekom Malaysia in South Africa. CK and his wife, Rosalind, were ethnic Chinese Malaysians but considered that their fluency in *bahasa Malaysia* (the formalized version of the Malay language used in Malaysia) made them in some ways 'more Malay' than the so-called 'Malays' of South Africa. As CK would have been well aware, however, Islam was the pre-eminent marker of Malay-ness in Malaysia. Interview, Kuala Lumpur, 25 February 2008.

18 As was considered in Chapter 5, Mat Nor said, for example, that he had 'caught' Malaysian students trying to hide Singapore flags and logos when taking pictures in the clubhouse. Interview, Liverpool, 29 September 2004.

19 Interview, Liverpool, 29 September 2004.

20 Malaysian students and their families (some of whom travelled regularly between Manchester and Kuala Lumpur international airports) are an

important source of knowledge for descendants wishing to explore Southeast Asian routes (and roots).

21 Guy was also one of the three men that Singapore journalist Dewani Abbas met at the Malay Club in 1989, as mentioned in Chapter 5. See also: 'Tetap Melayu walau di bumi "Mat Saleh"', *Berita Minggu*, 3 October, 1989. She described him as looking 'rugged' (she uses the English term) in his denim jacket and dark glasses.

22 Interview with JJ, Liverpool, 3 September 2004.

23 An example of one exception is in recollections of the Youp family's boarding house on Upper Huskisson Street in Chapter 3.

24 This is certainly the case for Fadzil Mohamed, for example, whose increased religiosity after visiting Malaysia was considered in Chapter 6, as well as for Haji Ngah Musa (Musa), one of the two Malay men that the Malaysian journalist Ahmad Rodzi Yaakob met at the Al-Rahma mosque in 1989. Ahmad Rodzi Yaakob 'Melayu Liverpool tidak pernah lupakan tanahair' [Malays in Liverpool never forgot the homeland], *Berita Harian*, 12 July 1989; and see Chapter 5.

25 Interview with Fadzil Mohamed, Liverpool, 2 August 2006.

26 This had diasporic resonances that extended to Malaysia. When Joanne Higgins visited Malaysia in 2004, she found that it was very important to her relatives in Malacca that her grandfather, Youp bin Baba, had been buried as a Muslim. Interview, Liverpool, 12 September 2004.

27 Notes from conversation at 7 Jermyn Street, 10 October 2004.

28 Notes from conversation with Jaafar Mohamad, 10 October 2004.

29 The significance of this social positioning was reinforced to me back at the Malay Club when the British daughter of one ex-seaman described the students as 'parasitical and self-interested'.

30 As was reported in the *Liverpool Daily Post*, Raffles is best known as the supposed founder of Singapore. The 'Raffles: Spice of Life' display comprised material held by the British Library. 'Raffles coup for the city', *Liverpool Daily Post*, 9 August 2007, p. 3.

31 Referencing the much more famous (Petronas) twin towers in Malaysia which form part of the Kuala Lumpur City Centre, Crete and Candia were together known by students as KMCC (*Kampung Melayu Crete Candia*).

32 It was here that I got to meet former students who had experienced Liverpool during the Toxteth riots (and who had attended the Malay Club in earlier eras), and was able to forge links with others who had moved back to Malaysia.

33 Terengganu-born Musa was the man whose death was mentioned to Fadzil Mohamed during his 2008 trip to Malacca, which was recounted in Chapter 6.

34 Ciara Leeming, 'Low demand project update: Toxteth regeneration', *The Empty Homes Agency: Monthly News Bulletin*, February 2007, http://www.emptyhomes.com/documents/bulletin/feb07.doc (accessed 11 July 2008; no longer available). The remainder of this paragraph is drawn from the same bulletin. The Empty Homes Agency is a charity founded in London in 1992 to provide homes for homeless people. It seeks to highlight the

waste of empty properties in England and to bring some of these back into use.

35 As one long-time resident of Cairns Street, Hazel Tilley, put it: 'To people here this feels like a deliberate attempt to demoralize us and drive us out so young professionals can move in.' Council and housing association homes were said to have been emptied and boarded up, preventing the market from operating normally and leaving areas to rot until residents had little choice but to move out.

36 Amok (sometimes spelled amuk or even amuck) is a word brought into the English language from *bahasa Melayu.* The notion of running amok has been mentioned in passing in previous chapters as a specifically Malay affliction in both British colonial and Singaporean postcolonial imaginings. See Chapter 2 on descriptions of the 'vicious attributes' of Malay-ness in theories about Jack the Ripper, and Chapter 6 on Lee Kuan Yew's fears about the actions of pro-UMNO Malays in Singapore after separation from Malaysia.

37 Interview with Hazel Tilley, Liverpool 4 August 2008.

38 Notes from conversation with Farida Chapman, Liverpool, 12 July 2008.

9

Conclusion

Catching up with Kuala Lumpur?

As a boy I walked past the colossal, grand and grimy buildings of Liverpool and wondered what went on there. Now, as buddleia bushes grew from rooftops, the question could only be, what used *to go on there?*

Du Noyer (2007: 174)

For the reasons that were elaborated in the last chapter, no grand Malay or Malaysian and Singapore celebrations were organized as part of Liverpool's year as European capital of culture in 2008. The person seemingly most concerned to reassemble the diverse 'community' that had been brought together at the 2004 *Merdeka* celebrations was me. I sought an opportunity to present the findings of my research to the people about whom I was writing, and to get their individual and collective feedback. The opportunity that arose was one that involved piggybacking on Kelab (Club) UMNO Liverpool plans for *Merdeka* day celebrations among Malaysian students and professionals in the city. These were held in the recently opened Contemporary Urban Centre on Saturday 30 August, the day before the 51st anniversary of Malaysian independence. This date fell conveniently towards the end of my planned six months of sabbatical leave in the city, but the collaboration meant that my presentation on 'Malays in Liverpool' formed part of a schedule that also included patriotic Malaysian singing and a poetry recital.

From World City to the World in One City: Liverpool through Malay Lives,
First Edition. Tim Bunnell.

Whatever my reservations about such collaboration, I was at least able to share findings from my research over the previous four years with ex-seamen (including some who had not been invited to the 2004 street party) and their family members whom I personally invited to the Contemporary Urban Centre, as well as with scores of Liverpool-based Malaysian students and professionals, and members of their families. The Malay Club and what used to go on there – the social gatherings and long-distance linkages that the club once anchored – featured prominently in my presentation and in some of the conversations which preceded and followed it. Number 7 Jermyn Street, however, remained closed for the whole time I was based in Liverpool and, indeed, throughout 2008. The alternative Contemporary Urban Centre venue for the 2008 *Merdeka* gathering had opened the previous year following adaptive regeneration of a collection of seven-storey, nineteenth-century warehouses which included a renovation phase known as the Buddleia Project on account of 'the extensive growth of this plant over the building exterior' (Wake and Lau, 2008: n.p.). Vaunted in one media report as 'Europe's biggest black and minority ethnic community centre', the Contemporary Urban Centre was located in the old south docks area on Greenland Street, the street where Johan Awang (the man who ran Liverpool's Malay Club in its first site) had lived in the 1950s (see Chapter 2; and Figure 3.1).[1]

The second building to house the Malay Club, at 7 Jermyn Street in Liverpool 8, had joined the swathes of abandoned buildings whose decaying exteriors and rooftops now provide homes for exotic vegetation – evidence in its own right, of course, of Liverpool's transoceanic historical connections. Was it merely coincidence that the place that had sustained social interaction among Liverpool-based Malay men for more than four decades closed in the lead-up to civic celebration of Liverpool's ethnocultural diversity in 2008? To what extent was the 'death' of the Malay Club more actively bound up with wider processes of urban 'regeneration' in the city? On the one hand, it is important to recall that Liverpool's Malay Club began on St James Road in the 1950s primarily as a space of homosocial interaction, and that sustenance of its membership was initially dependent upon Liverpool's position in maritime commercial networks that brought seafaring men from the *alam Melayu* to and through the city. Relocation of the club from its initial home occurred at the tail end of a maritime world city era that was well and truly over by the 1970s. In addition, although scores of (ex-)seamen formed families in Liverpool, the fact that even the second clubhouse on Jermyn Street began as a space predominantly for interaction among adult males meant that it afforded little opportunity for a potential second generation to develop individual or collective senses of Malay-ness. In other words, the demise of the Malay Club as a social institution was in large part attributable to the composition of its membership and the wider demise of Liverpool as a maritime centre that had once brought seafarers from the *alam Melayu* to and through the city.

On the other hand, successive rounds of urban redevelopment, including the contemporary period of culture-led regeneration, contributed to the unsustainability of Liverpool's Malay Club. In the first place, the wave of demolition in the 1960s, which included the St James Road vicinity of the club's initial location, reduced possibilities for social interaction among (people who might have come to identify as) second- or third-generation 'Malays'. Dispersal of the population to so-called overspill estates outside the city (Chapter 4) made it less likely that they would attend the Malay Club or meet people of shared Malay ancestry in Liverpool 8 in ways that had occurred in the south docks and Chinatown in earlier decades (Chapter 3). Second, people growing up in other parts of Liverpool or in the wider Merseyside region often came to hold mainstream, negative perceptions of inner-city Liverpool 8, especially after the 'Toxteth' riots of 1981. This resulted in their social as well as spatial disconnection from the Malay Club – the 'place of community' – and the people associated with it, both (ex-)seamen and students from Malaysia. Third, during the ongoing phase of culture-led urban regeneration, the city council had, at best, neglected and allegedly sought more deliberately to run down buildings on and around Granby Street. This served to make Liverpool 8 even less attractive to descendants of Malay seamen and to Malaysian students whose attendance at the club might otherwise have extended its life beyond the first generation.

Against this wider historical backdrop, conflicts arising within the quasi-community assembled through the 2004 *Merdeka* celebrations in Liverpool put paid to any further grant-getting 'Malaysian and Singapore' community partnerships. During 2008 incorporation of Liverpool-based Malays into capital of culture celebrations was either as consumers or as residents responsible for ensuring the city's positive reception among visitors. In Liverpool, as elsewhere, urban elites have long been concerned to fashion and image the(ir) city in ways that align with their commercial interests, and to convince diverse members of city populations that elite visions are in the interests of all (Philo and Kearns, 1993: 3). One of the oft-cited defining characteristics of neoliberal urbanism is the way in which city residents are made responsible for their individual and collective economic well-being (Leitner *et al.*, 2007: 4). In the case of the European capital of culture

2008 process, this included the civic obligation to put on a good show, to make Liverpool 'great for 2008', especially in terms of urban cleanliness.[2] The *Liverpool Echo* began a campaign to tackle 'the city's chronic litter problem', demanding a 'sea-change in attitudes from residents and businesses'. The 'manifesto for a cleaner city' sought to foster as well as to work through Liverpudlians' 'basic sense of pride in their city' – urging them to take 'personal responsibility' for the image of Liverpool. Rather than performing Malay-ness as part of the world in one city, then, Liverpool Malays contributed to the success of (multi)cultural celebrations in 2008 through more generic modes of civic conduct – being 'a binner not a sinner', as the *Liverpool Echo* put it.

What did Liverpool's status as European capital of culture in 2008 mean for the vicinity of the Malay Club and the varied communities associated with it? Liverpool 8, more than any other part of Liverpool, had for at least half of the past century embodied the demographic diversity upon which the 'world in one city' tag line is founded.[3] It is therefore significant that a report in the lead-up to Liverpool's bid for *Impacts08* – the impact study that was commissioned by the Liverpool Culture Company and carried out by the two leading universities in the city – showed that young people in Toxteth (known colloquially as 'Tocky') and Croxteth ('Crocky')[4] felt excluded from the European capital of culture and that their local areas were likewise excluded. An important distinction between the perceptions of youths in Tocky as compared to those from overwhelmingly white Crocky, however, concerned experiences of racism by 'Tockyheads' (people from Tocky) outside their own neighbourhood and especially in the city centre. This mapped onto geographies of exclusion from capital of culture initiatives given that the European capital of culture 2008 was associated in the minds of youths from Tocky with 'L1' (the Liverpool 1 postal code designation which denotes the city centre). One boy was even reported as saying that 'L1 is Liverpool, Toxteth's not in Liverpool' (Marne and Parker, 2006: 10). Such imaginings suggest that three decades of urban policy responses to the riots of 1981 had done little to overcome the racialized processes of exclusion in Liverpool 8 (Frost and Phillips, 2011).[5] The *Impacts08* report did not specify the ethnic, racial or religious identities of the young people who were interviewed in Tocky. What is clear, though, is that this territorially defined group considered high-profile city-centre developments to be a world apart from Liverpool 8.

The single biggest investment in the lead-up to the European capital of culture 2008 was indeed in the city centre, redevelopment of which was overseen by Britain's first urban regeneration company, Liverpool

Vision (Meegan, 2003). Rebranded as 'Liverpool 1' in November 2005, what began as the Liverpool Paradise Street development area was a £950 million retail-led project which was vaunted as city-centre 'regeneration' and as a sign of Liverpool's wider economic 'renaissance' (Parker and Garnell, 2006).[6] The 42-acre (17-hectare) site connects the waterfront to the city's existing main shopping thoroughfare (see Figure 1.1). A visit to the site by Queen Elizabeth II and the Duke of Edinburgh – who took part in 'the traditional Topping Out ceremony for one of the highest buildings in Liverpool 1'[7] in May 2008 – heightened anticipation of the public launch. Phase 1 opened to great fanfare a week later. The opening dominated the first three pages of the *Liverpool Echo* on 29 May, with headlines including 'Open all ours' and 'It's here, it's ours and it's open.' Liverpool 1 was also the talk of the archivists at the Merseyside Maritime Museum. I walked through the site one afternoon after the maritime archives closed and it all felt uncannily familiar. At a barbeque I attended two days later a young Malay woman from Malaysia who was working as a surveyor in Liverpool pinpointed the sense of *déjà vu* felt by those of us familiar with cities in Southeast Asia. Liverpool, as she put it, was finally 'catching up with Kuala Lumpur'.[8] At one level, this comment inverts the imagined geography of uneven development that partly motivated young Malay seafaring men to travel from what are today the nation states of Malaysia and Singapore to *Eropah* in the late colonial period, placing Kuala Lumpur at the leading edge of urban (or at least retail) development and relegating Liverpool to shopping centre laggard.[9]

The notion of Liverpool 'catching up' with Kuala Lumpur in this context may also be understood as a form of everyday urban comparativism. No doubt the fact that I have come to see it in this way has to do with the resurgence of comparative urban studies – especially relational forms of comparative urbanism (e.g. Nijman, 2007; Ward, 2010; Robinson, 2011) – in the decade during which I have been carrying out the research for this book. My Malay Routes project was framed in terms of relational geographies from the outset, considering constitutive commercial linkages and associated social networks or 'webs' between Liverpool and the *alam Melayu*. As detailed in Chapter 1, from very early on the project also became attentive to the territorial grounding or anchoring of those historically shifting constitutive connections, particularly at the Jermyn Street home of the Malay Club. However, although my research (and, indeed, this book) was not conceived in comparative terms, the Liverpool–Kuala Lumpur comparison made at the barbeque I attended in Liverpool in May 2008, together with the rise of relational comparativism in academic urban studies, invite comparative reflection.

Comparative, Conceptual and Methodological Returns

In addition to returning to the conceptual and methodological contributions that were set out in Chapter 1, in this concluding section I draw together some of the previously implicit comparative and relational aspects of the book and add others based on observations made during and since Liverpool's European capital of culture year. The intention is to foreground insights from the study that extend beyond the case of a single city. Clearly much of the material in the preceding chapters *is* specifically about Liverpool and I hope that the book will be judged to have added something to the already impressive body of scholarship on this compelling city. But this book also has wider implications for ways of seeing cities and doing urban research. Even a city such as Liverpool, which has so often been narrated as unique and incommensurable, can be analysed comparatively alongside a range of other cities, ostensibly similar or different (see Belchem, 2000). What is more, as a city which (rightly or wrongly) has been cast as an exception to national-scale processes of urban transformation, economic development and demographic change in Britain, and especially in England (Allt, 2008), Liverpool lends itself particularly well to less territorially confined comparative framings. Studies of Liverpool and its constitutive connections, then, not only benefit from comparative perspectives, but also speak to efforts to revitalize comparative urban studies through consideration of relations across diverse urban and regional contexts (Robinson, 2011).

To the extent that Liverpool has been considered comparatively, this has tended to concern shared or overlapping structural economic positioning with other cities. I have made mention of several such instances in this book. First, in terms of British cities that have experienced post-imperial and postindustrial economic decline, Liverpool has been referred to alongside Glasgow. I have examined how proponents of culture-led regeneration in Liverpool drew upon Glasgow as a model for turning around negative (external) perceptions of the city through urban reimaging and material transformation in the city centre (Chapter 7). Academics have, in turn, seen Glasgow as an important reference point for critique of Liverpool's neoliberal culture-led regeneration policies. Second, as a city with a legacy of demographic diversity from an era of commercial pre-eminence, Liverpool has found a place among historical 'immigrant gateway' cities (Price and Benton-Short, 2008). Here the key comparative reference point was Birmingham (Chapter 7). Although Liverpool and Birmingham have rather different histories of migration, authorities in both cities have sought to capitalize upon the 'multicultural' demographic legacy of their immigrant gateway pasts. This is partly about marketing ethnocultural diversity as an attraction – the world in one city – but also has to do with efforts to profit from diasporic linkages. Just as Birmingham's economic worlding strategies have included harnessing that city's diasporic networks of 'people, cultures, commodities, and knowledges' (McEwan *et al.*, 2008: 130), public–private partnerships in Liverpool have invested in historical associations and community links with economically booming parts of the world, especially in China. The shifting geographies of development underlying such city-level 'diaspora strategies' (Larner, 2007) invoke mappings of the new international division of labour through which Liverpool may be located in further structural categories, including 'shrinking cities' (see Couch *et al.*, 2005) and, as mentioned in Chapter 7, 'downscaled' cities (Glick Schiller and Çağlar, 2011: 8). The latter term emerges from efforts to specify a range of political economic positions for cities in an era of neoliberal global restructuring, each of which implies different roles and possibilities for migrant populations. Notions of Liverpool's exceptionalism are unsettled when it is placed in this kind of political economy category, alongside other cities mostly in deindustrializing western Europe and North America.

In shuttling between historical political economic transformations, on the one hand, and lived geographies of Malay Liverpool, on the other, my research has encompassed a much wider range of comparative imaginings and relational (re)framings. These have included (in Chapter 6) comparisons of bathroom facilities across time and space – seemingly more meaningful measures of geohistorical transformation in the minds of Malay ex-seamen than the spectacular infrastructural and real estate (re)developments that dominate most urban scholars' views of urban and regional change – as well as the notion of Liverpool 'catching up' with Kuala Lumpur mentioned above. At one level, such casual comparisons may be dismissed as having no wider (academic) significance or relevance to urban studies. But apart from providing examples of how ordinary people experience and inhabit changing city landscapes in relation to diverse urban elsewheres – surely something that should be of interest to all but the most resolutely positivist or narrowly political economic conceptions of urban studies – I argue that everyday and lived forms of comparison are resources for expanding urban scholars' comparative framings. A combination of the way in which scholars categorize cities (developmentally and regionally) and 'the often unarticulated assumption that no comparison is possible across cities that are regarded as substantially differentiated' has profoundly restricted comparative imaginings (Robinson, 2011: 4–5; and 2006). It is revealing that despite having carried out extensive research on Kuala Lumpur (and, to a lesser extent, on Singapore) prior to embarking on my Malay Routes project, I did not initially consider these cities in comparative relation to Liverpool. Even in terms of the most basic foundations for comparison through shared characteristics, both Kuala Lumpur (Chapter 7) and Singapore (see Chang, 1997), like Birmingham, were bound up in forms of multicultural marketing prior to 'world in one city' Liverpool. Neither Kuala Lumpur nor Singapore, of course, formed part of a New Labour Britain concerned to re-examine its ethnocultural and economic links with the world during the 1990s (Chapter 5). However, as I showed in Chapters 7 and 8, students from territories that were formerly part of 'plural society' colonial British Malaya were very well equipped to perform Malay(sian) 'culture' while sojourning in Liverpool. This brings into view a relational postcolonial urban dimension to community-led performances of multicultural Liverpool that might otherwise be read merely in terms of a wider national policy context or even as manifesting a certain stage in capitalism and associated forms of (entrepreneurial, neoliberal) urban governance (Harvey, 1989). Attending to, and taking seriously, ordinary people's practices, imaginings, memories and worlds of connection opens largely unexplored ways of seeing cities in comparative and constitutive relation to elsewhere.

Alongside and sometimes intertwined with the lived worlds of connection that I have foregrounded in this book have been relational geographies expressed in material urban transformation. New York City, for instance, was the inspiration for the high-rise refashioning of Liverpool's waterfront skyline in the form of the Royal Liver Building which became the tallest building in Europe in 1911 (Chapter 2). At the other end of the twentieth century, in my previous research in Malaysia I examined New York City-inspired efforts to mark Kuala Lumpur on world maps through the construction of the tallest twin towers in the world – the Petronas Twin Towers (see Bunnell, 2004a; and Chapter 6). Although the (re)construction and 'regeneration' of Liverpool city centre in the lead-up to 2008, in contrast, made no impression on world building height charts, marketing material for the Liverpool 1 project made reference to an architectural collaboration involving the 'world famous' César Pelli, who designed the Petronas Twin Towers in Kuala Lumpur.[10] Pelli was also architect of the fourth Ocean Financial Centre in Singapore, which was completed in 2011 (Seet, 2011). The fact that a 'starchitect' such as Pelli, among other global urban experts, operates in multiple cities around the world today is so well established in urban studies by now as to be quite unremarkable (Rimmer, 1991; Olds, 2001). I make mention of my multi-sited research encounters with César Pelli here for a rather different reason: to demonstrate another way in which cities that are held apart by conventional urban studies categorizations and area studies partitions of knowledge production may be drawn together in a relational urban frame. To me, this is one of the key, but surprisingly little remarked upon, strengths of political economy work on transnationally mobile urban policies and actors (Bunnell, 2015).

In that one of the acknowledged weaknesses or blind spots of the same strand of urban studies research is its 'presentism' (McFarlane, 2011), it is also worth noting that Pelli's new Ocean Financial Centre in Singapore stands on the 'Blue Funnel Corner' site of earlier Ocean buildings. In the case of the second Ocean Building (completed in 1923), Liverpool-based architects were initially engaged to ensure transfer of Liverpool's Manhattan-style design to colonial Singapore (Chapter 2). Other cities during the same period show material evidence of efforts to emulate aspects of the Liverpool skyline. A recent historical profile of the city has noted that from the late nineteenth century, 'mayors, architects and engineers from round the world looked to Liverpool and its urban area for inspiration' and that the Bund waterfront in Shanghai is evidence that Liverpool's Pier Head was considered 'worthy of emulation into the 1920s' (Sykes *et al.*, 2013: 306–7). Twenty-first-century urban regeneration in Liverpool may have brought a 'global architect' (McNeill, 2009), César Pelli, to the city as part of transnational circuits that also include Kuala Lumpur and Singapore, but maritime world city Liverpool was bound up in spatially extensive circulations of urban imagery, ideas, aspirations and expertise more than a century ago.

Not only does relational examination of world city Liverpool provide evidence of historical antecedents to today's transnational networks of urban expertise and associated material transformation, but forms of comparison across time in this book unsettle the presentism of much scholarly deployment of the term 'world city' (and, relatedly, the 'global city'). Although long historical usage of both terms is acknowledged in the literature (e.g. Sassen, 2001; Taylor, 2004), this nonetheless emphasizes how nominal antecedents obscure the emergence of a distinct new city type from the last decades of the twentieth century. In academic urban studies, a world/global city has come to be seen as one with global 'command and control' expertise and capabilities made possible by new forms of technology (Sassen, 1991), as part of the new international division of labour (Friedmann, 1986). Material in this book shows that, in both respects, there are some historical continuities as well as differences between Liverpool in the first half of the twentieth century and world/global cities as they are conceived in urban studies research today. First, not only did the second Ocean Building stand as material evidence that Liverpool's commercial reach extended into the *alam Melayu*, but the building also functioned as the regional headquarters of the Liverpool-controlled Ocean Steamship Company (Chapter 2). In Liverpool itself, India Buildings in Water Street became the coordinating centre of a worldwide network of shipping routes. In addition, just as the importance of spatial proximity among the specialized service firms that produce the capacity for contemporary global economic control is recognized in the urban studies literature, historical work on Liverpool has noted how shipowners and providers of other kinds of service functions to mercantile activity clustered on specific streets (including Water Street), and that 'none of these clusters could be too far from any of the others' (Milne, 2006: 297). Geographically extensive command centre functions that are central to influential strands of world/global cities research over the last three decades thus have important historical antecedents, especially in the case of imperial commercial centres (see also King, 1990; Arrighi, 1996).

Second, in terms of labour, the Malay ex-seamen whose life geographies form the main contours and timeline of this book were part of a colonial seafaring workforce that sustained world city Liverpool. Although neither seafarers nor maritime linkages more generally are prominent in popular or academic imaginings of world cities today, there have been recent efforts to bring the maritime sector (back) into world city research and even to devise listings of contemporary 'world maritime cities' (Verhetsel and Sel, 2009). More widely, there is recognition that today's established world/global cities such as London and New York – and more recent or 'wannabe' world cities such as Kuala Lumpur or Singapore – contain, and are dependent upon, low-wage workforces of international migrants and sojourners (e.g. Sassen, 2001; Yeoh 2004; May *et al.*, 2007; Yeoh, 2014). Just as the men in my study undertook border-crossing work that serviced and sustained Liverpool during the colonial division of labour, seafaring continues to service world maritime cities today, albeit under very different global labour market conditions. In terms of the geography of urban and regional development, the most straightforward historical change, of course, is that the former imperial maritime centre of Liverpool does not find a place on twenty-first-century academic listings of world/global cities – even world *maritime* cities – while both Singapore and even Kuala Lumpur do.[11] This underscores a wider point that 'world city' denotes more than a hierarchically delimited set of cities in the present or a position for other cities to aspire to. It also invites historical comparison across shifting geographies of uneven development, analytically drawing together cities with very different, but nonetheless intertwined, developmental trajectories or pathways. Relational comparison of Liverpool and Kuala Lumpur (or Singapore) over time, for example, might include examination of shifting constitutive connections between cities on very different developmental pathways ('into' and 'out of' world city-ness respectively).

My work provides evidence of shifting social as well as economic interconnections between the *alam Melayu* and Liverpool from the tail end of an era when the city was an imperial maritime centre through a period during when it fell off (maritime) world city maps. The first of the three sets of arguments made in Chapter 1 was that maritime world city Liverpool sustained *transnational* Malay social linkages or 'webs' prior to the current era of economic globalization. These webs were spun along, without being reducible to, routes and infrastructures of imperial commerce. Maritime work enabled one man in my study to travel 'up and down' between Singapore and Liverpool (Chapter 2). For another man, Liverpool had become a 'second home' before he decided to settle and seek a shore job there (Chapter 6). Can the seafaring life stages of such men legitimately be considered as an historical form of subaltern transnationalism? In definitional terms, the answer to this question rests in part on the issue of how regularly – and over what period of time – connections need to be sustained in order to qualify as transnational. In empirical terms there are limits to the extent to which memories of mobile lives from half a century ago enable detailed analysis of the regularity of transborder connections or the depth of participation in dual social contexts, even when examined alongside shipping itineraries and other archival fragments. Important recent work on contemporary seafarers' international social linkages has raised the possibility of seafarers being doubly marginalized – from both the national social context in which they are based and, over time, from their society of origin (Sampson, 2013). This may reasonably be said to apply to the lives of Liverpool-based Malay men in the period of maritime decline which followed the initial post-Second World War boom in British shipping. However, I am not convinced that social and political marginality precludes transnationalism, unless subaltern transnationalism is itself an oxymoron. Some seafaring Malay men, for at least certain stages of their lives, had one foot (or at least a toe or two) in both Liverpool and their Malay world homeland. I maintain that such men may be counted among instances of proto-transnationalism from below. The limits to how far back this argument can be sustained historically concern not so much regularity of contact or degree of participation, but matters of political geography. Seafaring Malay lives were transnationalized by the inscription of nation-state boundaries across pre-existing maritime social webs connecting Liverpool and the *alam Melayu*, rather than through late twentieth-century advances in technologies of communication and transportation.

Whether transnational or translocal (or both), long-distance Malay social webs and the ways in which they changed over time are of significance not just to Liverpool, but to ways of seeing the constitutive social and economic connections of cities more widely. There is clearly a danger that my work, in highlighting Liverpool's extended maritime social connections in an era before the advances in technologies of communication and transportation that are commonly understood to have enabled transnationalism, could be construed as (further) evidence of Liverpool's territorial exceptionalism. That Liverpool subsequently became less relationally rich in maritime commercial terms may likewise be read as evidence of a city that has gone against the historical tide of technological and economic change in a late twentieth-century era of globalization, interconnectivity and interdependence. As such, it is important to recall that if Liverpool was a pre-globalization maritime world city, this was due to its position within much wider webs of commercial connections incorporating port towns and cities around the world. It was these extended connections, rather than anything territorially unique to Liverpool, that made possible subaltern social webs. In addition, although Liverpool does not appear on late twentieth-century world city maps, and has even fallen from lists of maritime world cities, my work makes clear that the city's long-distance social and economic connections to the *alam Melayu* are ongoing. Some, of course, are founded specifically upon demographic legacies of Liverpool's world city past. Examples include the transnational family (re)connections of Liverpool-based Malay ex-seamen made possible by international flights and/or increasingly ubiquitous technologies of long-distance communication. Other connections, such as those associated with the decision of Malaysian citizens to study in the city, however, may have nothing to do with the historical presence of Malay seafarers or their families in one-time world city Liverpool. In such cases, Liverpool appears not specifically as a post-world city, or even as a former immigrant gateway city, but as a non-world city. Like the overwhelming majority of cities in the world, Liverpool is not a global centre for advanced producer services, but it does form part of and is remade through a variety of other constitutive social as well as economic networks.

Awareness of a diverse range of historical and contemporary webs may serve to unsettle Liverpool's (post-)world city exceptionalism, but it also demands critical reflection on the territorial scaling and wider spatial framing of my study and in urban research more widely. In line with the second set of arguments outlined at the beginning of the book, I have shown that Malay Liverpool and its historically shifting connections were grounded or anchored in specific local, urban geographies.

These included not only the Liverpool 8 vicinity of the Jermyn Street Malay Club where I carried out much of my fieldwork, but also the earlier (broadly pre-Second World War) location of the 'other Liverpool' (Lane, 1997). During the tail end of Liverpool's period as a maritime world city, it was the south docks and contiguous Chinatown area which contained the demographic diversity that attested to embodied connections with far-flung littoral parts of the world (Chapter 3). Children of Malay seafarers grew up as part of a 'league of nations' in these spatially confined areas of the city, while their seafaring fathers traversed wider worlds of connection. Most Malay men who eventually settled and formed families in Liverpool embarked on oceanic seafaring work as a way of operating at the level of the world (*dunia*) – 'worlding' (Simone, 2001) – rather than with the intention of migrating. Ironically, although they worked along (and more actively spun) trans- and interoceanic webs that extended way beyond the *alam Melayu* (Malay world *region*), in terrestrial terms, 'Sailortown' (Hugill, 1967) rarely extended further inshore than docklands. The interweaving of highly localized dockland social geographies (in Liverpool as well as in other ports around the world), as part of a world-spanning Sailortown, raises important scalar and ontological questions. Most fundamentally, although 'Liverpool' features in the title of this book, to what extent is the city its primary spatial unit of analysis? Perhaps the interconnected world of Sailortowns may be regarded as an antecedent to contemporary forms of extended, even planetary, urbanization, with historical sea lanes and oceanic highways functioning as urban infrastructure (Brenner and Schmid, 2014). But there is also potential for specific connections to be differentiated as urban 'units of comparisons' in their own right (Robinson, 2011: 14).

Anchoring my study of Malay Liverpool and its worlds of connection in specific micro-scale club sites as well as in wider neighbourhood territories raises further issues about histories and geographies of transnationalism. I have sought to show that the Malay Club was a site of both worldly connections and local association across the lives of ex-seafaring men. This has included consideration of the changing composition of the people who met at 7 Jermyn Street and what took place there over time, as well as how the club thus became connected through different kinds of social webs back to the *alam Melayu*. But to what extent did the translocal *function* of the club site change over time? During the late colonial maritime era, Liverpool's Malay Club was clearly a significant node, along with similar institutions in London and New York City, in the Malay Atlantic and in wider maritime Malay social webs. At a time when overseas news was very difficult to obtain and when international telecommunications were prohibitively expensive to most people, such sites were vital nodes for the circulation of information, gossip and stories, carried by seamen, both in their heads and in material forms such as the Singapore newspapers that Hashim took to the Malay Club in New York (Chapter 2). In this way, seafaring men were perhaps not so much (proto-)transnationals in themselves, but part of the 'infrastructure' of long-distance social connectivity (Simone, 2004). Correspondingly, it was less mobile, locally based men – those who ran or were able to frequent clubs for visiting seamen – who inhabited what would now be termed 'transnational social spaces' (Faist, 2000) in the middle of the twentieth century. During my time in Liverpool after 2003, in contrast, the use of mobile phone (SMS) and internet-based technologies meant that some of the people whom I met there were much less dependent upon transnationally mobile visitors or the Malay Club site for their long-distance social connections. Although information and communication technologies are not the focus of my own study, their growing ubiquity, even during the course of my research, invites historical forms of comparative urban study. I have argued that mid-twentieth century maritime centres provide evidence of antecedents to the urban geographies of long-distance urban social linkages today. Yet it is also worth asking whether the micro-geographical anchoring of maritime social webs should be considered as an historically specific form of translocalism – one based on infrastructures of connection very different from those that have become commonplace in the twenty-first century.

Sites such as 7 Jermyn Street, and the people who met up there, provide clues to answering such questions of comparison over time as well as to expanding the ways in which we look at cities in the present. Above all, in line with my third set of arguments, this book serves as a demonstration of a certain way of doing or practising urban studies. That is, it advances a method that takes ordinary people and places seriously as both subjects and objects of urban research. If some people have appeared in the book as 'infrastructure' or as names from archival records that merely stand for wider phenomena, others have been heard as voices providing insights into historical relational geographies, legacies of those pasts and ways in which they continue to be inhabited and remade. Clearly these are not the kinds of people whose city-making practices and mobilities are examined in work on starchitects, roving international consultants or policy experts, who have been the focus of influential recent strands of urban studies research. Non-experts, ordinary people in cities, thus expand the 'material' of relational/territorial urban geographies. They do so as living archives for worlds of connection, and by drawing attention to often unnoticed sites which have sustained as well as reflected those worlds.

The building on Jermyn Street that housed the Malay Club before it closed in 2007 is visually unspectacular. It is doubtful whether many people have stopped to wonder what used to go on there in the way that author Paul Du Noyer did when walking past much grander empty buildings in Liverpool as a boy. Fewer still are likely to have reflected on the wider geographies that the site articulated, even as Liverpool continues to be marketed and consumed as the World in One City. The prospect of its demolition has receded, but not due to any civic value afforded to Jermyn Street's Malay world connections. Liverpool City Council's 'homesteading' plan for the so-called Four Streets of Liverpool 8 made national headline news in 2014 because it included the sale of 20 houses for only £1 each.[12] Subsequent renovation efforts also grabbed the headlines when the work of one architectural collective in the area was shortlisted for Britain's most prestigious art prize.[13] As important and interesting as these initiatives are, media coverage of them has focused largely on localized issues of neighbourhood and community development. In contrast, to the extent that urban transformation in Liverpool has been an occasion for recent imaginings of wider worlds, this has concerned plans for a much more spectacular project reportedly inspired by high-rise developments facing the Bund in Shanghai.[14] Pitched at investors from China, at one level the proposed Shanghai Tower is a product of emergent geographies of global economic development and investment. Yet, as I have shown in this book, there are ordinary urban localities that have long been constituted through social as well as economic connections with former colonial territories in Asia and other distant elsewheres.

Notes

1 The electoral register for 1950 shows that 'Awang, Johan B.' was living at 37 Greenland Street in 1950.

2 'Tidy up Liverpool: Be a binner not a sinner', *Liverpool Echo*, 6 May 2008.

3 As television scriptwriter Jimmy McGovern put it, Liverpool 8 is 'the only place which you can really describe as "The World in One City"' (cited in Murden, 2006: 483).

4 Croxteth is another area of the city suffering from high levels of social and economic deprivation.

5 Indeed, precisely because of the notoriety assumed by 'Toxteth' as a result of the riots, this area – and by extension the people associated with it – may have been further marginalized, including in the minds of people with Malay ancestors. One contributor to a BBC web forum on the 25th anniversary of the riots considered that there had been no improvement in conditions on Granby Street and suggested that 'it has been like all the other areas outside of the city centre, robbed of funding to pay for capital of culture in the city centre' (cited in Frost and Phillips, 2011: 116).

6 Liverpool 1 has also been subjected to much more critical academic scrutiny, particularly in terms of the neoliberal privatization of some 35 city-centre streets. Roy Coleman (2010: 150) has noted that the project 'confers responsibility for the new city centre to organized capital to be privately policed with "quartermasters" and 400 surveillance cameras'.
7 Liverpool Private Sector Development Association, Press Release, May 2008, http://www.liverpoolpsda.co.uk/Press/PressReleases/05-2008/queen.htm (accessed 11 July 2008; no longer available).
8 Field notes, 31 May 2008.
9 The fact that this young woman had studied in Britain and was gaining professional work experience in Liverpool suggests that the wider economic or developmental inversion is far from complete.
10 One of the 'interesting facts' in the 'Your guide to Liverpool One' leaflet which I collected in 2008, is that 'Local architects, Brock Carmichael, have collaborated with world famous Cesar Pelli who have [*sic*] designed some of the tallest buildings in the world.'
11 Kuala Lumpur is included on Verhetsel and Sel's list of 'world maritime cities' as part of a wider metropolitan region extending way beyond the formal boundaries of the city and, most importantly, incorporating Port Klang (formerly Port Swettenham).
12 'Why selling off homes for just £1 in derelict area of Liverpool makes sense', *The Guardian*, 20 February 2013.
13 'The street that might win the Turner Prize: how Assemble are transforming Toxteth', *The Guardian*, 15 May 2015.
14 'Liverpool reaches to the sky to thrive', *Financial Times*, 12 March 2012.

Key Lifepaths

Ali (Ali Kechil) was born in 1932 in Perak, Malaya, but his family subsequently moved to the island of Penang. Ali worked as a *peon* (servant boy) for an Indian shipping company in George Town and then as a chandler before beginning seafaring work with the Straits Steamship Company. He started oceangoing work as a quartermaster with the Blue Funnel Line in the mid-1950s. Ali signed off from Blue Funnel in Liverpool in 1958, by which time the city had already become his 'second home'. He worked initially at the Adelphi Hotel and then as a bus driver until his retirement in 1997. Ali first returned to what had by then become Malaysia in 1994.

Bahazin (Bahazin Bin-Kassim) was born in Kuala Kangsar, Perak, Malaya in 1924. He first arrived in Britain as a seaman in 1949, and was based in North Shields before moving to Liverpool. Bahazin became the first president of Liverpool's Malay Club at 7 Jermyn Street, and assumed the all-important role of cook. He lived next door to the club with his English family. Bahazin died in the 1980s but his family home continued to provide lodging for Liverpool-based and visiting Malay men.

Ben Youp (Youp bin Baba) was born in 1892 in Tanjung Keling, Malacca. He arrived in Liverpool as a seaman before the Second World War. Ben Youp was unable to find seafaring employment immediately after the war and so worked as a road digger before returning to sea. He married Priscilla who was, as a result, disowned by her Protestant parents. Ben and Priscilla Youp lived at 144 Upper Huskisson Street and their home provided lodging to visiting Malay seamen. Ben Youp moved into

From World City to the World in One City: Liverpool through Malay Lives,
First Edition. Tim Bunnell.

Bahazin's house on Jermyn Street in the early 1970s and was a regular at the club next door in the years prior to his death in 1978.

Carrim (Haji Quigus Carrim Rahim) was born on Belitung, an island in what is today Indonesia, in 1919. He fled to Singapore with a friend after angering Belitung's raja, leaving behind a wife and a young daughter. Carrim obtained oceangoing seafaring work in Singapore, arrived at London in March 1948 and eventually moved to Liverpool. He married a local woman named Vera and the couple took in Malaysian student lodgers into their home on Pickwick Street, Liverpool 8, in the 1970s. Carrim made a return visit to Singapore and Indonesia with Vera in 1989. He died in Liverpool in August 2004.

Dol was born in Singapore in 1929 and began work at sea as a teenager, initially with the Straits Steamship Company, and then with other companies operating regional routes. He was recruited in Singapore to work with the Moller Line (which was looking for seafarers who were British subjects) and flown to London where he joined the *Gladys Moller*. Dol arrived in Liverpool in December 1950 and continued to work at sea until 1966. He struggled to find a 'shore job', so moved to Glasgow, then to Preston (to be close to his wife's parents) and to London, before moving back to Liverpool in 2003. Dol made his first return visit to Singapore in 1990 after almost four decades away.

Fadzil (Fadzil Mohamed) was born in Muar in Johor in 1931 and moved to Malacca, and then on to Kuala Lumpur where he worked briefly as a *peon* for a British family after the Japanese occupation. After returning to Johor in 1946 he walked over the causeway to Singapore, from where he began seafaring work with the Straits Steamship Company. Fadzil gained his first extra-regional seafaring experience on the Blue Funnel Line ship, the MV *Charon*. In 1948, he worked on a Moller Line ship which took him to Boston, USA. Although he subsequently spent time living in Cardiff and London, by the mid-1950s Fadzil had come to call Liverpool home. He continued to work at sea until he retired, and was able to make short visits to Singapore as a seaman (the last one in 1973). It was only in 2004 that he first returned to Malaysia after his daughters had reconnected with family there in the 1990s. Fadzil made several return visits to Southeast Asia thereafter before passing away in Liverpool in June 2012.

Hashim was born in 1925 in Kampong Glam, Singapore, where his Ambonese grandfather ran a boarding house. Hashim worked on Prince Line's 'round the world' service in the 1950s and 1960s, becoming very familiar with many port cities, especially New York where his uncle lived and worked as a barber. He also had a relative living in Liverpool, on Nile

Street, near to the Anglican Cathedral. Hashim was based in Liverpool from 1959, working out of the city as a seafarer, until the mid-1980s. He remitted money back to Singapore, including payment for his mother to perform the *hajj*, but never made a return visit after his retirement.

Jaafar (Jaafar Mohamad) was born in Singapore in 1931 and spoke Boyanese at home with his mother, who was born on the Indonesian island of Bawean. Jaafar worked on various regional shipping lines, including the Sarawak Steamship Company and the Singapore-based MV *Charon*, before securing oceangoing employment as a cook on Blue Funnel Line ships (including those that operated on pilgrim routes to Jeddah) in the 1950s. He travelled 'up and down, up and down' between Liverpool and Singapore with Blue Funnel and eventually decided to stay in Liverpool in 1960 after the ship he was working on was dry-docked there following a collision in the Suez Canal. Jaafar first returned to Singapore in 2000, after four decades away, and thereafter made regular return visits to Southeast Asia, usually to avoid the winter months in Liverpool.

JJ was born in the town of Kuala Pilah, Negeri Sembilan, Malaya, in 1928 of mixed Portuguese and Ceylonese ancestry. He moved to Singapore with his mother during the Second World War and served on Japanese boats with Malay crew. After the war, JJ began training as a wireless operator in Singapore before joining Malay seafaring friends to return to work at sea. He jumped ship in London in 1950 but subsequently moved to North Shields where he married his first wife. Although he had visited Liverpool many times, he only moved there in 1984 after separating from his second wife in Newcastle. After more than 40 years away, he visited Singapore and Malaysia in 1992. JJ converted to Islam in Liverpool and subsequently married a Malay woman in Jelebu, Negeri Sembilan, in 1995. Thereafter, he travelled back and forth between Negeri Sembilan and Liverpool.

Johan (Johan Awang) was born in Telok Mas, Malacca in about 1900. He moved to Liverpool from New York after the Second World War and lived on Greenland Street in the south docks area of the city with his wife 'Filipina Alice' in the 1950s. Johan founded and ran Liverpool's Malay Club at its first site on St James Road. He worked in a halal butcher's shop on Granby Street and became the first Malay man in the city to open a shop of his own, on North Hill Street in Liverpool 8. After the death of his wife, Johan returned to Malacca in the 1970s and passed away there.

Majid was born in Kampung Serkam, Malacca in 1917. Majid first visited Liverpool prior to the Second World War, but returned to Malacca.

He shipped out of Singapore in early 1942, just before the Japanese invasion, and jumped ship in Australia, eventually finding work with three other Malay men cutting sugar cane in Cairns. Majid left Australia in 1946 as a fireman on board one of the few Larrinaga Line steamships that survived the war. He arrived back in Liverpool in the summer of 1947 and was based in the city thereafter, except for a short period in Cardiff in the 1950s. After almost half a century away, Majid made a first return visit to Malacca in 1995. He died in Liverpool in 2005.

Mat Nor (Mohamed Nor Hamid) was born in Tanjung Keling, Malacca in 1933, but was sent for schooling in Singapore. Mat Nor worked on Straits Steamship Company and other regional ships, and then on Blue Funnel Line's Western Australia service before being flown to Colombo to begin his first oceangoing work. He arrived in Liverpool on a Prince Line ship in 1952, and lodged in the house next door to the home of his uncle, Ben Youp. Mat Nor married in 1959 and stopped work as a seafarer in 1965. He subsequently worked as a crane driver on the docks in Liverpool and redundancy money from that work funded his first trip back to Malacca (with his British family) in 1978. He made many subsequent return trips to Singapore as well as Malaysia. Mat Nor became the president of the Malay Club from the early 1990s and oversaw its registration as the Merseyside Malaysian and Singapore Community Association.

Musa (Ngah Musa) was born in Losong, Kuala Terengganu, Malaya in 1929. His first seafaring work was on a Straits Steamship vessel, the *Empire Seascape.* He first visited Britain in 1948, and subsequently jumped ship on both sides of the Atlantic. Musa was based in Liverpool from 1956 when he married a local woman. From 1980 Musa volunteered at the local mosque and subsequently opened a stall there selling Islamic literature. He made many return trips to Malaysia, sometimes together with members of his Liverpool family. He died in Liverpool in December 2007 and was buried in his home village in Terengganu.

Rahman was born in Singapore in 1931 and first arrived in Britain by aeroplane in 1952, having been recruited for seafaring work in Singapore. Back in Singapore in the late 1950s, Rahman was detained for his involvement in Angkatan Revolusi Tentera Islam Singapura (ARTIS, Singapore Islamic Revolutionary League). On his release, he returned to working at sea, as a bosun, and was based in Liverpool from the early 1960s. Rahman made the first of several return visits to Singapore in the early 1980s with his two Liverpool-born children.

Archival and Documentary Sources

Full citation details are provided in chapter endnotes.

Main archives and collections

The British Library (BL), London
  India Office Records (IOR)
Liverpool Record Office, Central Library, Liverpool
Maritime Archives and Library, Merseyside Maritime Museum, Liverpool
  Ocean Steamship Co. Archive (OA)
The National Archives of the United Kingdom, Kew
  Board of Trade records (BT)
  Colonial Office records (CO)
National University of Singapore
  Central Library, Singapore/Malaysia Collection

Other depositories

Butetown History and Arts Centre, Cardiff
Cardiff Central Library
London City Mission Archives
Main Library, University of Manchester

From World City to the World in One City: Liverpool through Malay Lives,
First Edition. Tim Bunnell.

National Archives of Singapore
National Archives of Malaysia, Kuala Lumpur
School of Oriental and African Studies Library, University of London
Singapore Press Holdings Information Resource Centre
Sydney Jones Library, University of Liverpool

References

Abdul Rahman Embong (1996) 'Social transformation, the state and the middle class in post-independence Malaysia', *Southeast Asian Studies*, 34(3): 56–79.

Abu Hasan Adam (2000) *Dari Malaysia Hall London…: Sebuah Memoir*, Kuala Lumpur: Premier Line.

Alibhai-Brown, Yasmin (2001) 'After multiculturalism', in Bernard Crick (ed.), *Citizens: Towards a Citizenship Culture*, Oxford: Blackwell, pp. 47–56.

Aljunied, Syed Muhd Khairudin (2009) *Colonialism, Violence and Muslims in Southeast Asia: The Maria Hertogh Controversy and its Aftermath*, London: Routledge.

Aljunied, Syed Muhd Khairudin (2011) 'Malay identity in postcolonial Singapore', in Maznah Mohamad and Syed Muhd Khairudin Aljunied (eds), *Melayu: The Politics, Poetics and Paradoxes of Malayness*, Singapore: NUS Press, pp. 145–67.

Allt, Nicky (ed.) (2008) *The Culture of Capital*, Liverpool: Liverpool University Press.

Amin, Ash (2002) 'Ethnicity and the multicultural city: living with diversity', *Environment and Planning A*, 34(6): 959–80.

Aminurrashid, H. (1961) *Terbang ka-Barat*, Singapore: Pustaka Melayu.

Anderson, Jon and Kimberley Peters (eds) (2014) *Water Worlds: Human Geographies of the Ocean*, Farnham: Ashgate.

Arrighi, Giovanni (1996) *The Long Twentieth Century: Money, Power, and the Origins of Our Times*, London: Verso.

Balachandran, G. (2007) 'South Asian seafarers and their worlds c. 1870–1930s', in Jerry H. Bentley, Renate Bridenthal and Kären Wigen (eds), *Seascapes: Maritime Histories, Littoral Cultures, and Transoceanic Exchanges*, Honolulu: University of Hawaii Press, pp. 186–202.

Bald, Vivek (2013) *Bengali Harlem and the Lost Histories of South Asian America*, Cambridge, MA: Harvard University Press.

From World City to the World in One City: Liverpool through Malay Lives, First Edition. Tim Bunnell.

Ballantyne, Tony (2006) *Between Colonialism and Diaspora: Sikh Colonial Formations in an Imperial World*, Durham, NC: Duke University Press.

Barnard, Timothy P. and Hendrik M.J. Maier (2004) 'Melayu, Malay, Maleis', in Timothy P. Barnard (ed.), *Contesting Malayness: Malay Identity Across Boundaries*, Singapore: Singapore University Press, pp. ix–xiii.

Barrell, John (1991) *The Infection of Thomas De Quincey: A Psychopathology of Imperialism*, New Haven: Yale University Press.

Baucom, Ian (2005) *Specters of the Atlantic: Finance Capital, Slavery, and the Philosophy of History*, Durham, NC: Duke University Press.

Beaverstock, Jon V., Richard G. Smith and Peter J. Taylor (1999) 'A roster of world cities', *Cities*, 16(6): 445–58.

Belchem, John (2000) *Merseypride: Essays in Liverpool Exceptionalism*, Liverpool: Liverpool University Press.

Belchem, John (2005) 'Comment: whiteness and the Liverpool-Irish', *Journal of British Studies*, 44(1): 146–52.

Belchem, John (2006) 'Celebrating Liverpool', in John Belchem (ed.), *Liverpool 800: Culture, Character and History*, Liverpool: Liverpool University Press, pp. 9–57.

Bell, David and Mark Jayne (eds) (2004) *City of Quarters: Urban Villages in the Contemporary City*, Aldershot: Ashgate.

Bentley, Jerry H., Renate Bridenthal and Kären Wigen (eds) (2007) *Seascapes: Maritime Histories, Littoral Cultures, and Transoceanic Exchanges*, Honolulu: University of Hawaii Press.

Ben-Tovim, Gideon (1988) 'Race, politics and urban regeneration: lessons from Liverpool', in Michael Parkinson, Bernard Foley and Dennis Judd (eds), *Regenerating the Cities: The UK Crisis and the US Experience*, Manchester: Manchester University Press, pp. 141–55.

Bhattacharyya, Gargi (2000) 'Metropolis of the Midlands', in Maria Balshaw and Liam Kennedy (eds), *Urban Space and Representation*, London: Pluto Press, pp. 162–74.

Bibby Line (1981) *Motor Vessel 'Derbyshire' 1976–80: In Memoriam*, Liverpool: Kershaw Publications.

Binnie, Jon, Julian Holloway, Steve Millington and Craig Young (2006) 'Introduction: grounding cosmopolitan urbanism: approaches, practices and policies', in Jon Binnie, Julian Holloway, Steve Millington and Craig Young (eds), *Cosmopolitan Urbanism*, London and New York: Routledge, pp. 1–34.

Boland, Philip (1999) 'Merseyside and Objective 1 Status, 1994–1999: implications for the next programming period', *Regional Studies*, 33(8): 788–92.

Boland, Philip, Michael Mannin and James Wallace (1995) 'Merseyside – implications of Objective 1 and the government office', *Regional Studies*, 29(7): 698–705.

Bowen, Phil (2008) *A Gallery to Play To: The Story of the Mersey Poets*, Liverpool: Liverpool University Press.

Brenner, Neil and Christian Schmid (2014) 'Planetary urbanization', in Neil Brenner (ed.), *Implosions/Explosions: Towards a Study of Planetary Urbanization*, Berlin: JOVIS, pp. 160–63.

Brown, Jacqueline Nassy (2005) *Dropping Anchor, Setting Sail: Geographies of Race in Black Liverpool*, Princeton, NJ: Princeton University Press.

Bunnell, Tim (2002) '(Re)positioning Malaysia: high-tech networks and the multicultural rescripting of national identity', *Political Geography*, 21(1): 105–24.

Bunnell, Tim (2004a) *Malaysia, Modernity and the Multimedia Super Corridor: A Critical Geography of Intelligent Landscapes*, London: RoutledgeCurzon.

Bunnell, Tim (2004b) 'Re-viewing the *Entrapment* controversy: megaprojection, (mis)representation and postcolonial performance', *Geojournal*, 59(4): 297–305.

Bunnell, Tim (2007) 'Post-maritime transnationalization: Malay seafarers in Liverpool', *Global Networks*, 7(4): 412–29.

Bunnell, Tim (2008) 'Multiculturalism's regeneration: celebrating *Merdeka* (Malaysian Independence) in a European Capital of Culture', *Transactions of the Institute of British Geographers*, 33(2): 251–67.

Bunnell, Tim (2015) 'Antecedent cities and inter-referencing effects: learning from and extending beyond critiques of neoliberalization', *Urban Studies*, 52(11): 1983–2000.

Bunnell, Tim, Sallie Yea, Linda Peake, Tracey Skelton and Monica Smith (2012) 'Geographies of friendships', *Progress in Human Geography*, 36(4): 490–507.

Burbidge, F.W. (1880) *The Gardens of the Sun; or, a Naturalist's Journal on the Mountains and in the Forests and Swamps of Borneo and the Sulu Archipelago*, London: John Murray.

Burgess, Jacqueline (1985) 'News from nowhere: the press, the riots and the myth of the inner city', in Jacqueline Burgess and John R. Gold (eds), *Geography, the Media and Popular Culture*, London: Croom Helm, pp. 192–228.

Burton, Antoinette (1998) *At the Heart of Empire: Indians and the Colonial Encounter in Late-Victorian Britain*, Berkeley: University of California Press.

Caradog Jones, D. (1940) *The Economic Status of Coloured Families in the Port of Liverpool*, Liverpool: University Press of Liverpool.

Cartier, Carolyn (1998) 'Megadevelopment in Malaysia: from heritage landscapes to "leisurescapes" in Melaka's tourism sector', *Singapore Journal of Tropical Geography*, 19(2): 151–76.

Chamberlain, Mary and Selma Leydesdorff (2004) 'Transnational families: memories and narratives', *Global Networks*, 4(3): 227–41.

Chandler, George (1960) *Liverpool Shipping: A Short History*, London: Phoenix House.

Chang, T.C. (1997) 'From "instant Asia" to "multifaceted jewel": urban imaging strategies and tourism development in Singapore', *Urban Geography*, 18(6): 542–62.

Chong, Terence (2005) 'The construction of the Malaysian Malay middle class: the histories, intricacies and futures of the Melayu Baru', *Social Identities*, 11(6): 573–87.

Chua Beng Huat (2011) 'Singapore as model', in Ananya Roy and Aihwa Ong (eds), *Worlding Cities: Asian Experiments and the Art of Being Global*, Oxford: Wiley-Blackwell, pp. 29–54.

Clarke, Nick (2012) 'Urban policy mobility, anti-politics, and histories of the transnational municipal movement', *Progress in Human Geography*, 36(1): 25–43.

Clarkson, John, Bill Harvey and Roy Fenton (1998) *Ships in Focus: Blue Funnel Line*, Preston: Ships in Focus Publications.

Clifford, James (1997) *Routes: Travel and Translation in the Late Twentieth Century*, Cambridge, MA: Harvard University Press.

Cochrane, Allan, Jamie Peck and Adam Tickell (1996) 'Manchester plays games: exploring the local politics of globalization', *Urban Studies*, 33(8): 1319–36.

Cohen, Phil (1999) 'In visible cities: urban regeneration and place-building in the era of multicultural capitalism', *Communal/Plural*, 7(1): 9–28.

Cohen, Robin (1997) *Global Diasporas: An Introduction*, London: University College of London Press.

Cohen, Sara (2007) *Decline, Renewal and the City in Popular Music Culture: Beyond the Beatles*, Aldershot: Ashgate.

Coleman, Roy (2010) 'The imagined city: power, mystification and synoptic surveillance', in Kirstie Ball and Laureen Snider (eds), *The Surveillance-Industrial Complex: A Political Economy of Surveillance*, London: Routledge, pp. 141–58.

Collins, Francis Leo (2012) 'Transnational mobilities and urban spatialities: notes from the Asia-Pacific', *Progress in Human Geography*, 36(3): 316–35.

Comber, Leon (1983) *13 May 1969: A Historical Survey of Sino-Malay Relations*, Singapore: Graham Brash.

Conan Doyle, Arthur (1986) [1891] 'Adventure VI – "The man with the twisted lip"', *The Complete Illustrated Sherlock Holmes*, Ware: Omega Books, pp. 166–80.

Connolly, Mark Gerard (2013) 'The "Liverpool model(s)": cultural planning, Liverpool and Capital of Culture 2008', *International Journal of Cultural Policy*, 19(2): 162–81.

Cook, Ian G., Phil Cubbin and Matt Tucker (2008) '"Don't go down there": Liverpool Chinatown through the decades', unpublished mimeo.

Cornelius, John (1991) *Liverpool 8*, Liverpool: Liverpool University Press.

Couch, Chris (2003) *City of Change and Challenge: Urban Planning and Regeneration in Liverpool*, Aldershot: Ashgate.

Couch, Chris, Jay Karecha, Henning Nuissl and Dieter Rink (2005) 'Decline and sprawl: an evolving type of urban development observed in Liverpool and Leipzig', *European Planning Studies*, 13(1): 117–36.

Craggs, Susan and I. Loh Lynn (1985) *A History of the Chinese Community*, Liverpool: Merseyside Community Relations Council.

Cresswell, Tim (2004) *Place: A Short Introduction*, Oxford: Blackwell.

Daniels, Stephen and Catherine Nash (2004) 'Lifepaths: geography and biography', *Journal of Historical Geography*, 30(3): 449–58.

Daunton, M.J. (1977) *Coal Metropolis: Cardiff 1870–1914*, Leicester: Leicester University Press.

De Quincey, Thomas (1985) [1821] *Confessions of an English Opium-Eater and Other Writings*, edited and introduced by Grevel Lindop, Oxford: Oxford University Press.

Dick, Howard W. and Peter J. Rimmer (2003) *Cities, Transport and Communications: The Integration of Southeast Asia since 1850*, New York: Palgrave Macmillan.
Dicken, Peter (2003) *Global Shift: Reshaping the Global Economic Map in the 21st Century*, 4th edn, London: Sage.
Dickens, Charles (1911) [1875] *The Uncommercial Traveller*, London: J.M. Dent and Sons.
Dobbs, Stephen (2003) *The Singapore River: A Social History, 1819–2002*, Singapore: Singapore University Press.
Drabble, John (2000) *An Economic History of Malaysia, c. 1800–1990: The Transition to Modern Economic Growth*, Basingstoke: Macmillan.
Driver, Felix and David Gilbert (1999) 'Imperial cities: overlapping territories, intertwined histories', in Felix Driver and David Gilbert (eds), *Imperial Cities: Landscape, Display and Identity*, Manchester: Manchester University Press, pp. 1–17.
Du Noyer, Paul (2007) *Liverpool: Wondrous Place, From the Cavern to the Capital of Culture*, London: Virgin Books.
Duffy, Katherine and Jo Hutchison (1997) 'Urban policy and the turn to community', *Town Planning Review*, 68(3): 347–62.
Duruz, Jean and Gaik Cheng Khoo (2015) *Eating Together: Food, Space and Identity in Malaysia and Singapore*, Petaling Jaya: Strategic Information and Research Development Centre.
Eccles, David (2005) *Larrinaga Line, 1863–1974*, Windsor: World Ship Society.
European Commission (2010) Summary of the European Commission Conference 'Celebrating 25 Years of European Capitals of Culture', Brussels, 23–4 March, available at http://ec.europa.eu/culture/tools/actions/documents/conclusions_ecoc_en.pdf (last accessed on 15 June 2011).
Evans, Neil (1980) 'The South Wales race riots of 1919', *Journal of Welsh Labour History*, 3(1): 5–29.
Faist, Thomas (2000) 'Transnationalization in international migration: implications for the study of citizenship and culture', *Ethnic and Racial Studies*, 23(2): 189–222.
Falkus, Malcolm (1990) *The Blue Funnel Legend*, Basingstoke: Macmillan.
Featherstone, David (2007) 'Spatial politics of the past unbound: transnational networks and the remaking of political identities', *Global Networks*, 7(4): 430–52.
Featherstone, David, Richard Phillips and Johanna Waters (2007) 'Introduction: spatialities of transnational networks', *Global Networks*, 7(4): 383–91.
Federation of Malaya (1956) *Annual Report of the Federation of Malaya*, Kuala Lumpur: Government Press.
Ferguson, James (1999) *Expectations of Modernity: Myths and Meanings of Urban Life on the Zambian Copperbelt*, Berkeley: University of California Press.
Fischer, Johan (2008) *Proper Islamic Consumption: Shopping Among the Malays in Malaysia*, Copenhagen: NIAS Press.
Fischer, Johan (2011) *The Halal Frontier: Muslim Consumers in a Globalized Market*, New York: Palgrave Macmillan.
Fish, Stanley (1997) 'Boutique multiculturalism, or why liberals are incapable of thinking about hate speech', *Critical Inquiry*, 23: 378–95.

Florida, Richard (2002) *The Rise of the Creative Class*, New York: Basic Books.

Fisher, Michael H. (2004) *Counterflows to Colonialism: Indian Travellers and Settlers in Britain 1600–1857*, Delhi: Permanent Black.

Friedmann, John (1986) 'The world city hypothesis', *Development and Change*, 17(1): 69–83.

Frost, Diane (1999) *Work and Community among West African Migrant Workers since the Nineteenth Century*, Liverpool: Liverpool University Press.

Frost, Diane (2008) 'The maligned, the despised and the ostracized: working-class white women, interracial relationships and colonial ideologies in nineteenth- and twentieth-century Liverpool', in Sheryllynne Haggerty, Anthony Webster and Nicholas J. White (eds), *The Empire in One City: Liverpool's Inconvenient Imperial Past*, Manchester: Manchester University Press, pp. 143–64.

Frost, Diane and Richard Phillips (eds) (2011) *Liverpool 81: Remembering the Riots*, Liverpool: Liverpool University Press.

Fryer, Peter (1984) *Staying Power: The History of Black People in Britain*, London: Pluto Press.

Ghosh, Amitav (2008) 'Of fanás and forecastles: the Indian Ocean and some lost languages of the age of sail', *Economic and Political Weekly*, 21 June: 56–62.

Gielis, Ruben (2009) 'A global sense of migrant places: towards a place perspective in the study of migrant transnationalism', *Global Networks*, 9(2): 271–87.

Gifford, Tony, Wally Brown and Ruth Bundey (1989) *Loosen the Shackles: First Report of the Liverpool Inquiry into Race Relations in Liverpool*, London: Karia Press.

Gilroy, Paul (1993) *The Black Atlantic: Modernity and Double Consciousness*, Cambridge, MA: Harvard University Press.

Glick Schiller, Nina and Ayse Çağlar (2009) 'Towards a comparative theory of locality in migration studies: migrant incorporation and city scale', *Journal of Ethnic and Migration Studies*, 35(2): 177–202.

Glick Schiller, Nina and Ayse Çağlar (eds) (2011) *Locating Migration: Rescaling Cities and Migrants*, Ithaca: Cornell University Press.

Glick Schiller, Nina, Ayse Çağlar and Thaddeus C. Guldbrandsen (2006) 'Beyond the ethnic lens: globality, locality, and born-again incorporation', *American Ethnologist*, 33(4): 612–33.

Goh, Daniel P.S. (2010) 'Multiculturalism and the problem of solidarity', in T. Chong (ed.), *Management of Success: Singapore Revisited*, Singapore: Institute of Southeast Asian Studies, pp. 561–78.

Gomez, Edmund Terence and Jomo K.S. (1997) *Malaysia's Political Economy: Politics, Patronage and Profits*, Cambridge: Cambridge University Press.

Green, Anthony (2006) *Our Journey: 30 Years of Haj Services in Singapore*, Singapore: Islamic Religious Council of Singapore.

Griffiths, Matthew (2006) *Kirkby & Knowsley*, Stroud: Nonsuch Publishing.

Gullick, J.M. (1983) *The Story of Kuala Lumpur, 1857–1939*, Singapore: Eastern Universities Press.

Haggerty, Sheryllynne, Anthony Webster and Nicholas J. White (eds) (2008) *The Empire in One City: Liverpool's Inconvenient Imperial Past*, Manchester: Manchester University Press.

Hall, David (2003) 'Images of the city', in Ronaldo Munck (ed.), *Reinventing the City? Liverpool in Comparative Perspective*, Liverpool: Liverpool University Press, pp. 191–210.

Halliday, Fred (2010) *Britain's First Muslims: Portrait of an Arab Community*, London: I.B. Tauris.

Hamzah Sendut (1965) 'The structure of Kuala Lumpur: Malaysia's capital city', *Town Planning Review*, 36: 49–66.

Hanna, Willard A. (1966) *The Malays' Singapore*, New York: American Universities Field Staff.

Hannerz, Ulf (1996) *Transnational Connections: Culture, People, Places*, London: Routledge.

Harley, J.B. (1988) 'Maps, knowledge and power', in Denis Cosgrove and Stephen Daniels (eds), *The Iconography of Landscape*, Cambridge: Cambridge University Press, pp. 277–312.

Haron, Muhammed (2005) 'GAPENA and the Cape Malays: initiating connections, constructing images', *Sari*, 23: 47–66.

Harvey, David (1989) 'From managerialism to entrepreneurialism: the transformation in urban governance in late capitalism', *Geografiska Annaler. Series B, Human Geography*, 71(1): 3–17.

Hayden, Dolores (1995) *The Power of Place: Urban Landscapes as Public History*, Cambridge, MA: MIT Press.

Henderson, Joan C. (2003) 'Tourism promotion and identity in Malaysia', *Tourism Culture and Communication*, 4(2): 71–81.

Herson, John (2008) '"Stirring spectacles of cosmopolitan animation": Liverpool as a diasporic city, 1825–1913', in Sheryllynne Haggerty, Anthony Webster and Nicholas J. White (eds), *The Empire in One City: Liverpool's Inconvenient Imperial Past*, Manchester: Manchester University Press, pp. 55–77.

Hirschman, Charles (1986) 'The making of race in colonial Malaya: political economy and racial category', *Sociological Forum*, 1(2): 330–61.

Huff, W.G. (1994) *The Economic Growth of Singapore: Trade and Development in the Twentieth Century*, Cambridge: Cambridge University Press.

Huff, W.G. (1995) 'The developmental state, government and Singapore's economic development since 1960', *World Development*, 38(8): 1421–38.

Hugill, Stan (1967) *Sailortown*, London: Routledge and Kegan Paul.

Hunt, Tristram (2014) *Ten Cities that Made an Empire*, London: Allen Lane.

Hussin Mutalib (1993) *Islam in Malaysia: From Revivalism to Islamic State*, Singapore: Singapore University Press.

Hyde, Francis E. (1956) 'The expansion of Liverpool's carrying trade with the Far East and Australia 1860–1914', *Transactions of the Royal Historical Society*, 6: 139–60.

Hyde, Francis E. (1957) *Blue Funnel: A History of Alfred Holt & Company of Liverpool, 1865–1914*, Liverpool: Liverpool University Press.

Imperial War Graves Commission (1952) *Naval Memorials in the UK: Introduction to the Registers*, London: Imperial War Graves Commission.

Iskandar Mydin (1989) 'City lights: pre-war Singapore's allure for rural migrants', *The Heritage*, 10: 5–12.

Jackson, A. and C.E. Wurtzburg (1952) *The History of Mansfield & Company: Part 1, 1868–1924*, Singapore: Mansfield.

Jacobs, Jane M. (1996) *Edge of Empire: Postcolonialism and the City*, London: Routledge.

Jacobs, Jane M. (2012) 'Urban geographies I: still thinking relationally', *Progress in Human Geography*, 36(3): 412–22.

Jehom, Welyne Jeffrey (2008) 'Ethnic pluralism and ethnic relations in Sarawak', in Zawawi Ibrahim (ed.), *Representation, Identity and Multiculturalism in Sarawak*, Kajang: Persatuan Sains Sosial Malaysia, pp. 93–109.

Jennings, Eric (1973) *Mansfields: Transport and Distribution in South-East Asia*, Singapore: Meridian Communications.

Jomo K.S. (1995) 'Introduction', in K.S. Jomo (ed.), *Privatizing Malaysia: Rents, Rhetoric, Realities*, Boulder: Westview Press, pp. 1–10.

Jones, Paul and Stuart Wilks-Heeg (2004) 'Capitalising Culture: Liverpool 2008', *Local Economy*, 19(4): 341–60.

Jones, Phil and James Evans (2008) *Urban Regeneration in the UK: Theory and Practice*, London: Sage.

Kahn, Joel S. (2006) *Other Malays: Nationalism and Cosmopolitanism in the Modern Malay World*, Singapore: Singapore University Press.

Keith, Michael (2005) *After the Cosmopolitan: Multicultural Cities and the Future of Racism*, London: Routledge.

Kemp, Paul (1989) *Liverpool: The Battle of the Atlantic*, London: Hyperion Books.

Kennerley, Alston (1989) 'British Seamen's Missions and Sailors' Homes 1815 to 1870: Voluntary Welfare Provision for Serving Seafarers', PhD thesis, Council for National Academic Awards.

Kerr, Madeline (1958) *The People of Ship Street*, London: Routledge and Kegan Paul.

Keshvani, Nazir (1999) 'One for the road: Hishamuddin Rais in profile', *Cinemaya*, 44: 16–18.

Kessler, Clive (1999) 'A Malay diaspora? Another side of Dr Mahathir's Jewish problem', *Patterns of Prejudice*, 33(1): 23–42.

Khan-Cheema, Muhammad Akram (1979) 'Islam and the Muslims in Liverpool', MA dissertation, University of Liverpool.

Khoo Boo Teik (1995) *Paradoxes of Mahathirism: An Intellectual Biography of Mahathir Mohamad*, Kuala Lumpur: Oxford University Press.

Khoo Gaik Cheng (2009) 'Koptiam: discursive cosmopolitan spaces and national identity in Malaysian culture and media', in Amanda Wise and Selvaraj Velayutham (eds), *Everyday Multiculturalism*, Basingstoke: Palgrave Macmillan, pp. 87–104.

King, Anthony D. (1990) *Global Cities: Post-Imperialism and the Internationalization of London*, London: Routledge.

King, Anthony D. (1996) 'Worlds in the city: Manhattan transfer and the ascendance of spectacular space', *Planning Perspectives*, 11: 97–114.

King, Anthony D. (2004) *Spaces of Global Cultures: Architecture, Urbanism, Identity*, London: Routledge.

King, Ross (2008) *Kuala Lumpur and Putrajaya: Negotiating Urban Space in Malaysia*, Singapore: NUS Press.

Krishnan, Sanjay (2006) 'Opium and empire: the transports of Thomas de Quincey', *boundary 2*, 33(2): 203–34.

Kua Kia Soong (2007) *May 13: Declassified Documents on the Malaysian Riots of 1969*, Petaling Jaya: Suaram Komunikasi.

Kymlicka, Will (2003) 'Immigration, citizenship, multiculturalism: exploring the links', *The Political Quarterly*, 74(3): 195–208.

Lai Chee Kien (2007) *Building Merdeka: Independence Architecture in Kuala Lumpur, 1957–1966*, Kuala Lumpur: Galeri Petronas.

Lamont, Michèle and Sada Aksartova (2002) 'Ordinary cosmopolitanisms: strategies for bridging racial boundaries among working-class men', *Theory, Culture and Society*, 19(4): 1–26.

Lane, Tony (1997) *Liverpool: City of the Sea*, Liverpool: Liverpool University Press.

Larner, Wendy (2007) 'Expatriate experts and globalizing governmentalities: the New Zealand diaspora strategy', *Transactions of the Institute of British Geographers*, 32(3): 331–45.

Law, Ian and June Henfrey (1981) *A History of Race and Racism in Liverpool, 1660–1950*, Liverpool: Merseyside Community Relations Council.

Lawless, Dick (1994) 'The role of seamen's agents in the migration and employment of Arab seafarers in the early twentieth century', *Immigrants and Minorities: Historical Studies in Ethnicity, Migration and Diaspora*, 13(2–3): 34–58.

Lawson, Will (1927) *Pacific Steamers*, Glasgow: Brown, Son & Ferguson.

Lawton, Richard (1964) 'Liverpool and the tropics', in Robert W. Steel and R. Mansell Prothero (eds), *Geographers and the Tropics: Liverpool Essays*, London: Longmans, pp. 349–75.

Lee, Gregory Barry (1998) 'Paddy's Chinatown: a short (hi)story of a Liverpool hybridity', *Interventions*, 1(1): 97–124.

Lee Kuan Yew (1998) *The Singapore Story: Memoirs of Lee Kuan Yew*, Singapore: Marshall Cavendish.

Lee Kuan Yew (2000) *From Third World to First: The Singapore Story: 1965–2000*, Singapore: Marshall Cavendish.

Lee, Robert (2013) 'The seafarers' urban world: a critical review', *International Journal of Maritime History*, 25(1): 23–64.

Lees, Loretta (2003) 'Visions of "urban renaissance": the Urban Task Force report and the Urban White Paper', in Robert Imrie and Mike Raco (eds), *Urban Renaissance? New Labour, Community and Urban Policy*, Bristol: Policy Press, pp. 61–82.

Leifer, Michael (1964) 'Communal violence in Singapore', *Asian Survey*, 4(10): 1115–21.

Leitner, Helga, Eric S. Sheppard, Kristin Sziarto and Anant Maringanti (2007) 'Contesting urban futures: decentering neoliberalism', in Helga Leitner, Jamie Peck and Eric S. Sheppard (eds), *Contesting Neoliberalism: Urban Frontiers*, New York: Guilford Press, pp. 1–25.

Leonard, Mark (1997) *Britain™: Renewing Our Identity*, London: Demos.

Levitas, Ruth (2000) 'Community, utopia and New Labour', *Local Economy*, 15(3): 188–197.

Linebaugh, Peter and Marcus Rediker (2012) *The Many-Headed Hydra: Sailors, Slaves, Commoners, and the Hidden History of the Revolutionary Atlantic*, London: Verso.

Little, Kenneth (1948) *Negroes in Britain: A Study of Racial Relations in English Society*, London: Routledge and Kegan Paul.

Liverpool City Council (2002) *The Cultural Strategy for Liverpool*, Liverpool: Liverpool City Council.

Liverpool Culture Company (2002) *Liverpool 2008: European Capital of Culture Bid*, Liverpool: Liverpool Culture Company.

Loo Yat Ming (2013) *Architecture and Urban Form in Kuala Lumpur: Race and Chinese Spaces in a Postcolonial City*, Burlington: Ashgate.

McKay, Benjamin (2011) 'Taking identity on the road: two recent Malaysian films', in Yeoh Seng Guan and Julian C.H. Lee (eds), *Fringe Benefits: Essays and Reflections on Malaysian Arts and Cinema*, Petaling Jaya: Strategic Information and Research Development Centre, pp. 3–29.

MacKenzie, John M. (1986a) 'Introduction', in John M. MacKenzie (ed.), *Imperialism and Popular Culture*, Manchester: Manchester University Press, pp. 1–16.

MacKenzie, John M. (1986b) '"In touch with the infinite": the BBC and the Empire, 1923–53', in John M. MacKenzie (ed.), *Imperialism and Popular Culture*, Manchester: Manchester University Press, pp. 165–91.

MacKenzie, John M. (1999) '"The Second City of the Empire": Glasgow – imperial municipality', in Felix Driver and David Gilbert (eds), *Imperial Cities: Landscape, Display and Identity*, Manchester: Manchester University Press, pp. 215–37.

Mahathir Mohamad (1970) *The Malay Dilemma*, Singapore: Times Books.

Mahathir Mohamad (1986) *The Challenge*, Petaling Jaya: Pelanduk Publications.

Mandal, Sumit K. (2013) 'Global conjunctions in the Indian Ocean – Malay world textual trajectories', *Indonesia and the Malay World*, 41: 143–5.

Mangan, J.A. (1986) '"The grit of our forefathers": invented traditions, propaganda and imperialism', in John M. MacKenzie (ed.), *Imperialism and Popular Culture*, Manchester: Manchester University Press, pp. 113–39.

Mansor Puteh (1983) 'Menjengah ke teratak Melayu di Pulau Manhattan', *Dewan Budaya*, February, pp. 38–39.

Marne, Pauline and Sara Parker (2006) '"It's our world isn't it?" Engaging with young people in Liverpool', *Impacts 08 – The Liverpool Model, European Capital of Culture Research Programme*, Liverpool: University of Liverpool.

Marsh, Bryn J. and Sue Almond (1993) *The Home Port: Bootle, the Blitz and the Battle of the Atlantic*, Bootle: Sefton Council.

Martinez, Patricia (2004) 'Perhaps he deserved better: the disjuncture between vision and reality in Mahathir's Islam', in Bridget Welsh (ed.), *Reflections: The Mahathir Years*, Washington, DC: Southeast Asia Studies Program, Johns Hopkins University, pp. 28–39.

Massey, Doreen (1993) 'Power-geometry and a progressive sense of place', in Jon Bird, Barry Curtis, Tim Putnam, George Robertson and Lisa Tickner (eds), *Mapping the Futures: Local Cultures, Global Change*, London: Routledge, pp. 57–69.

May, Jon, Jane Wills, Kavita Datta, Yara Evans, Joanna Herbert and Cathy McIlwaine (2007) 'Keeping London working: global cities, the British state and London's new migrant division of labour', *Transactions of the Institute of British Geographers*, 32(2): 151–67.

May, Roy and Robin Cohen (1974) 'The interaction between race and colonialism: A case study of the Liverpool race riots of 1919', *Race and Class*, 16(2): 111–26.

Mbembe, Achille and Sarah Nuttall (2004) 'Writing the world from an African metropolis', *Public Culture*, 16(3): 347–72.

McCann, Eugene (2010) 'Urban policy mobilities and global circuits of knowledge: toward a research agenda', *Annals of the Association of American Geographers*, 101(1): 107–30.

McCann, Eugene and Kevin Ward (2010) 'Relationality/territoriality: toward a conceptualization of cities in the world', *Geoforum*, 41(2): 175–84.

McEwan, Cheryl, Jane Pollard and Nick Henry (2008) 'The non-"global city" of Birmingham, UK: a gateway through time', in Marie Price and Lisa Benton-Short (eds), *Migrants to the Metropolis: The Rise of Immigrant Gateway Cities*, Syracuse, NY: Syracuse University Press, pp. 128–49.

McFarlane, Colin (2011) *Learning the City: Knowledge and Translocal Assemblage*, Oxford: Wiley-Blackwell.

McLellan, A. (1953) *The History of Mansfield and Company: Part 2, 1920–1953*, Singapore: Mansfield.

McManus, Kevin (1994) *Nashville of the North: Country Music in Liverpool*, Liverpool: Institute of Popular Music.

McNeill, Donald (2009) *The Global Architect: Firms, Fame and Urban Form*, New York: Routledge.

Meegan, Richard (1999) 'Urban development corporations, urban entrepreneurialism and locality: the Merseyside Development Corporation', in Rob Imrie and Huw Thomas (eds), *British Urban Policy: An Evaluation of the Urban Development Corporations*, London: Sage, pp. 64–105.

Meegan, Richard (2003) 'Urban regeneration, politics and social cohesion: the Liverpool case', in Ronaldo Munck (ed.), *Reinventing the City? Liverpool in Comparative Perspective*, Liverpool: Liverpool University Press, pp. 53–79.

Meegan, Richard and Alison Mitchell (2001) '"It's not community round here, it's neighbourhood": neighbourhood change and cohesion in urban regeneration policies', *Urban Studies*, 38(12): 2167–94.

Melville, Herman (1983) [1849]) *Redburn: His First Voyage*, New York: The Library of America.

Merrifield, Andy (1996) 'Social justice and communities of difference: a snapshot from Liverpool', in Andy Merrifield and Erik Swyngedouw (eds), *The Urbanization of Injustice*, London: Lawrence and Wishart, pp. 200–22.

Milne, Graeme J. (2006) 'Maritime Liverpool', in John Belchem (ed.), *Liverpool 800: Culture, Character and History*, Liverpool: Liverpool University Press, pp. 257–310.

Milner, Anthony (2008) *The Malays*, Chichester: John Wiley & Sons, Ltd.

Mitchell, Katharyne (1993) 'Multiculturalism, or the united colours of capitalism?' *Antipode*, 25(4): 263–94.

Mitchell, Katharyne (1997) 'Different diasporas and the hype of hybridity', *Environment and Planning D: Society and Space*, 15(5): 533–53.

Mitchell, Katharyne (2004) 'Geographies of identity: multiculturalism unplugged', *Progress in Human Geography*, 28(5): 641–51.

Modood, Tariq (2007) *Multicultural Politics: Racism, Ethnicity and Muslims in Britain*, Edinburgh: Edinburgh University Press.

Mokhtar Naim (1973) 'Merantau: Minangkabau Voluntary Migration', PhD dissertation, University of Singapore.

Mooney, Gerry (2004) 'Cultural policy as urban transformation? Critical reflections on Glasgow, European City of Culture 1990', *Local Economy*, 19(4): 327–40.

Muhammad Haniff Bin Hassan (2007) 'Explaining Islam's special position and the politic of Islam in Malaysia', *The Muslim World*, 97(2): 287–316.

Muhammad Muhd Taib (1993) *Melayu Baru*, Kuala Lumpur: ITC Book Publisher.

Muhammad Mumtaz Ali (1996) *The Muslim Community in Britain: An Historical Account*, Kelana Jaya: Pelanduk.

Muir, Ramsay (1907) *A History of Liverpool*, London: Williams and Norgate.

Murden, Jon (2006) '"City of change and challenge": Liverpool since 1945', in John Belchem (ed.), *Liverpool 800: Culture, Character and History*, Liverpool: Liverpool University Press, pp. 393–485.

Murray, Nicholas (2008) *So Spirited a Town: Visions and Versions of Liverpool*, Liverpool: Liverpool University Press.

Murtagh, Brendan and Stephen McKay (2003) 'Evaluating the social effects of the EU URBAN Community Initiative Programme', *European Planning Studies*, 11(2): 193–211.

Nagata, Judith (1974) 'What is a Malay? Situational selection of ethnic identity in a plural society', *American Ethnologist*, 1(2): 331–50.

Nathan, S.R. (2005) 'The changing nature of seamen's welfare efforts in Singapore', in Aileen Lau and Laure Lau (eds), *Maritime Heritage of Singapore*, Singapore: Suntree Media, pp. 185–93.

Nijman, Jan (2007) 'Introduction: comparative urbanism', *Urban Geography*, 28(1): 1–6.

O'Brien, Dave (2010) '"No cultural policy to speak of": Liverpool 2008', *Journal of Policy Research in Tourism, Leisure and Events*, 2(2): 113–28.

Olds, Kris (2001) *Globalization and Urban Change: Capital, Culture, and Pacific Rim Mega-Projects*, Oxford: Oxford University Press.

Ong, Aihwa (2011) 'Introduction: worlding cities, or the art of being global', in Ananya Roy and Aihwa Ong (eds), *Worlding Cities: Asian Experiments and the Art of Being Global*, Oxford: Wiley-Blackwell, pp. 1–26.

Ormond, Meghann (2015) '*En route*: transport and embodiment in international medical travel journeys between Indonesia and Malaysia', *Mobilities*, 10(2): 285–303.

Oswin, Natalie and Brenda S. Yeoh (2010) 'Introduction: mobile city Singapore', *Mobilities*, 5(2): 167–75.

Paddison, Ronan (2001) 'Communities in the city', in Ronan Paddison (ed.), *Handbook of Urban Studies*, London: Sage, pp. 194–205.

Parekh, Bhikhu (2006) *Rethinking Multiculturalism: Cultural Diversity and Political Theory*, Basingstoke: Macmillan.

Parker, Charlie and Catherine Garnell (2006) 'Regeneration and retail in Liverpool: a new approach', *Journal of Retail and Leisure Property*, 5: 292–304.

Parkinson, Michael and Franco Bianchini (1993) 'Liverpool: a tale of missed opportunities?' in Franco Bianchini and Michael Parkinson (eds), *Cultural Policy and Urban Regeneration: The Western European Experience*, Manchester: Manchester University Press, pp. 155–77.

Peck, Jamie and Nik Theodore (2012) 'Follow the policy: a distended case approach', *Environment and Planning A*, 44(1): 21–30.

Peet, George L. (1985) *Rickshaw Reporter*, Petaling Jaya: Eastern Universities Press.

Philo, Chris and Gerry Kearns (1993) 'Culture, history, capital: an introduction to the selling of places', in Gerry Kearns and Chris Philo (eds), *Selling Places: The City as Cultural Capital, Past and Present*, Oxford: Pergamon Press, pp. 1–32.

Pile, Steve (1999) 'What is a city?', in Doreen Massey, John Allen and Steve Pile (eds), *City Worlds*, London: Routledge, pp. 5–50.

Pooley, Colin G. (1977) 'The residential segregation of migrant communities in mid-Victorian Liverpool', *Transactions of the Institute of British Geographers*, 2(3): 364–82.

Portes, Alejandro, Luis E. Guarnizo and Patricia Landolt (1999) 'Introduction', Special Issue: Transnational Communities, *Ethnic and Racial Studies*, 22(2): 217–37.

Price, Marie and Lisa Benton-Short (eds) (2008) *Migrants to the Metropolis: The Rise of Immigrant Gateway Cities*, Syracuse, NY: Syracuse University Press.

Rahim, Lily Zubaidah (2009) *Singapore in the Malay World: Building and Breaching Regional Bridges*, Abingdon: Routledge.

Ramwell, Dave and Tim Madge (1992) *A Ship Too Far: The Mystery of the Derbyshire*, London: Hodder and Stoughton.

Reynolds, Henry (2003) *North of Capricorn: The Untold Story of the People of Australia's North*, Crows Nest, NSW: Allen and Unwin.

Rigg, Jonathan (1994) 'Redefining the village and rural life: lessons from South East Asia', *The Geographical Journal*, 160(2): 123–33.

Rimmer, Peter J. (1991) 'The global intelligence corps and world cities: engineering consultancies on the move', in Peter W. Daniels (ed.), *Services and Metropolitan Development: International Perspectives*, London: Routledge, pp. 66–106.

Robinson, Jennifer (2006) *Ordinary Cities: Between Modernity and Development*, London: Routledge.

Robinson, Jennifer (2011) 'Cities in a world of cities: the comparative gesture', *International Journal of Urban and Regional Research*, 35(1): 1–23.

Roy, A.L. (1888) *Reminiscences England and American, Part II: England and India*, Calcutta: Royal Publishing House.

Roy, Ananya (2009) 'The 21st-century metropolis: new geographies of theory', *Regional Studies*, 43(6): 819–30.

Runnymede Trust (2000) *The Future of Multi-ethnic Britain: The Parekh Report*, London: Profile Books.

Said, Edward W. (1993) *Culture and Imperialism*, London: Chatto and Windus.

Salter, Joseph (1873) *The Asiatic in England: Sketches of Sixteen Years' Work Among Orientals*, London: Jackson and Halliday.

Salter, Joseph (1896) *The East in the West: Or Work among the Asiatics and Africans in London*, London: S.W. Partridge and Co.

Sampson, Helen (2013) *International Seafarers and Transnationalism in the Twenty-First Century*, Manchester: Manchester University Press.

Sandhu, Kernial Singh and Paul Wheatley (1983) *Melaka: The Transformation of a Malay Capital c.1400–1980*, vols 1 and 2, Kuala Lumpur: Oxford University Press.

Sassen, Saskia (1991) *The Global City*, Princeton: Princeton University Press.

Sassen, Saskia (2001) *The Global City* (revised edn), Princeton: Princeton University Press.

Saunier, Pierre-Yves (2002) 'Taking up the bet on connections: a municipal contribution', *Contemporary European History*, 11: 507–27.

Schottmann, Sven (2011) 'The pillars of "Mahathir's Islam": Mahathir Mohamad on being-Muslim in the modern world', *Asian Studies Review*, 35(3): 355–72.

Seet, K.K. (2011) *Prime: Pride of Passage*, Singapore: Straits Times Press.

Sekula, Allan (2000) 'Freeway to China (Version 2, for Liverpool)', *Public Culture*, 12(2): 411–22.

Shaari Isa (2009) *Kirkby: The Life and the Loves*, Auckland: The Right Connection.

Shamsul A.B. (1999) 'From *Orang Kaya Baru* to *Melayu Baru*: cultural construction of the Malay "new rich"', in Michael Pinches (ed.), *Culture and Privilege in Capitalist Asia*, London: Routledge, pp. 86–110.

Shamsul Baharin and Lee Boon Thong (1988) *FELDA: 3 Decades of Evolution*, Kuala Lumpur: FELDA.

Sherry, Norman (1966) *Conrad's Eastern World*, Cambridge: Cambridge University Press.

Silk, Michael (2002) '"Bangsa Malaysia": global sport, the city and the mediated refurbishment of local identities', *Media, Culture and Society*, 24(6): 775–94.

Simone, AbdouMaliq (2001) 'On the worlding of African cities', *African Studies Review*, 44(2): 15–41.

Simone, AbdouMaliq (2004) 'People as infrastructure: intersecting fragments in Johannesburg', *Public Culture*, 16(3): 407–29.

Sin Chih Hoong (2003) 'The politics of ethnic integration in Singapore: Malay "regrouping" as an ideological construct', *International Journal of Urban and Regional Research*, 27(3): 527–44.

Sloane, Patricia (1999) *Islam, Modernity and Entrepreneurship Among the Malays*, Houndmills: Macmillan.

Smith, Michael Peter (2001) *Transnational Urbanism: Locating Globalization*, Oxford: Wiley-Blackwell.

Smith, Michael Peter (2005) 'Transnational urbanism revisited', *Journal of Ethnic and Migration Studies*, 31(2): 235–44.

Smith, Michael Peter and Luis Eduardo Guarnizo (eds) (1998) *Transnationalism from Below: Comparative Urban and Community Research*, New Brunswick: Transaction Publishers.

Söderström, Ola (2014) *Cities in Relations: Trajectories of Urban Development in Hanoi and Ouagadougou*, Chichester: John Wiley & Sons, Ltd.

Spencer, Ian R.G. (1997) *British Immigration Policy since 1939: The Making of Multi-racial Britain*, New York: Routledge.

Stammers, Michael (1991) *Liverpool: The Port and Its Ships*, Stroud: Alan Sutton Publishing.

Steele, Murray (2008) 'Transmitting ideas of empire: representations and celebrations in Liverpool, 1886–1953', in Sheryllynne Haggerty, Anthony Webster and Nicholas J. White (eds), *The Empire in One City: Liverpool's Inconvenient Imperial Past*, Manchester: Manchester University Press, pp. 123–42.

Stivens, Maila (2006) '"Family values" and Islamic revival: gender, rights and state moral projects in Malaysia', *Women's Studies International Forum*, 29: 354–67.

Stockwell, A.J. (2008) '*Merdeka!* Looking back at independence day in Malaya', *Indonesia and the Malay World*, 36(106): 327–44.

Studwell, Joe (2007) *Asian Godfathers and Power in Hong Kong and South-East Asia*, London: Profile Books.

Sykes, Olivier, Jonathan Brown, Matthew Cocks, David Shaw and Chris Couch (2013) 'A city profile of Liverpool', *Cities*, 35: 299–318.

Tabili, Laura (1994) *We Ask for British Justice: Workers and Racial Difference in Late Imperial Britain*, Ithaca: Cornell University Press.

Tagliacozzo, Eric (2013) *The Longest Journey: Southeast Asians and the Pilgrimage to Mecca*, Oxford: Oxford University Press.

Tan Sooi Beng (1992) 'Counterpoints in the performing arts of Malaysia', in Joel S. Kahn and Francis Loh Kok Wah (eds), *Fragmented Vision: Culture and Politics in Contemporary Malaysia*, Sydney: Allen and Unwin, pp. 282–305.

Tan Tai Yong (2008) *Creating 'Greater Malaysia': Decolonization and the Politics of Merger*, Singapore: Institute of Southeast Asian Studies.

Taylor, Peter J. (2004) *World City Network: A Global Urban Analysis*, London: Routledge.

Taylor, T.K. (2006) *Sunset of the Empire in Malaya: A New Zealander's Life in the Colonial Education Service*, London: The Radcliffe Press.

Thompson, Eric C. (2007) *Unsettling Absences: Urbanism in Rural Malaysia*, Singapore: NUS Press.

Tomizawa, Hisao (2010) 'Old and new aspects of Malayness in the contemporary Dunia Melayu movement', in Hashim Ismail (ed.), *Tinta di Dada Naskhah: Melakar Jasa Dato' Dr Abu Hassan Sham*, Kuala Lumpur: Jabatan Penerbitan Akademi Pengajian Melayu, Universiti Malaya, pp. 29–44.

Tomlinson, H.M. (1950) *Malay Waters: The Story of Little Ships Coasting out of Singapore and Penang in Peace and War*, London: Hodder & Stoughton.

Tooke, Jane (2003) 'Spaces for community involvement: processes of disciplining and appropriation', *Space and Polity*, 7(3): 233–46.

Tregonning, K.G. (1967) *Home Port Singapore: A History of Straits Steamship Company Limited, 1890–1965*, Singapore: Oxford University Press.

Uduku, Ola (2003) 'Ethnic minority perspectives', in Ronaldo Munck (ed.), *Reinventing the City? Liverpool in Comparative Perspective*, Liverpool: Liverpool University Press, pp. 122–43.

Verhetsel, Ann and Steve Sel (2009) 'World maritime cities: from which cities do maritime decision-makers operate?', *Transport Policy*, 16(5): 240–50.

Vertovec, Steven (2001) 'Transnational challenges to the "new" multiculturalism', Paper presented to the ASA Conference, University of Sussex, 30 March–2 April.

Visram, Rozina (1986) *Ayahs, Lascars and Princes: The History of Indians in Britain, 1700–1947*, London: Pluto Press.

Visram, Rozina (2002) *Asians in Britain: 400 Years of History*, London: Pluto Press.

Vredenbregt, Jacob (1962) 'The Haddj: some of its features and functions in Indonesia', *Bijdragen tot de Taal-, Land- en Volkenkunde*, 118: 91–154.

Vredenbregt, Jacob (1964) 'Bawean migrations', *Bijdragen tot de Taal-, Land- en Volkenkunde*, 120(1): 109–39.

Wain, Barry (2009) *Malaysian Maverick: Mahathir Mohamad in Turbulent Times*, Basingstoke: Palgrave Macmillan.

Wake, Michael and Terry Lau (2008) *Contemporary Urban Centre: North West*, London: Novas Scarman Group.

Ward, Kevin (2010) 'Towards a relational comparative approach to the study of cities', *Progress in Human Geography*, 34(4): 471–87.

Werbner, Pnina (1999) 'Global pathways: working class cosmopolitans and the creation of transnational ethnic worlds', *Social Anthropology*, 7(1): 17–35.

Westhuizen, Janis van der (2004) 'Marketing Malaysia as a model Muslim state: the significance of the 16th Commonwealth Games', *Third World Quarterly*, 25(7): 1277–91.

White, Nicholas J. (2004) *British Business in Post-Colonial Malaysia, 1957–70: 'Neo-colonialism' or 'Disengagement'?* London: RoutledgeCurzon.

White, Nicholas J. (2008) 'Liverpool shipping and the end of empire: the Ocean group in East and Southeast Asia', in Sheryllynne Haggerty, Anthony Webster and Nicholas J. White (eds), *The Empire in One City: Liverpool's Inconvenient Imperial Past*, Manchester: Manchester University Press, pp. 165–87.

Wigen, Kären (2007) 'Introduction', in Jerry H. Bentley, Renate Bridenthal and Kären Wigen (eds), *Seascapes: Maritime Histories, Littoral Cultures, and Transoceanic Exchanges*, Honolulu: University of Hawaii Press, pp. 1–18.

Wilks-Heeg, Stuart (2003) 'From world city to pariah city? Liverpool and the global economy, 1850–2000', in Ronaldo Munck (ed.), *Reinventing the City? Liverpool in Comparative Perspective*, Liverpool: Liverpool University Press, pp. 36–52.

Wong, Maria Lin (1989) *Chinese Liverpudlians: A History of the Chinese Community in Liverpool*, Birkenhead: Liver Press.

World Bank (1993) *The East Asian Miracle: Economic Growth and Public Policy*, New York: Oxford University Press.

Yeoh, Brenda S.A. (2004) 'Cosmopolitanism and its exclusions in Singapore', *Urban Studies*, 41(12): 2431–45.

Yeoh, Brenda S.A., Shirlena Huang and Katie Willis (2000) 'Global cities, transnational flows and gender dimensions; the view from Singapore', *Tijdschrift voor Economische en Sociale Geografie*, 91(2): 147–58.

Yeoh Seng Guan (ed.) (2014) *The Other Kuala Lumpur: Living in the Shadows of a Globalising Southeast Asian City*, London: Routledge.

Yip, Andrew Kam-Tuck (2009) 'Islam and sexuality: orthodoxy and contestations', *Contemporary Islam*, 3(1): 1–5.
Zawawi Ibrahim (1998) *The Malay Labourer: By the Window of Capitalism*, Singapore: Institute of Southeast Asian Studies.
Žižek, S. (1997) 'Multiculturalism, or the cultural logic of late capitalism', *New Left Review*, 225: 28–51.

Index

From World City to the World in One City: Liverpool through Malay Lives,
First Edition. Tim Bunnell.